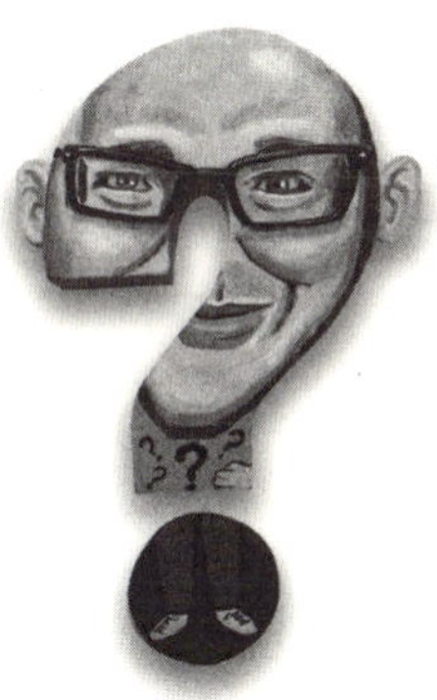

A veteran nerd with unbound enthusiasm for everything you love, **Marshall Julius** is a film critic, blogger, broadcaster, quizmaster and collector of colourful plastic things. Though his lifestyle appears sedentary, actually he's wildly active on Twitter: @marshalljulius.

VINTAGE GEEK

The Quiz Book

MARSHALL JULIUS

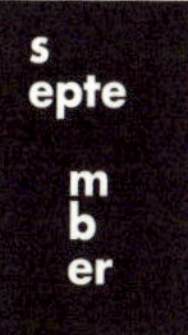

1 3 5 7 9 10 8 6 4 2

First published in 2019 by September Publishing

Typeset by Ed Pickford

Printed in Poland on paper from responsibly managed, sustainable sources by L&C Printing Group

ISBN 978-1-912836-02-4

September Publishing
www.septemberpublishing.org

With love, and gratitude, to my wife, and producer, Ruta –

You are the answer to all the most important questions.

Contents

The Answers

FOREWORD

By
Mike Reiss

Except for his black-rimmed glasses, Marshall Julius looks like he's composed entirely of meringue. He resembles a near-sighted Jewish snowman. He could be a stunt double for Dr Bunsen Honeydew. (If you're reading this book, I assume you know who Dr Bunsen Honeydew is.)

Marshall's wife, Ruta, however, is absolutely gorgeous. When I first met her, I instantly heard a film noir narrator in my head:

NARRATOR (V.O.)
The second I laid eyes on this dame I knew I would have to murder Marshall and make her my own.

My point, if indeed I have one, is this: when a woman who looks like Ruta loves a guy who looks like Marshall, he must really be something special. (This is a self-serving belief: my wife is constantly mistaken for Nicole Kidman, while I resemble a pile of wet garbage.)

In fact, Ruta loves Marshall enough to let him turn an entire room of their cosy home into a Simpsons shrine: it is packed from floor to ceiling with pop-eyed yellow figurines. Marshall Julius has bought so much Simpsons stuff, he put Matt Groening's children through college. And bought him a boat. It's a forty-foot yacht called *Thanks, Marshall!*

The depth of Marshall's knowledge about the series is astounding. I only knew the answers to half the questions in his chapter about *The Simpsons*, and I wrote the book on the show. (Literally. It's called *Springfield Confidential*, and it's now out in paperback.)

Every chapter in this book is like that – you will learn four amazing things on every page. Who lit the submarine set on the James Bond film *The Spy Who Loved Me*? Stanley Kubrick? No way! You're making that up! (Maybe he did make it up – who's going to check?) There's none of those half-baked trivia questions you'll find in most quiz books, like, What's the name of the incredible, hulking monster in Marvel Comics movies? (ANSWER: Jon Favreau.)

This book is like the best Simpsons episodes (the ones I wrote). It's funny. It's smart. It's packed with great material and loaded with guest stars. And, it can be unexpectedly touching, in Marshall's candid autobiographical segments that open each chapter.

It is truly, to quote something Comic Book Guy never said, "The best pop culture quiz book…EVER!" If you're reading this book in the store, buy it. (If you've already bought it, buy my book, *Springfield Confidential*, instead.)

NARRATOR (V.O.)

And so I finished Marshall's Foreword. And soon I would finish Marshall himself…and make his wife my own.

Mike Reiss

INTRODUCTION

There's a scene in Barry Levinson's period bromance *Diner* where sports-mad Eddie (Steve Guttenberg) sets his fiancée (Sharon Ziman) a football quiz. The stakes? Either she proves she knows enough about the things he loves, or the wedding's off. Though that's obviously wildly eccentric behaviour, there was something about that scene that triggered the crazy in fifteen-year-old me. Within days, I'd devised a quiz of my own, and soon after, forced the few friends I had to take it.

It wasn't about sports, of course, because, well, I had no interest in that sort of stuff, and still don't. Instead, it covered the things all right-minded people treasure: *Star Wars*, *Star Trek* and *Superman*, Bond and *Battlestar Galactica*, *Flash Gordon*, *Logan's Run* and, well, there was a question in there about *Manimal* too.

The DNA of that original quiz runs strong in the book you now hold in your hands. To paraphrase *Jurassic Park*, questions found a way.

I've always felt that to completely grow up, to turn your back on the things that once meant the most to you, would be the most terrible betrayal of the child you once were. Almost like murdering your juvenile self. To that end, I still love all the same things that I did as a kid, only ever adding to my interests – never subtracting.

As a collector, film critic and, for want of a better title, a professional appreciator, my mission in life is to both celebrate, and maintain, the memory of everything I can't think about without getting a lump in my throat. Which is a lot. My nostalgia knows no bounds and my enthusiasm has no brakes.

This calling of mine hardly materialised from thin air.

My mother was a nerd before the term existed. When I was small, every Saturday afternoon, we'd pull the sofa close to the TV

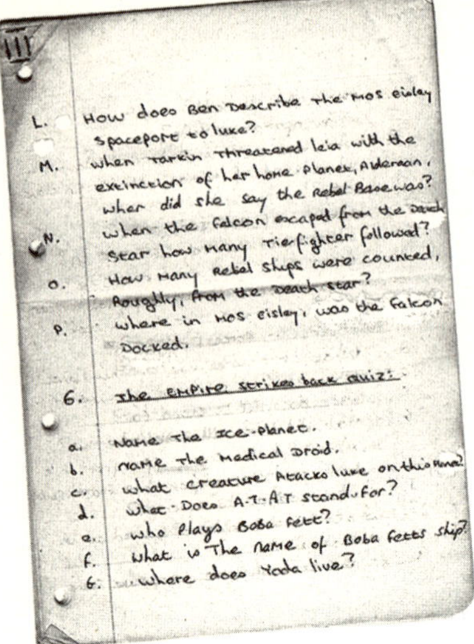

III

L. How does Ben Describe the Mos eisley spaceport to luke?
M. when Tarkin Threatened leia with the extinction of her home planet, Alderaan, wher did she say the Rebel Base was?
N. when the falcon escaped from the Death star how many Tie fighter followed?
O. How many Rebel ships were counted, Roughly, from the Death star?
P. where in Mos eisley, was the falcon Docked.

6. The Empire strikes back quiz:

a. Name the Ice-planet.
b. name the medical Droid.
c. what creature Atacks luke on this planet?
d. what Does A-T-A-T stand for?
e. who plays Boba fett?
f. what is The name of Boba fetts ship?
G. where does Yoda live?

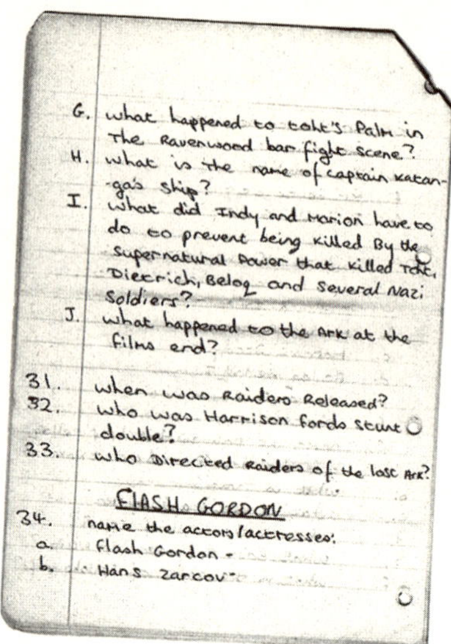

G. what happened to toht's Palm in The Ravenwood bar fight scene?
H. what is the name of captain katanga's ship?
I. what did Indy and Marion have to do to prevent being Killed By the supernatural power that killed Toht, Dietrich, Belog and several Nazi soldiers?
J. what happened to the Ark at the films end?

31. when was Raiders Released?
32. who was Harrison fords stunt double?
33. who Directed Raiders of the lost Ark?

FLASH GORDON

34. name the actors/actresses:
a. flash Gordon -
b. Hans Zarcov -

It begins! Pages from the quiz that started it all. The great-granddaddy of the book you now hold in your hands.

and sit, cuddled up, eating snacks and watching old movies. It was my favourite time of the week. My mum loved musicals, comedies, thrillers...Really anything good. She introduced me to Humphrey Bogart, Cary Grant and Bette Davis, to Katharine Hepburn, Bob Hope and Gene Kelly. Also directors – unveiling the worlds of Alfred Hitchcock, Billy Wilder, Michael Curtiz and the like.

And while we watched those fine old films, long before the invention of commentary tracks, she'd tell me about the casts – from the stars to the supporting players – sharing stories from their lives and the making of their movies. She brought cinema from the age of serials and newsreels to life, and honestly, it intoxicated me. I hung on her every word and though at school lessons rarely sank in, at home, with my mum, I retained every word. I was eight-and-a-half when *Star Wars* came along, and having been primed for geekery by my mother, and further encouraged to embrace the dorky arts by my collector cousin Ronald, I fully embraced my destiny: by nature and nurture a nerd, and proud of it.

I've never really liked the word trivia. It's so judgemental. The facts and information I've so eagerly absorbed over the years are of value to me, and important to me, and I know I'm not alone in this. So a noun defining such choice nuggets as fun, yes, and interesting, certainly, but also largely worthless and inconsequential, has no place in a quiz book of mine. Take them separately and, I'll concede, they might not seem like anything more than amusing fripperies, but stack a whole bunch on top of one another and you begin to build a picture of how the things we love came to be. And that's not trivial.

So these facts, then, were first of use to me, and my friends, in those long-distant days of pre-Internet yore. Invariably I'd get a call from a mate who, for the life of him, couldn't remember the name of something, or who made such-and-such, or what happened at the end of that thing. And I'd know, and they'd be grateful, I'd feel good about myself, and all would be right with the world. Pub quizzes, too, were my thing. Just don't ask me sports questions. Or pop questions. Or geography questions. Or really

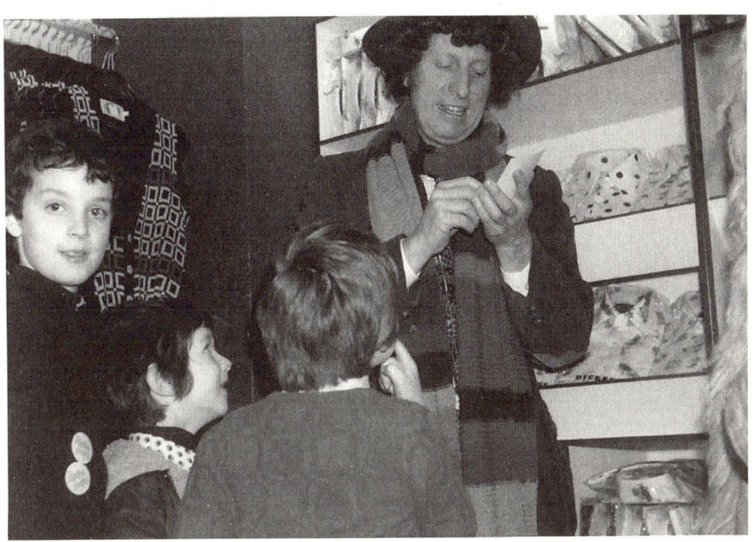

A glorious shot from 1975 of me, age six, gazing with love and awe at the Doctor.

anything about the real world. But if the questions concern comic-books, films, TV shows, videogames or any other fun, cool stuff like that...I'm in like Flynn.

When, however, the Internet made the sum of all human knowledge available to everyone, around the clock and around the globe, my capacity for fascinating facts lost some of its cachet. Still, you can't trust everything you read online: I've lost count of how many times, while interviewing an actor or filmmaker, that I've referred to something I read about them online and they've flatly refuted it.

There's also value in actually knowing things. You could, for example, write a quiz book. Or better still, buy a quiz book, to test yourself, your friends and your loved ones, finally determining who among you rules your particular nerd roost.

I'm not saying I wrote this book off the top of my head. The web was certainly useful. Back when I wrote a book about action movies in the mid-Nineties, I spent days at the British Film Institute's reference library, using an old microfilm reader to trawl through even older magazine cuttings. Honestly, I much prefer the IMDb! I've also collected a dizzying number of reference books over the years, lots of making-ofs and episode guides I was able to press into service for the first time in forever.

To write *Vintage Geek*'s 1,000 questions and answers, I spent six months disappearing down the nerdiest and most labyrinthine rabbit holes I could unearth, barely coming up for air as one fact led to another, then to another until – Holy Cow! I didn't know that! Many wild things were discovered, and corralled into the pages ahead.

It's been a significant voyage of discovery for me, and I've loved the process, although walking around with a head swirling with facts and figures makes it pretty much impossible to focus on anything in the real world. Now the book's finished – this introduction was the last thing I wrote for it – a period of real-life readjustment is certainly in order as I reacquaint myself with my family, my friends, and the outside world.

My hope for this book is that while, yes, I expect you'll be able to answer many of the questions, several, I think, will take you by surprise. You will, fingers crossed, learn several amazing new things,

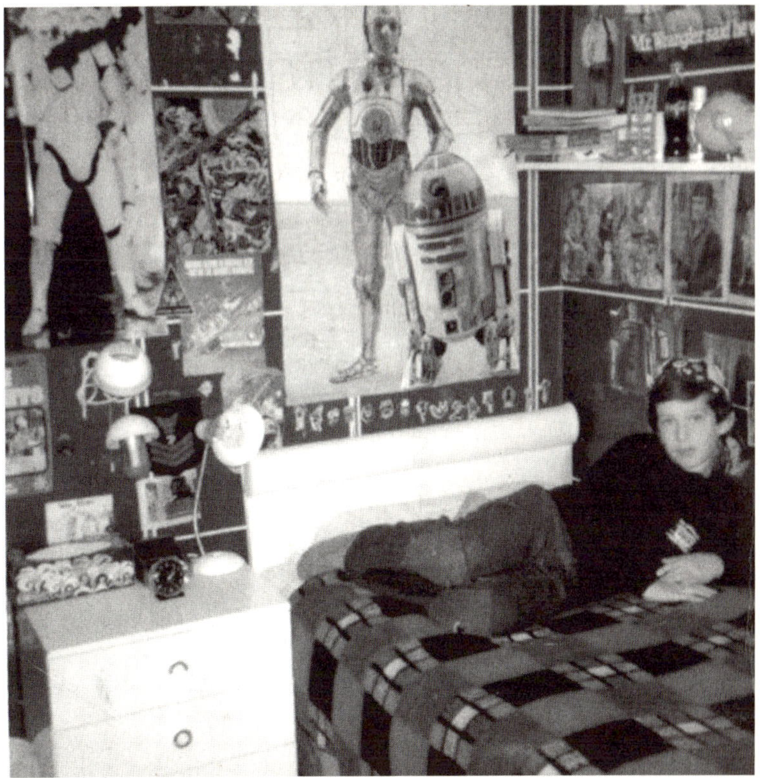

It's been more than 40 years since this pic was taken and I still love all the same things.

about several amazing old things, as we trawl through such beloved 20th-century fandoms as Fifties' Sci-Fi Cinema, Sixties' *Star Trek*, Seventies' Stephen King, Eighties' Actioners, Nineties' *Simpsons* and a whole lot of other goodness besides.

To cram, then, or not to cram? Well, *Vintage Geek* is meant to be fun, so the last thing I'd want you to do is treat each quiz like an exam. That said, it would surely be no hardship to spend a day watching, say, George Romero's first three Dead flicks or John Carpenter's Apocalypse Trilogy, and certainly, you'll get more of the answers right if the films are fresh in your mind. Make a day of it, I say!

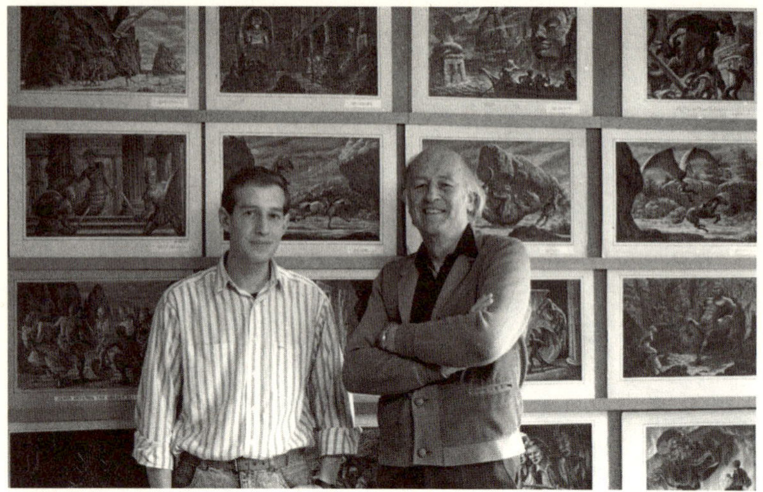

Hangin' with Harryhausen in 1988. I was 19 and had hair that I didn't appreciate. What I did appreciate was being in the presence of my hero.

Along the way, you'll encounter fifty fantastic guest stars: writers, artists, musicians, actors, filmmakers...All now quizzers, too, and absolute legends. I'm privileged to have befriended many of them on Twitter, my natural online habitat. If you've not yet joined my great, geeky community, come say hello at @marshalljulius – I'm not hard to find and I don't bite.

Good luck then, my friends, my Vintage Geeks!

May the Answers be with you all.

Marshall.

The Questions

James Bond: The Roger Moore Years

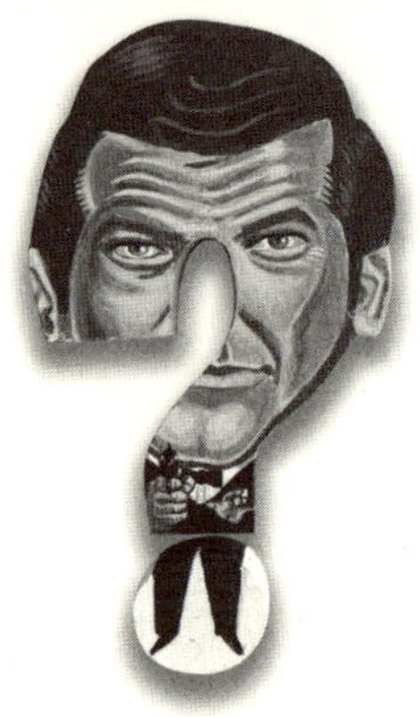

"Who's your favourite Bond?"

When I was a kid, the choice was between Sean Connery and Roger Moore. As far as I'm concerned, it still is.

Connery was my TV Bond. I was too young to go see the first wave of 007s at the cinema, but they were on the box all the time, and being allowed to stay up late to watch one was a very special treat.

Roger was my Big Screen Bond. *The Spy Who Loved Me* was the first film of his that I saw at the cinema and, to paraphrase sweet Sandy Olsson, I was hopelessly devoted to Mr Moore from that point on.

When pressed by my schoolmates to pick a favourite, I'd refuse. Why pick one side of the same shiny coin over the other?

Sean was the man I dreamed of becoming one day. Tough and capable. Confident and magnetic. An alpha dad who'd protect you while preparing you for the world.

Roger was my brother, though. Smooth and amusing. Stylish and kind. He'd teach me about girls and gambling and how to drink bourbon without making a face.

Both had a hand in raising me, so don't Sophie's Choice me, OK? I love them both.

So why pick Roger for this chapter, over Sean? Actually, that was an easy decision: because he's the fun one. Fun, I approve of. Fun's what I want this book to be.

Much like the man himself, Moore's Bond loved his work. There was a lightness and a joy to him, a smile and a sparkle, and if I've managed to capture even an ounce of that life and levity in these next few pages, hooray for us all!

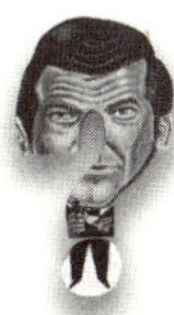

1. What does the sign say on the gate of Kananga's crocodile farm?

2. Hugo Drax's Viennese laboratory is opened by playing which famous 5-note movie theme on a touchtone keypad?

3. Which actor who played one of Moore's Bond villains was related to Ian Fleming?

4. "Bond! What do you think you're doing?"

5. What card represents Bond (Roger Moore) in Solitaire's (Jane Seymour) tarot deck?

6. Which long-time Bond villain finally receives his comeuppance in *For Your Eyes Only* (1981)? Also, how does Bond despatch him?

007. The sheep's eyeball enthusiastically gobbled by Louis Jourdan in *Octopussy* (1983) was the real thing: True or false?

8. Which Eighties action star made his acting debut in *A View to a Kill* (1985) – cast at the last minute by director John Glen to play a henchman while he happened to be on set, visiting girlfriend Grace Jones?

9. Moore was the youngest actor to debut as James Bond: True or false?

10. What is Jaws' sole line of dialogue?

11. After Bond seduces double agent Rosie Carver (Gloria Hendry), then pulls a gun on her, demanding information, she pleads, "But you couldn't. You wouldn't. Not after what we've just done?" How does Bond respond?

12. Which director helmed more of Moore's Bonds than any other?

13. Prior to shooting *The Man with the Golden Gun* (1974), where in Los Angeles did Hervé "Nick Nack" Villechaize reside?

14. As a result of his failing eyesight, cinematographer Claude Renoir was unable to see to the end of the supertanker set in *The Spy Who Loved Me* (1977). Who was secretly enlisted by designer Ken Adam to supervise the lighting in Renoir's place?

GUEST STAR: Mark Millar

Comicbook writer best known for *Kick-Ass, Kingsman: The Secret Service*, *Wanted*, *Superior, Nemesis*, *Superman: Red Son*, *Civil War*, *Old Man Logan* and much more besides.

15. Which Bond movie was promised next in the closing credits of *The Spy Who Loved Me* (1977)?

16. Early on in *For Your Eyes Only* (1981), the movie establishes a more serious, less gadgety tone by making which grand gesture?

17. While posing as a snake charmer, how does MI6 agent Vijay (Vijay Amritraj) attract Bond's attention in *Octopussy* (1983)?

18. Which one of Moore's Bond movies was known as *Moving Target* in Italy, *Dangerously Yours* in France and *Murder in the Eyes* in Israel?

19. Who played Bond's CIA chum Felix Leiter in *Live and Let Die* (1973), and how many times did the character return during Moore's tenure as Bond?

20. Which fellow Bond star first met Moore at the Royal Academy of Dramatic Arts in the mid-Forties, sharing a class with him in 1944?

21. Which one of his Bond films did Moore like best? Also, which was his least favourite?

22. With which four shiny elements did Scaramanga (Christopher Lee) construct his signature golden gun?

23. What is the one movie in which Moore got to drive Bond's iconic 1964 silver birch Aston Martin DB5?

24. Of which Bond actress would Roger Moore only comment, "My mother once said if you have nothing good to say about someone, say nothing at all!"?

25. When asked why he accepted the role of Bond, given his distaste for guns and violence, master of self-deprecation Moore revealed that as a young actor at RADA, he'd been approached by a famous English writer, director, actor and wit, who gave him the following advice: "Young man, with your devastating good looks and your disastrous lack of talent, you should take any job ever offered you. In the event that you're offered two jobs simultaneously, take the one that offers the most money."

This, said Moore, is why he played Bond. But who was it that gave him this advice?

26. Which of Moore's Bond girls was born Joyce Penelope Wilhelmina Frankenberg and, in the Eighties, dubbed Queen of the Miniseries?

27. Moore suffered from which unusual phobia?

28. How, famously, did Roger Moore describe his acting range?

29. Besides the Log Cabin Girl (Sue Vanner), who else needs James?

GUEST STAR: Sanjeev Bhaskar

Comedian and actor best known for *Goodness Gracious Me* (1998–2000) and *The Kumars at No. 42* (2001–2006).

30. Which is the only Bond film to feature the singer of the title song in the opening credits?

31. Q (Desmond Llewelyn) appears as a field agent for the first time in which Roger Moore Bond film?

32. Who composed the score for *Live and Let Die* (1973)?

33. What year did Roger Moore first play James Bond?

34. Which of Moore's Bonds holds the record for the most-watched film ever broadcast on British television?

35. The first stunt ever calculated by computer modelling, the 360° corkscrew car jump in *The Man with the Golden Gun* (1974), was performed by uncredited British stuntman Loren "Bumps" Willard as eight cameras simultaneously captured the action. How many takes, though, did it take to get it right?

36. Swedish actress Maud Adams appeared in which three Roger Moore Bond films?

37. Moore's Bond contract provided him with an unlimited supply of which brand of Cuban cigar?

38. James Bond appeared in a trio of features in 1983. What were they, and who played him in each film?

39. Which of Moore's Bonds has the lowest body count?

40. Having worked previously with Moore in *Sherlock Holmes in New York* (1976) and *The Sea Wolves* (1980), which actor took a role in *A View to a Kill* (1985), not because he liked the Bond films, but to work with his old mate Sir Roger again?

41. Which one of Moore's Bond girls was a doctor? Also, what was her qualification and who played her?

42. How was Bond's bayou boat chase originally described in the screenplay for *Live and Let Die* (1973)?

43. Originally created to house the epic supertanker set for *The Spy Who Loved Me* (1977), Pinewood Studio's colossal 007 Stage was destroyed by a fire in 1984 during the production of which movie?

44. Which one of Moore's Bond films featured Bernard Lee's final appearance as M?

45. Which item of clothing had to be custom-made for *The Man with the Golden Gun* (1974), at an apparent cost of $10,000?

46. After starring together in *The Spy Who Loved Me* (1977), Barbara Bach and Richard Kiel appeared alongside one another in which two additional movies?

47. Desmond Llewellyn appeared in all but one of Moore's Bond films as the irascible Q. Which one did he miss?

48. Which three Moore 007 movies feature fighting sequences aboard trains? Also, who did Bond battle in each of them?

49. Which of Moore's Bonds is the only film in the franchise to feature two boat chases?

50. What were the three functions of Bond's Rolex Submariner in *Live and Let Die* (1973)?

Answers on page 150

The Simpsons: The First Ten Years

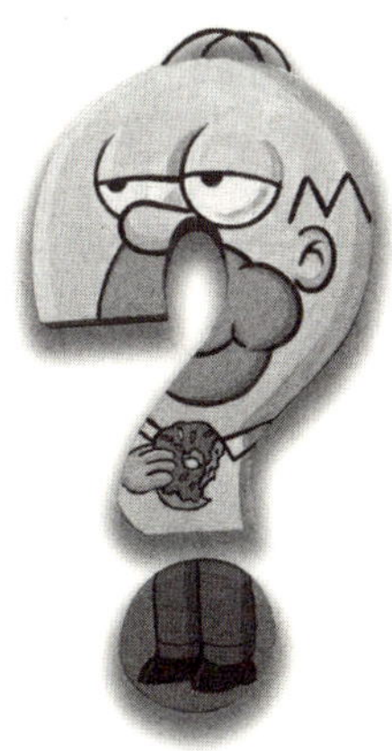

If an asteroid hit Earth with the same impact as *The Simpsons*, we'd all be specks of space dust right now.

Even in 1987, when early versions of Springfield's first family appeared on our screens in raw but striking shorts on *The Tracey Ullman Show*, there was a sense that special new ground was being broken.

Cut to Christmas 1989, and a gift that hasn't stopped giving since: *The Simpsons*. The first time I saw it, I could hardly believe how funny it was. How irresistible the characters were. How sharply it parodied everything I loved. How quotable every single line was. Here was a show that seemed to be speaking directly to me. But it wasn't just me who felt that way. Somehow it seemed to connect deep down with pretty much everyone.

Certainly my friends were as obsessed with it as I was. In Britain, at first, you could only see it on Sky TV, a satellite channel, so since my friend Sal was the only one of us back then with a dish, every Sunday night we'd congregate at his house to watch it en masse.

He'd also record it, of course, so we could watch each new episode over and over (and over and over and over again), building an enviable VHS collection with which we invented binge watching. You're welcome!

The Simpsons' first decade was wall-to-wall wonderful. Every show was an event. No one took it for granted. Back then, particularly on Sundays, 90% of everything we said was a quote from *The Simpsons*. The other 10% we devoted to discussing the show, and quizzing one another on obscure points of Simpsonian trivia.

To paraphrase those last few lines tapped out by Richard Dreyfuss in *Stand By Me* (1986), I never had any friends later on like the ones I used to watch *The Simpsons* with. Jebus, does anyone?

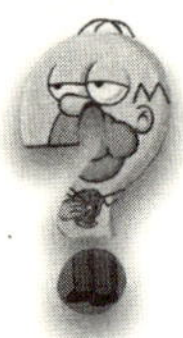

1. Matt Groening named the five core members of Springfield's first family after his own relatives. True or false?

2. What were Bart (Nancy Cartwright), Lisa (Yeardley Smith) and Maggie's first words?

3. Homer (Dan Castellaneta) was destined to lead which secret society? Also barred from joining which subsequent secret society?

4. What did Kirk Van Houten (Hank Azaria) sing to try to woo his wife back?

5. What was the name of Abraham Simpson's (Dan Castellaneta) army unit?

6. What is Radioactive Man's catchphrase?

7. How, in 1992, was *The Simpsons* credited with saving the life of an 8-year-old boy?

8. Name four of the Seven Duffs.

9. Who shot Mr Burns (Harry Shearer)?

GUEST STAR: Yeardley Smith

The voice of Lisa Simpson!

10. What is Lisa Simpson's middle name and who is she named after?

11. Who is Maggie's arch-enemy?

12. What's the address of the Simpsons' residence?

13. What is Homer's (Dan Castellaneta) official job title at the nuclear power plant?

14. What is Krusty the Clown's (Dan Castellaneta) real name?

15. Who did Bart (Nancy Cartwright) sell his soul to, and for how much?

16. Which word, invented by *The Simpsons* and first featured in "Lisa the Iconoclast" (S07E16), was added to the Merriam-Webster dictionary in 2018?

17. What did Mr Burns (Harry Shearer) steal from the US government in 1945?

18. Who is Homer (Dan Castellaneta) mistaken for after getting lost in the woods in "The Call of the Simpsons" (S01E07)?

19. What's the one thing Homer (Dan Castellaneta) can offer Marge that no one else can?

20. How did Matt Groening work his initials into Homer's (Dan Castellaneta) design?

21. How old are Homer (Dan Castellaneta), Marge (Julie Kavner), Bart (Nancy Cartwright), Lisa (Yeardley Smith) and Maggie?

22. What is Homer's (Dan Castellaneta) favourite donut filling?

23. Name any two Kent Brockman (Harry Shearer) shows.

24. Who, in 1990, remarked that *The Simpsons* single "Do the Bartman" was a slap in the face to rappers everywhere?

GUEST STAR: Josh Weinstein

Writer/producer on *The Simpsons*, *Mission Hill*, *Futurama* and *Disenchantment*. Writer on *Gravity Falls*.

25. What episode in the first eight seasons has the most ad-libbed lines from any actor?

26. What's Patty and Selma's (both voiced by Julie Kavner) favourite brand of cigarette?

27. What is Reverend Lovejoy's (Harry Shearer) hobby?

28. What's the name of Flanders' (Harry Shearer) stupid shop?

29. Who voiced both Lionel Hutz and Troy McClure?

30. What does it mean, to "Pull a Homer"?

31. What did Mr Burns (Harry Shearer) call his autobiography?

32. How and why does Homer (Dan Castellaneta) get himself declared disabled?

33. What was the name of Homer's (Dan Castellaneta) bowling team, and who were the founding members?

34. Which member of *The Simpsons* cast voices the most characters in the show?

35. What's the secret ingredient of a Flaming Moe (formerly a Flaming Homer)?

36. What does Smithers (Harry Shearer) collect?

37. What's the name of Springfield's baseball team?

38. What does Springfield have in common with Ogdenville, Brockway and North Haverbrook?

39. How does the phrase "D'oh!" appear in *Simpsons* scripts?

GUEST STAR: Michael Price

Writer/producer on *The Simpsons*, *F is for Family*, *LEGO Star Wars: The Yoda Chronicles* and *LEGO Star Wars: Droid Tales.*

40. "Simpsons Roasting on an Open Fire" (S01E01) was the first episode of the series that aired in December of 1989, but it wasn't originally slated to be the premiere. What episode, which aired later in season one, was the original "pilot"?

41. What was the name of Homer's (Dan Castellaneta) barbershop quartet, and who else was in the group?

42. Where does Bart (Nancy Cartwright) find Mr Burns' (Harry Shearer) cherished teddy bear Bobo?

43. What is Homer's (Dan Castellaneta) middle initial, and what does it stand for?

44. Krusty (Dan Castellaneta), although illiterate, subscribes to which magazine?

45. What were the names of Bart's (Nancy Cartwright) elephant and Homer's (Dan Castellaneta) lobster?

46. Who composed *The Simpsons*' memorable theme tune?

47. Which *Simpsons* character is a parody of Arnold Schwarzenegger, and what's the name of his death-dealing alter ego?

48. In the "Dial 'Z' for Zombies" segment of "Treehouse of Horror III" (S04E05), how does Homer (Dan Castellaneta) respond after Bart (Nancy Cartwright) exclaims, "Dad, you killed the zombie Flanders!"?

49. "We wanted to do an episode where the thinking was, 'What if a real-life, normal person had to enter Homer's [Dan Castellaneta] universe and deal with him?'" Which episode, and what person, is *Simpsons* writer/producer Josh Weinstein referring to?

50. Where in Springfield might you find the latest issues of *Manboy*, *Batchick*, *Birdguy*, *Dog Kid*, *Lava Lady* and *The Human Bee*?

Answers on page 159

George A. Romero: *Night*, *Dawn* and *Day*

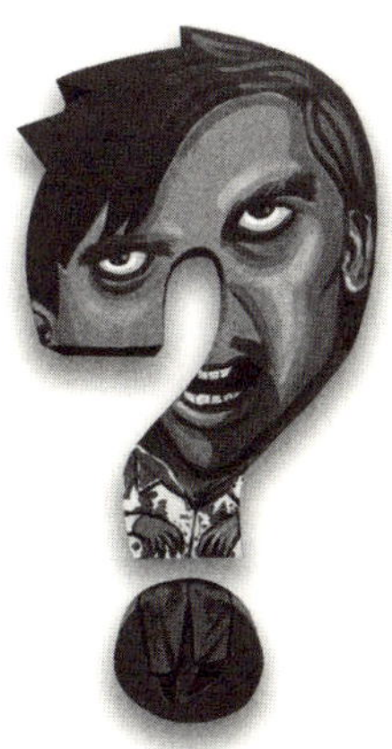

I was ten years old when I first learned of *Dawn of the Dead*. It was 1979 and the film had just been released in England. It had an X certificate, which is like an 18 today, only much more forbidden-sounding. It was the first night of Passover and a holy night for me, not because of the religious stuff, but because I got to stay up really late and hang out with my cousin Ronald, who was four years older than me, a fantastic nerd, and really just my hero.

Ronald had been trying for a few years already to get into X films. He once, famously, rocked up to a local cinema with his freckles covered in talc, and sunglasses on, in the hopes of appearing mature enough to see one. Alas, he was foiled on that occasion. At 14, though, he'd managed to sneak in to a showing of *Dawn of the Dead*, and on that fateful Passover night, his face flushed with the success of his venture, he described to me, in thrilling, gory detail, every last thing he remembered about the film.

Though I wasn't sure I was brave enough at ten to see it, even if I'd somehow been able, I considered myself a fan from that moment on. And when, thanks to the magic of VHS, I finally caught up with *Dawn of the Dead* (1978) and Romero's earlier effort, *Night of the Living Dead* (1968), regardless of the years of anticipation that preceded them, I was totally blown away.

A low-budget, black-and-white shocker shot in Pittsburgh by filmmaker George A. Romero and co-writer John A. Russo, *Night of the Living Dead* changed the public's perception of zombies from spooky, slavish drones reanimated by voodoo sorcery to relentless flesh-eating monsters halted only by a blow to the brain.

A decade later, with a larger budget, colour film and buckets of bloody animal organs, Romero stepped up the pace with *Dawn of the Dead* and finally *Day of the Dead* (1985), crafting a classic cult trilogy that set the current zombie standard, and though, yes, he ended up making a bunch more, it's his original trilogy that I'll be quizzing you about here.

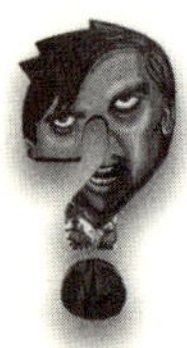

1. Whose grave are Johnny (Russell Streiner) and Barbra (Judith O'Dea) visiting in *Night of the Living Dead*?

2. "When there's no more room in Hell..."

3. What's the headline on the newspaper that blows up against the trashcans in *Day of the Dead*?

4. Who is first to die in *Night of the Living Dead*?

5. What happens to the zombie (Jim Krut) that sneaks up behind Roger (Scott H. Reiniger) while he's refuelling the chopper in *Dawn of the Dead*?

6. What animal is seen on the steps of the First National Bank at the beginning of *Day of the Dead*?

7. What does Barbra (Judith O'Dea) lose before making it to the relative safety of the house in *Night of the Living Dead*?

8. When Peter (Ken Foree) and Roger (Scott H. Reiniger) first go shopping in *Dawn of the Dead*, which two items are at the top of Peter's list?

9. What is Dr Logan's (Richard Liberty) nickname in *Day of the Dead*? Also, what is his mad dream?

GUEST STAR: John A. Russo

Co-writer of *Night of the Living Dead*.

10. How many "Ben's Trucks" were used in *Night of the Living Dead*?

11. When the boys first head down into the mall in *Dawn of the Dead*, which iconic zombie heads up the stairs after Fran (Gaylen Ross)?

12. Who's the only clean-shaven soldier in *Day of the Dead*?

13. What's the first thing Barbara (Judith O'Dea) manages to say to Ben, in *Night of the Living Dead*?

14. Where is Roger (Scott H. Reiniger) bitten when he's caught between the trucks, in *Dawn of the Dead*?

15. According to Dr Logan's (Richard Liberty) calculations in *Day of the Dead*, what's the ratio of zombie to human survivor?

16. What, according to TV reports in *Night of the Living Dead*, is likely responsible for corpses reanimating around the globe?

17. Which film in Romero's Dead Trilogy was both the lowest grossing and the filmmaker's favourite?

18. What book does Dr Logan (Richard Liberty) give Bub in *Day of the Dead*?

19. Though hired by Romero to create the make-up effects for *Night of the Living Dead*, why was Tom Savini ultimately unable to work on the movie?

20. What are the creatures called in *Night of the Living Dead*?

21. What does Bub (Howard Sherman) do to Rhodes (Joe Pilato) after shooting him and leaving him in the clutches of his zombie brethren, in *Day of the Dead*?

22. How many people are hiding out in the house in *Night of the Living Dead*?

23. After killing all the mall zombies in *Dawn of the Dead*, what do Stephen (David Emge) and Peter (Ken Foree) do with their rotting corpses?

24. In *Day of the Dead*, what does Rhodes (Joe Pilato) scream at the zombie horde who rip him in half and feast on his entrails?

GUEST STAR: Tom Savini

The Godfather of Gore! Actor and director, but above all else, make-up effects maestro whose credits include *Dawn of the Dead* (1978), *Friday the 13th* (1980), *Creepshow* (1982) and *Day of the Dead* (1985).

25. Whose head was blown off at the beginning of *Dawn of the Dead* when the SWAT team shows up?

26. What's most important to Harry (Karl Hardman), according to his long-suffering wife Helen (Marilyn Eastman), in *Night of the Living Dead*?

27. Which actor's hobbling, stumbling zombie walk did Romero single out as his all-time favourite?

28. What does Harry (Karl Hardman) call the TV aerial in *Night of the Living Dead*?

29. How do Peter (Ken Foree) and Fran (Gaylen Ross) accidentally attract the attention of the motorcycle raiders in *Dawn of the Dead*?

30. What's the one thing that frightens Romero's zombies?

31. Who played the first creature that makes it into the house, only to be bashed in the head with a tyre iron by Ben (Duane Jones), in *Night of the Living Dead*?

32. As shooting didn't start till late most nights on *Dawn of the Dead*, made-up zombie extras often drank, sometimes heavily, at local bars. What alcohol-fuelled incident cost the production $7,000?

33. Regarding the main casts only, which film in Romero's Dead Trilogy sees the most survivors at the end?

34. How do Tom (Keith Wayne) and Judy (Judith Ridley) die in *Night of the Living Dead*?

35. What's the title of the polka, by British composer Herbert Chappell, that plays so dissonantly over *Dawn of the Dead*'s closing credits?

36. What did the filmmakers primarily use for blood in *Night of the Living Dead*?

37. What's the real-life name of the mall featured in *Dawn of the Dead*?

38. How does Sheriff McClelland (George Kosana) respond to being asked by the reporter (Bill "Chilly Billy" Cardille) if the creatures are slow-moving, in *Night of the Living Dead*?

39. From where in the mall, in *Dawn of the Dead*, does Stephen (David Emge) attempt to destroy the Starship *Enterprise*?

GUEST STAR: Howard Berger

Oscar-winning make-up effects legend whose credits include *The Chronicles of Narnia: The Lion, the Witch and the Wardrobe* (2005), *Day of the Dead* (1985), *Evil Dead II* (1987), *Hitchcock* (2012) and lots more!

40. What was Greg Nicotero's nickname in *Day of the Dead*?

41. How does Harry (Karl Hardman) die, in *Night of the Living Dead*?

42. Which noted US film critic wrote that *Dawn of the Dead* was "one of the best horror films ever made", adding that while it was undeniably "gruesome, sickening, disgusting, violent, brutal and appalling, nobody ever said art had to be in good taste"?

43. Who grabs Barbra and drags her outside when the creatures finally make it into the house, in *Night of the Living Dead*?

44. How many times does Romero appear in his Dead Trilogy?

45. What's Peter's (Ken Foree) nickname for Stephen (David Emge) in *Dawn of the Dead*?

46. What's the real-life name of the cemetery featured in *Night of the Living Dead*?

47. What's unusual about the zombie kids who attack Peter in the airport hangar office, in *Dawn of the Dead*?

48. A huge fan of *Night of the Living Dead*, who helped Romero and producer Richard P. Rubinstein secure financing for *Dawn of the Dead* in exchange for international distribution rights?

49. What do *Dawn of the Dead*'s motorcycle raiders throw in the zombies' faces?

50. Who's the only character in Romero's Dead Trilogy to use the word "zombies"?

Answers on page 165

The Mighty Marvel Age of Comics

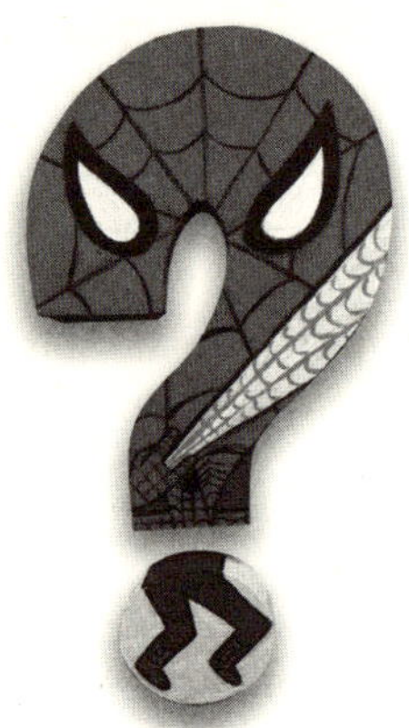

Greetings, True Believers!

As surely as mortal man from aeons past regarded their gods with reverence and gratitude for the bounties of life, nerds today have no less an impressive line-up of deities to praise for the parts they've played in building our universes and lavishing us with treats. And should we dare scale our modern Mount Olympus for a peek at the legends within, there on the throne once occupied by Zeus, Jupiter and Odin, flanked by an army of supers with a typewriter on his lap, would be perched Stan Lee.

The foundations of nerd culture are built on comicbooks and no one in the whole history of geek did more than Stan to build the multiverses we dwell in, and dwell on, today. I'm not saying he did it alone. Jack Kirby, Steve Ditko...I revere them almost equally. But it was Stan who saw comics as they were, imagined how they might be, and through sheer force of will, made that happen. It was Stan's naturalistic approach that made his characters as human and relatable as titans could possibly be. And it was Stan who welcomed us into his worlds with open arms and awesome alliterations, bringing us into the folds of his marvellous comicbooks, letting us in on the gags and making us one of the gang.

Within a single, spectacular decade, Stan, with Jack, Steve and a handful of others, created so much of what we love today that their achievements are no easier to comprehend than infinite space. For Marvel, their Big Bang was 1961's The Fantastic Four. Then planet after planet formed in quick succession: The Incredible Hulk. The Mighty Thor. The Amazing Spider-Man. Iron Man. The Avengers. The X-Men. Dr. Strange. Daredevil. The Silver Surfer...Is your mind blown yet?

The questions here relate strictly to that tumultuous, pioneering era. To the comicbook company that both reflected and shaped the 1960s. To the Marvel Age of yore...Excelsior!

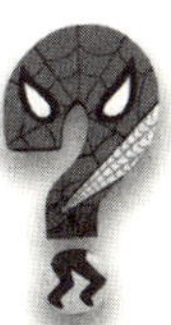

1. Inspired by the success of DC's Justice League of America (*The Brave and the Bold* #28, March 1960), Marvel Comics publisher Martin Goodman directed editor Stan Lee to create their own superhero team. What was the result?

2. When Namor the Sub-Mariner grumpily encounters an isolated tribe of Eskimos in *The Avengers* #4 (March 1964), what strange object are they praying to?

3. Thirties radio drama *Chandu the Magician* inspired the creation of which enchanting Marvel Comics character?

4. What message is inscribed in the side of Thor's hammer, Mjölnir?

5. What's the official name of Professor X's mutant academy?

6. According to artist Don Heck, what did Jack Kirby used to call superheroes?

7. What does the acronym S.H.I.E.L.D. stand for?

8. The Incredible Hulk was inspired by which iconic Universal Monster and what chilling Victorian novel?

9. What, in 1965, did Stan Lee name Marvel's brand new, "honest-to-gosh, far-out fan club in the mixed-up Marvel manner"?

GUEST STAR: Dan Slott

Creator of the Spider-Verse and writer on *The Amazing Spider-Man, Silver Surfer, She-Hulk, The Mighty Avengers, Fantastic Four* and more!

10. Vulture, Lizard, Green Goblin, Gog, Kraven: which one of these characters has never been a member of the Sinister Six?

11. Which comicbook series was born from a bet between Stan Lee and publisher Martin Goodman, after Goodman scoffed at Lee's bold claim that the new Marvel style could be applied to and benefit any genre of comic, even one with "a horrible title" and a dated WWII theme?

12. What's the first thing Mary Jane Watson ever says to Peter Parker?

13. What are the alliterative real names of Marvel supervillains Doctor Octopus, The Lizard, The Leader and The Absorbing Man?

14. Rather than clarifying every last detail with exhaustive scripts and layouts, Stan Lee would either hand his artists a synopsis, or even just talk them through a story, then leave them to create its art. "I never restricted them or said they had to follow what I gave them to the letter," said Lee, who'd write the dialogue and captions at the very end of the process to suit the finished art. What did this innovative practice come to be called?

15. Hulk is to Smash what Thing is to…?

16. Those who've studied their cosmic history understand the Silver Surfer heralds the arrival of which planet-consuming cosmic entity?

17. *The Fantastic Four* #1 (November 1961), *The Incredible Hulk* #1 (May 1962), *The Amazing Spider-Man* #1 (March 1963) and *The X-Men* #1 (September 1963): Which is the odd one out?

18. Debuting in August 1967, what was Marvel's satirical "Comic Magazine for Non-Believers Who Hate Comic Magazines"?

19. "The publisher said if we gave him more action and treated him like a normal superhero, sales would pick up," said Stan Lee. "I didn't want to change him, so I said, let's just drop the book." Which hero's comicbook did Lee cancel rather than change?

20. In *The Amazing Spider-Man* #1 (March 1963), why does Spidey break into the Fantastic Four's headquarters and then pick a fight?

21. Who, in 1963, designed and first drew Iron Man's original, cumbersome suit of armour, and what artist streamlined it into a slick red and gold affair later that same year?

22. While freelancing for DC in the 1960s, what artist drew Marvel's *Tales to Astonish* and *Tales of Suspense* on the side, under the pseudonym Adam Austin, later joining Marvel full-time, under his real name, to work on Captain America, Dr. Strange and Daredevil?

23. What was Stan Lee's original title for The X-Men?

24. While holidaying in windy Norway, frail Doctor Don Blake flees in terror from invading aliens, stumbling into a cave where he discovers a gnarled wooden stick that he strikes against a boulder in frustration. What reaction does this provoke?

GUEST STAR: Fabian Nicieza

Co-creator of Deadpool and X-Force, writer on *X-Men*, *New Warriors*, *Cable* & *Deadpool*, *Thunderbolts* and lots more!

25. Who was the first African-American character to regularly appear in a Marvel Comic?

26. "I think they're the greatest team in comics ever," said artist John Buscema of which legendary partnership?

27. Who is mankind's only hope against The Toad Men?

28. Which two superhero series debuted in September 1963, and what were their original line-ups?

29. Complete these three crazy Dr. Strange incantations:

A) By the ***** ***** of Hoggoth!
B) By the ******** ***** of Watoomb!
C) By the **** ***** of Raggadorr!

30. What could readers hope to win if they spotted an error in a Marvel comic and wrote to tell Stan Lee about it?

31. During their first encounter with Doctor Doom in *The Fantastic Four #5* (July 1962), Doom holds The Invisible Girl hostage so the others will do his bidding. To secure Sue's safe return, what does he demand of Reed, Johnny and Ben?

32. What was the title of Henry Pym's debut adventure in *Tales to Astonish #27* (January 1962)?

33. "Slowly, the figure speaks...In a voice which is not a voice... Mouthing words which are more than words...Expressing thoughts no mortal has ever gleaned before!" What momentous Marvel meeting does this grand caption precede?

34. What grand comicbook occasion did Stan Lee describe as "the world's most colossal collection of costumed characters, crazily cavorting and capering in continual combat!"?

35. Who was the first supervillain faced by Spider-Man?

36. Whose early adventures involved scuffles with the likes of The Absorbing Man, The Wrecker, The Destroyer, Lava Man, Radioactive Man, Mister Hyde, The Enchantress and The Grey Gargoyle?

37. What is Daredevil's signature weapon and which key function was added by artist Wally Wood in *Daredevil* #7 (April 1965)?

38. Jack Kirby's original concept art for Black Panther revealed that he and Stan Lee originally had a very different name in mind for the character. What was it?

39. Who are The Fantastic Four and what are their superhero names?

GUEST STAR: Rob Bruce

Comic Book Man, pop culturalist and co-founder of the New Jersey Horror Con.

40. Before he turned green, The Incredible Hulk was originally what colour?

41. What was Stan Lee's real name?

42. Mister Fantastic, Spider-Man, Iron Man, Daredevil: who's the odd one out?

43. Where in the world was Tony Stark injured, and by whom was he subsequently captured, triggering the creation of Iron Man, in his original origin tale?

44. What were Stan "The Man" Lee's nicknames for Jim Steranko, Jack Kirby and John Buscema?

45. How do The Fantastic Four acquire their powers?

46. Dormammu, Kingpin, Loki, Magneto: rearrange this alphabetical list of classic supervillains in order of their arrival in the Marvel Universe.

47. Best known for creating Golden Age antihero Namor the Sub-Mariner (*Marvel Comics* #1, October 1939), and co-creating Daredevil (*Daredevil* #1, April 1964) with Stan Lee, writer/artist "Wild" Bill Everett was a descendant of which iconoclastic English poet and artist?

48. After fooling the Skrulls into cancelling their first invasion by showing them clippings of monsters from old Marvel comics and convincing them those horrors awaited them on Earth, how does Reed Richards deal with the three remaining Skrulls left stranded among the humans?

49. Which three Marvel heroes might you bump into in Queens, Hell's Kitchen and Greenwich Village?

50. After Peter Parker dumps his Spidey costume in the trash in angsty Stan Lee/John Romita Sr. tale *Spider-Man No More*, an excited kid charges with it into J. Jonah Jameson's office, expecting a reward from the beaming newsman. What is he offered?

Answers on page 174

The Force is Strong with These Three: *Star Wars*/*Empire*/*Jedi*

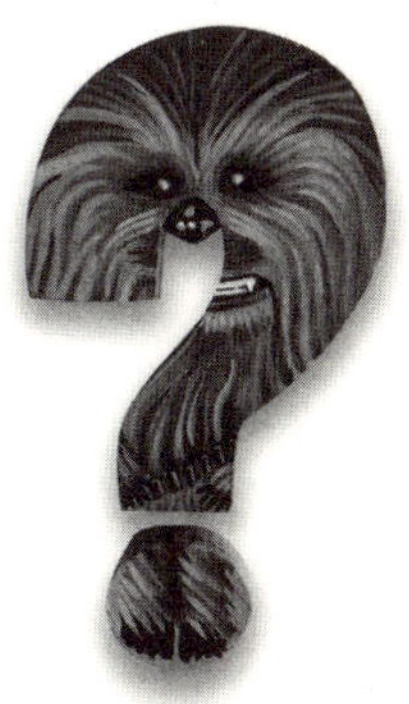

I was eight years old when *Star Wars* (1977) enslaved my generation. And by *Star Wars* I mean the first and finest film in the long-running franchise. The first third of the greatest trilogy ever filmed. The most perfect and personally meaningful movie ever made. The film that, back in the Seventies, we simply called *Star Wars*. Not *Episode IV*. Not *A New Hope*. Just *Star Wars*. So please, when I say *Star Wars*, don't ask me, "Which one?"

Star Wars opened our eyes as to what movies were capable of. Filled our dreams with robots, aliens and space travel. Excited us more than a night alone in Hamleys – "The Most Expensive Toy Store on Earth" – ever could. We wore the t-shirts, hung the posters and played with the action figures, which we tore from their packaging without a second thought and played with until they were worn and clearly loved.

Also, obviously, we returned to the cinema with religious devotion, seeing the movie over and over until we knew every creature by name, the layout of every ship and every line of dialogue – down to R2-D2's distinctive bleeps and blurps – by heart. *The Empire Strikes Back* (1980) and *Return of the Jedi* (1983) we likewise dedicated our childhoods to. No disrespect to the Father, the Son and the Holy Spirit, but these three films were our Holy Trinity, and man, our faith could move mountains.

In terms of what those movies mean to my generation, I can only equate their impact with such profound, life-changing events as cavemen stumbling across fire for the first time, the invention of grilled cheese sandwiches and how it must have felt for that audience of naïve 19th-century clucks who, according to urban legend, ran screaming from the screen when the train fast approached them in the Lumière brothers' plainly titled short film *Train Pulling into a Station* (1896).

For the record, the questions below strictly relate to the original theatrical releases of *Star Wars*, *The Empire Strikes Back* and *Return of the Jedi*.

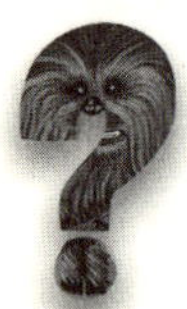

1. What's the name of Lucasfilm's special effects division?

2. Name any three of the six bounty hunters hired by the Empire to hunt Luke, Han and Leia.

3. Name two lifeforms indigenous to Hoth.

4. To throw fans and press off the scent, *Return of the Jedi* was shot under what false title?

5. Right up until the first day of filming *Star Wars*, what was Luke Skywalker's (Mark Hamill) original surname?

6. Which of Luke's (Mark Hamill) hands gets sliced off by Darth Vader?

7. Where, on Tatooine, does the Sarlacc reside?

8. How does Obi-Wan Kenobi describe Mos Eisley Spaceport to Luke?

9. What does Yoda have in common with Miss Piggy and Albert Einstein?

GUEST STAR: Mark Hamill

Star of *Star Wars, The Empire Strikes Back, Return of the Jedi* and the voice of The Joker in *Batman: The Animated Series* (1992–1994) and various spin-offs.

10. What's the first thing Luke ever said to Leia?

11. Who's taller – Peter Mayhew or David Prowse?

12. Who says "I have a bad feeling about this" in *Star Wars, Empire* and *Jedi*?

13. Which of George Lucas' filmmaker friends insisted on editing the text of *Star Wars*' iconic opening crawl?

14. Two of the asteroids in the asteroid sequence were a potato and a shoe: True or false?

15. What was the original title of *Return of the Jedi*, and why did George Lucas change it?

16. Dave Prowse's heavy Bristol accent earned him what cruel but hilarious nickname from the crew and his fellow cast mates?

17. How did Peter Mayhew win the role of Chewbacca? Also, what was his profession prior to being cast?

18. It took three actors to play Darth Vader in *Return of the Jedi*. Who were they, and what was their contribution?

19. What's unusual about a Tatooine sunset?

20. Meco's disco version of John Williams' *Star Wars* score, matter-of-factly titled "Star Wars Theme and Cantina Band", is the third best-selling instrumental single of all time: True or false?

21. How many times is Luke (Mark Hamill) upside down in *The Empire Strikes Back*?

22. What's the name of the *Star Wars* simulator ride that's been a staple at Disney parks since 1987?

23. Famously uncommunicative as a director, while shooting *Star Wars*, George Lucas guided his actors with which two stock phrases?

24. A, B, D, X, Y: Which is the odd one out?

GUEST STAR: Bonnie Burton

Author of *The Star Wars Craft Book*, *You Can Draw: Star Wars*, *Crafting With Feminism* and founder of Grrl.com.

25. Which well-known actor from Eighties' TV sitcom *Cheers* made an appearance in *The Empire Strikes Back*?

26. Fish-faced rebel hero Admiral Ackbar (Tim Rose/Erik Bauersfeld) is a member of which species?

27. Why was TK-421 (Stephen Bayley) not at his post?

28. The day Mark Hamill filmed the scene where Luke makes it out of his snowspeeder just before it's crushed by an Imperial Walker was particularly memorable for the actor for what two reasons?

29. Besides Luke (Mark Hamill), only one other X-Wing pilot survives all three movies. Who's the character and the actor who played him?

30. What's the first line spoken in *Star Wars*, and who delivers it?

31. What's the name of Darth Vader's (David Prowse/James Earl Jones) flagship destroyer in *The Empire Strikes Back*?

32. Which two *Star Wars* cast members have won Academy Awards, and what for?

33. Although "It's a trap" is famously Admiral Ackbar's (Tim Rose/Erik Bauersfeld) signature line in *Return of the Jedi*, it was spoken by which other character in which earlier movie?

34. How many languages does C-3PO (Anthony Daniels) speak?

35. Before landing the role of Lando Calrissian, Billy Dee Williams first auditioned for which role in *Star Wars*?

36. Which member of *Star Wars*' cast wore fluffy slippers while filming anything that didn't show his feet, and why?

37. Leia (Carrie Fisher) strangling Jabba (Larry Ward) in *Return of the Jedi* was a homage to which character's murder in what movie?

38. What's the name of the holographic chess game played by Chewbacca (Peter Mayhew) and the droids aboard the *Millennium Falcon* in *Star Wars*?

39. Where's Cloud City and what's mined there?

GUEST STAR: Ben Palmer

One of Europe's leading conductors of films in concert, including *Jurassic Park*, *E.T.*, *Raiders of the Lost Ark*, *Jaws*, *Home Alone* and *Star Wars*.

40. The recording of Alfred Newman's "20th Century Fox Fanfare" which opened *Star Wars* was borrowed from the soundtrack of which 1954 western?

41. What are Darth Vader's (Sebastian Shaw) final words in *Return of the Jedi*?

42. "Staggering as spectacle and technically brilliant, exciting, very noisy and warm-hearted. The battle scenes at the end go on for five minutes too long, and some of the dialogue is excruciating and much of it is lost in noise, but it remains a vivid experience." Which member of *Star Wars*' cast described the film this way?

43. Who owned the *Millennium Falcon* before Han Solo?

44. How far apart were the US and UK cinema releases of *Star Wars*?

45. Who's a feisty little one?

46. What does the TIE in TIE Fighter stand for?

47. Who directed each of the three original movies?

48. George Lucas accepted a lower salary for making *Star Wars* in exchange for what two requests that, at the time, seemed like small potatoes to Fox executives eager to save money on a film they were convinced would fail?

49. What was the name of the Official *Star Wars* Fan Club's newsletter?

50. Who shot first?

Answers on page 184

DOCTOR WHO: THE TOM BAKER YEARS

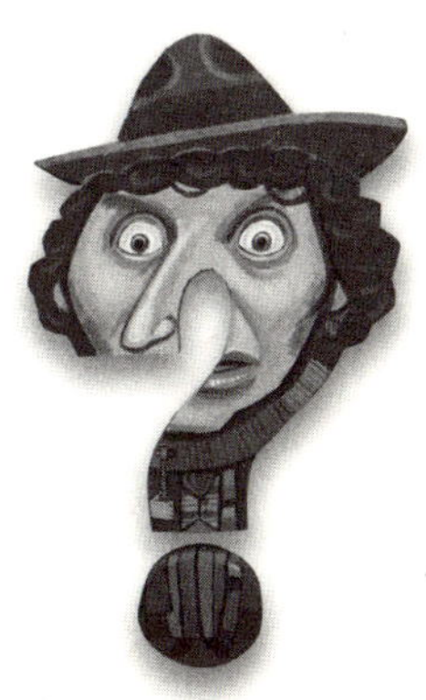

"Would you care for a jelly baby?"

I cared. I cared very much. I would have loved for the Doctor to give me a jelly baby. I would have loved it even more if he'd invited me into the TARDIS for a tour, and maybe swept me off on an adventure or two alongside Sarah and Harry. What fun that would have been.

I thought about that a lot when I was five years old, and Baker's Doctor was new to TV. I'd sit on the floor right in front of the telly, my face not a foot from the screen, and watch with wide-eyed wonder as my hero, and his loyal companions, dashed about, forever saving time and space.

My brothers – all much older than me – often teased me while I watched the programme, as they knew I believed it was real. That it was, in fact, some incredible documentary series, and nothing they ever said convinced me otherwise.

My glorious delusion reached its peak several months into 1975, when my father, who owned a chain of clothes shops called Austin's Menswear, opened a grand new store and, to pull in the punters and wring some plugs from the papers, hired my hero to make the mother of all personal appearances.

When we arrived at the shop, a crowd had already gathered outside. And no wonder, because there was the TARDIS, parked in the street for all to see. And suddenly, there too was the Doctor, waving to everyone from the roof, flashing that famous, infectious smile of his, dressed exactly as he did in the documentaries I watched him in every Saturday night.

Inside, later, I stood beside him and, gazing worshipfully as he signed autographs, asked him question after question about his incredible adventures. Where had he been before he came to my dad's shop? How difficult was it to drive the TARDIS? Where were Sarah and Harry? And didn't he ever get hot wearing that scarf?

The shop was heaving with people, all eager to snatch a moment with the Doctor, and yet there I was, glued to his side, conducting my first interview. I remember him looking at me, then the crowd, and then shrugging, booming to the room, "WHO IS THIS KID?!" It was all very good-natured, of course, and I didn't mind when everyone burst out laughing. I rather enjoyed the attention, to be honest. And the Doctor was just as wonderful as I'd anticipated. It was pretty much the most magical thing that could ever have happened to a kid, and a memory I wouldn't trade for anything.

Though I don't remember when, the time eventually arrived, of course, when I had to concede he was an actor, but it didn't make me love him any less. Far from it. Baker's Doctor was a glowing presence in my childhood. I learned from him, and his jelly babies, his mischievous grin and his sparkling eyes, that getting older didn't necessarily mean you had to grow up. That playing, embracing silliness and finding joy in life need never take a back seat to more traditional adult pursuits.

No one ever had more fun, in the entire history of fun, than Tom Baker did while playing the Doctor. Gosh, that inspired me.

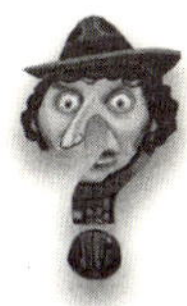

1. What role, in which movie, convinced producer Barry Letts that Tom Baker was the right man to succeed Jon Pertwee?

2. To supplement his meagre earnings as an actor, what was Tom Baker doing for work when he was cast as the Doctor?

3. Which of his companions did Baker's Doctor call "a clumsy, ham-fisted idiot"?

4. In which story did John Cleese and Eleanor Bron guest star as art critics who mistake the TARDIS for modern art?

5. What episode of which serial saw the very first appearance of Baker's fourth Doctor?

6. What is the name of the Experimental Prototype Robot built by Professor J.P. Kettlewell (Edward Burnham) in "Robot" (Season 12, Serial 1, 1974–1975)?

7. What was Tom Baker's only two-part *Doctor Who* serial?

8. What was the real-life reason for the Doctor banging his face on the TARDIS's console in "The Pirate Planet" (Season 16, Serial 2, 1978)?

9. When the script for "The Face of Evil" (Season 14, Serial 4) called for the Doctor to threaten one of the tribesmen with a weapon, Tom Baker objected. What did he use instead?

10. Which serial saw the first appearance of K9 and how many actors have voiced the character?

11. What was the name of the unproduced film Baker wrote with co-star Ian Marter during breaks in filming *Doctor Who*?

12. What's the final line spoken in "Genesis of the Daleks" (Season 12, Serial 4, 1975)?

13. In which serial did Tom Baker don an Inverness cape and deerstalker hat, foreshadowing his later role as Sherlock Holmes in a BBC TV adaptation of *The Hound of the Baskervilles* (1982)?

14. "The Ark in Space" (Season 12, Serial 2, 1975), "The Sontaran Experiment" (Season 12, Serial 3, 1975) and "The Ribos Operation" (Season 16, Serial 1, 1978): Which is the odd one out?

GUEST STAR: Louise Jameson

Best known for playing Leela in *Doctor Who* from 1977 to 1978. Also starred in *Tenko* (aired 1981–1984), *Bergerac* (1981–1991) and *EastEnders* (1985–present).

15. In which story did Leela's eyes transform from brown to blue? Also, what was the real-life reason behind the change?

16. The fourth and final part of which Tom Baker serial had the largest viewing figures for any episode of *Doctor Who* in the history of the series?

17. "We were deliriously happy for weeks," said Tom Baker of his short-lived marriage to which of his *Doctor Who* co-stars?

18. It's revealed, in "The Deadly Assassin" (Season 14, Serial 3, 1976), that the Doctor belongs to which Gallifreyan Chapter?

19. What six serials comprised Season 16's "Key to Time" arc?

20. Who does the Doctor say made his signature scarf? Also, how does he describe her?

21. Sometimes when the Doctor was required to rattle off TARDIS coordinates, Tom Baker would recite what real-life number?

22. In "The Stones of Blood" (Season 16, Serial 3, 1978), after Romana (Mary Tamm) casually tells K9 to "forget it" in response to a question, what does K9 remove all knowledge of from his memory banks?

23. Tom Baker's final serial as the Doctor, "Logopolis" (Season 18, Serial 7, 1981), was the first serial for which companion?

24. Actor Michael Spice menaced Baker's fourth Doctor as the eponymous villains of which two serials?

25. What was Begonia Pope's wonderful mistake?

26. "The Deadly Assassin" (Season 14, Serial 3, 1976) was the first and only televised series in the show's original run to ditch which key *Doctor Who* element?

27. What is Romana I's (Mary Tamm) full name, and how does the Doctor respond, in "The Ribos Operation" (Season 16, Serial 1, 1978), when she uses it to introduce herself?

28. What was the final piece of the Key to Time disguised as?

29. What was the name of the French cabaret singer, comedian and nightclub owner who inspired the fourth Doctor's bohemian look? Also, who painted his famous portraits?

GUEST STAR: Dave Johns

Veteran stand-up comedian and actor best known for playing the title role in Palme d'Or-winning drama *I, Daniel Blake* (2016).

30. Which three actors played the Master during Tom Baker's era?

31. What's the only *Doctor Who* television serial to feature a Rutan? Also, who are their mortal enemies?

32. Which writer penned three *Doctor Who* serials, all for Tom Baker's Doctor, and all broadcast in 1977?

33. According to the 1980 Prime Computer commercial featuring Tom Baker and Lalla Ward, how long is the Doctor's scarf?

34. What pocket universe is the Doctor trapped in after the TARDIS accidentally passes through a Charged Vacuum Emboitement?

35. "[He] found it physically impossible to buy a drink. He liked the idea of big sums of money for voiceovers, so I would say in [his] earshot that someone had offered me £15,000 for a voiceover, but I turned it down because it was going to take a whole hour. This wasn't true, but I could hear [his] heart pounding. In fact, he died of a heart attack shortly after that. I think that's why." Who is Tom Baker talking about?

36. What English synth-pop band released the instrumental tribute track "Tom Baker" in 1981?

37. What unflattering string of adjectives does Romana I (Mary Tamm) hurl at the Doctor in "The Armageddon Factor" (Season 16, Serial 6, 1979)?

38. What's the last thing Sarah Jane (Elisabeth Sladen) says to the Doctor when they finally part company at the end of "The Hand of Fear" (Season 14, Serial 2, 1976)?

39. What is the Doctor's term for robophobia, mentioned in "The Robots of Death" (Season 14, Serial 5, 1977)?

40. Season 16 of *Doctor Who* saw the series celebrate which trio of major milestones?

41. In which *Doctor Who* serial is Davros (Michael Wisher) introduced?

42. Which author wrote "The Pirate Planet" (Season 16, Serial 2, 1978) while simultaneously pitching what additional project about characters who, like the Doctor, tool through time and space?

43. Who is the last of the Osirans? Also, what gift does he have for humanity, in "Pyramids of Mars" (Season 13, Serial 3, 1975)?

44. Which part of the Doctor does mad scientist Mehendri Solon (Philip Madoc) want to complete his Frankensteinian creation with in "The Brain of Morbius" (Season 13, Serial 5, 1976)?

45. What colour jelly baby is the Doctor's favourite?

46. What sad, real-life event occurred between the original UK broadcast of episodes' one and two of "Revenge of the Cybermen" (Season 12, Serial 5, 1975)?

47. "Some of the stories of my era were latched onto as being more frightening, but I don't think we ever overstepped the mark. The ratings were very high, [so] people seemed to like it." Which real-life *Doctor Who* hero is speaking here?

48. How many series, serials and episodes comprise Tom Baker's record-setting run as the Doctor?

49. Which companions were with Tom Baker's Doctor when he regenerated?

50. Two years after quitting the show, Tom Baker agreed to appear in its 20th-anniversary special, "The Five Doctors" (1983). When he later changed his mind, how did producer John Nathan-Turner compensate for his absence, both in the special itself, and the accompanying publicity photocall?

Answers on page 191

JOHN CARPENTER'S APOCALYPSE TRILOGY

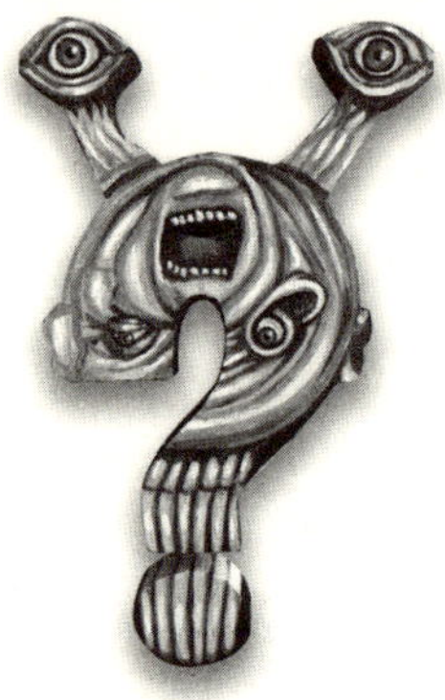

Besides eternal nothingness, what frightens a lot of us about death is the notion that we might face it alone. In this regard, John Carpenter's darkest films provide, perhaps, an odd sort of comfort as they suggest that regardless of whether the end comes via science, superstition or some unholy union of the two, we're all going to die together. Yay!

"I suppose my fascination with apocalyptic films started when I was growing up in the 1950s," reflects Carpenter. "Regardless of what you've heard, the Fifties were insane. Everyone was insane. And I was just a little kid trying to make sense of it all.

"The first thing that happened to me was I went to school in an era when they still read the Bible to you. They started in first grade, reading it to us every day until, by the third grade, they got to Revelation, and it was the most confusing thing I'd ever heard in my life. The imagery was sensational, and I was mesmerised by it, but what the hell was going on? I didn't understand it and I still don't, but it got me fascinated with the end of things."

As the name suggests, the trio of films that John Carpenter now considers his Apocalypse Trilogy – 1982's *The Thing*, 1987's *Prince of Darkness* and 1994's *In the Mouth of Madness* – are about the end of things. Regardless of their differences, it's a theme that bonds these classic horrors tightly together.

"By end of things," clarifies the filmmaker, "I don't just mean the end of a character. I'm talking about the end of everything: The world we know and all life on it. Each of my movies offers a very different take on the end."

It's an end that could easily arrive, apparently, independent of extra-terrestrial intervention, or the evil machinations of Great, Old Lovecraftian Gods.

"The second thing about the Fifties that pointed me in the direction of my Apocalypse Trilogy was the atomic bomb. I found out that human beings have the capacity to destroy ourselves. Somebody could push a button and these missiles would rain down on us. That got me really upset and thinking about the end."

Best hurry up now and get on with the quiz as who knows how much time we have left?

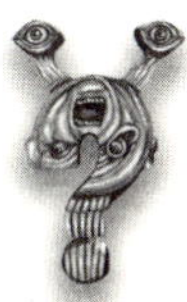

1. According to *The Thing*'s MacReady (Kurt Russell), what's a hard thing to come by these days?

2. According to Brian (Jameson Parker) in *Prince of Darkness*, what's a hard thing to come by these days?

3. According to *In the Mouth of Madness*'s Simon (Wilhelm von Homburg), what's not what it used to be?

4. *The Thing* was the first of John Carpenter's feature films not to be at least co-scored by the director. Who composed the soundtrack instead?

5. What's the first shot in *Prince of Darkness*?

6. Immediately after being thrown into his asylum cell in *In the Mouth of Madness*, Trent (Sam Neill) issues what desperate apology to the limping orderly?

7. Who shoots the trigger-happy Norwegian who storms into camp chasing the dog, in *The Thing*?

8. On the subatomic level, what does Professor Birack (Victor Wong) say classical reality collapses into, in *Prince of Darkness*?

9. What single item does Trent (Sam Neill) ask for in the asylum? Also, what does he use it for, in *In the Mouth of Madness*?

GUEST STAR: John Carpenter

The one and only! Director of *Dark Star* (1974), *Assault on Precinct 13* (1976), *Halloween* (1978), *The Fog* (1980), *Escape From New York* (1981), *The Thing* (1982), *Christine* (1983), *Big Trouble in Little China* (1986), *Prince of Darkness* (1987), *They Live* (1988), *In the Mouth of Madness* (1994) and more besides.

10. *The Thing* was shot on the Juneau icefields adjacent to what glacier?

11. What cartoon does Walter (Dennis Dun) watch in the kitchen in *Prince of Darkness*?

12. What's the name of Sutter Cane's (Jürgen Prochnow) publisher in *In the Mouth of Madness*?

13. Who delivers the first line of dialogue in *The Thing*?

14. What does Etchinson (Thom Bray) see at the foot of the alley stairs, shortly before being impaled by the Street Schizo (Alice Cooper), in *Prince of Darkness*?

15. According to Sutter Cane's (Jürgen Prochnow) editor Linda (Julie Carmen), what effect has his writing been known to have on his less stable readers?

16. According to Dr Blair's (Wilford Brimley) computer projection, how long would it take for the entire world to be infected after *The Thing*'s intruder organism reaches civilised areas?

17. What year is the dream broadcast from in *Prince of Darkness*?

18. Where does Trent (Sam Neill) believe the map he made from Sutter Cane (Jürgen Prochnow) book covers will lead, in *In the Mouth of Madness*?

19. What two characters, from which two movies in John Carpenter's Apocalypse Trilogy, wake from a dream, though really they're still dreaming, and it takes another scare to actually wake them from their dream?

20. What was *The Thing*'s primary source material?

21. Why did John Carpenter write the screenplay for *Prince of Darkness* under the pseudonym Martin Quatermass?

22. *The Thing*'s ruined Norwegian camp set cost more to build than the film's main American camp: True or false?

23. Where would *The Thing*'s Garry (Donald Moffat) rather not spend the rest of the winter?

24. According to Trent (Sam Neill) in *In the Mouth of Madness*, what should one never, never, never do?

GUEST STAR: Sandy King

Script supervisor on *Prince of Darkness* (1987) and *They Live* (1988), producer of *In the Mouth of Madness* (1994), *Village of the Damned* (1995), *Vampires* (1998) and *Ghosts of Mars* (2001). Also married to John Carpenter since 1990.

25. What actor first worked with John Carpenter on *Prince of Darkness* before appearing in six more of his films?

26. What attacks the villagers outside the Black Church after Simon (Wilhelm von Homburg) angrily demands the return of his son?

27. What's MacReady's (Kurt Russell) job at U.S. Outpost 31 in *The Thing*?

28. What's the name of the secret sect who for centuries kept the lid on Satan, the Anti-God and Alien Jesus in *Prince of Darkness*?

29. What's under the counter at reception in the Pickman Hotel, in *In the Mouth of Madness*?

30. *The Thing* was released on the same day as which other sci-fi favourite, a film that was likewise poorly reviewed but is regarded by many as a classic?

31. What's on the crazy Bag Lady's (Joanna Merlin) face when Professor Birack (Victor Wong) first notices her? Also, what's in her cup when she hassles the Priest (Donald Pleasence), in *Prince of Darkness*?

32. What film's playing on the TV in Trent's (Sam Neill) motel room after he flees Hobb's End in *In the Mouth of Madness*?

33. Who's the only U.S. Outpost 31 crew member killed by a human in *The Thing*?

34. How is Susan (Anne Howard) repeatedly described in *Prince of Darkness*?

35. Name any three of the seven Sutter Cane (Jürgen Prochnow) books featured in *In the Mouth of Madness*.

36. What song is Nauls (T.K. Carter) listening to when George (Peter Maloney) grumpily complains about the noise, in *The Thing*?

37. What phrase does Calder (Jessie Lawrence Ferguson) watch Lisa (Ann Yen) type repeatedly in *Prince of Darkness*?

38. Though the lion's share of *The Thing*'s iconic make-up effects were created by Rob Bottin, who stepped in to make the nightmarish "Kennel-Thing" when Bottin was briefly hospitalised with exhaustion?

39. "I've got a message for you and you're not going to like it…" What's the message? Also, do they like it, in *Prince of Darkness*?

GUEST STAR: Sam Neill

Star of *Dead Calm* (1989), *Memoirs of an Invisible Man* (1992), *Jurassic Park* (1993), *In the Mouth of Madness* (1994) and much more besides.

40. While making *In the Mouth of Madness*, who thought that playing The Carpenters' music all day and night would be a good maddening idea in the madhouse?

41. How many spider-like legs burst from the head-thing in *The Thing*?

42. What's the name of the abandoned LA church where the horror happens in *Prince of Darkness*?

43. Which member of the crew is revealed as The Thing during the tense blood test sequence?

44. What's written on the cinema marquee in Linda's (Julie Carmen) vision, and again later, when Trent goes to the movies, in *In the Mouth of Madness*?

45. Though long regarded as a classic, and of all his films, John Carpenter's personal favourite, *The Thing*'s original critical reception was frosty at best. Who cruelly dismissed the movie out of hand, saying, "If you want blood, go to the slaughter-house. All in all, it's a terrific commercial for J&B Scotch."

46. Which parts of Satan's body does the Priest (Donald Pleasence) hack off in *Prince of Darkness*?

47. What's the inscription on the doors of the Black Church in *In the Mouth of Madness*?

48. How long does Vance (Charles Hallahan) estimate the crashed alien spaceship has been in the ice, in *The Thing*?

49. How many people make it out of the church alive at the end of *Prince of Darkness*?

50. What is Sutter Cane's (Jürgen Prochnow) favourite colour, in *In the Mouth of Madness*?

Answers on page 201

THE 2600: ATARI'S ELECTRIC DREAM

In the beginning Nolan Bushnell and Ted Dabney created Atari, Inc.

And the Earth was without arcades; and quite dull; and darkness was upon the face of geeks.

And they said, Let there be Pong: and there was Pong.

And they played Pong, and it was good; and it divided nerds from their quarters.

And Atari created a home version; and the word good barely did it justice: more like divine.

And everyone who plugged Pong into their TV sets, for the first time experiencing godlike control of the image that appeared on their screens, went, Whoa; this is freaking cool!

And cool it freaking was; and a cool new faith was born.

Cut to: London, Christmas, 1982. I was 13 years old and though I don't remember being particularly good that year, I guess I pulled the furry trim over Santa's eyes because come December

25, he left me an Atari 2600 – the console previously known as the Atari VCS. It was the "woody" unit with the four front switches that was designed to look more like furniture than a console or computer.

Besides the copy of *Combat* that came in the box, I got *Adventure*, *Asteroids* and *Outlaw*, and if you think I spent more than five minutes with my family from the moment I tore the paper off that iconic box, until that cold January morning in 1983 when I was dragged back to school, you're bloody mad.

Atari's console changed everything. It was, for the longest time, everything. Though today it might seem quaint and unsophisticated, to me it was a portal into worlds that, the occasional visit to an arcade aside, I'd mainly only experienced passively before. But here, now, I was jetting, nay pew-pewing through space; slaying dragons in mazes loaded with treasure; squaring off against friends in ground, air and cowboy-themed combat, and really just having the time of my life.

1. Which VCS launch game was an unofficial port of 1976 arcade hit *Blockade*, the grandfather of all Snake games?

2. What flag flies in the centre of John Enright's cover art for 1978 strategy game *Flag Capture*?

3. Name any five of the nine Atari VCS launch games.

4. What are the names of the four ghosts in *Ms. Pac-Man* (1982)?

5. What classic 1982 game was recognised by *Softline* magazine as having "earned the ominous distinction of being the game with the most ways to die"? Ways you could croak included being run over on a busy motorway, drowning in a river, being eaten by alligators or riding a log off the side of the screen.

6. How many option switches were at the front of the first manufactured version of the Atari VCS? Also, what were they for?

7. *Video Olympics* (1977) offered 50 variants of which classic game, first produced by Atari in 1972?

8. How much did you have to win to break the bank in *Blackjack* (1977)?

9. The Atari VCS originally shipped with which game and accessories?

10. "The controls of this game may be a little more complicated than the actual problems," wrote *Video Magazine* of which VCS launch game?

11. What are the three main vehicles featured in *Combat* (1977)?

12. What was the North American launch date of the Atari VCS?

13. How many balls could you end up playing with at once in the cavity game mode of *Super Breakout* (1978)?

14. What colour dragon is featured in Susan Jaekel's iconic box art for *Adventure* (1979)? Also, what is it holding?

15. Which three of the Man of Steel's powers are used in 1979 adventure *Superman*?

16. What's the famous Easter egg hidden in *Adventure* (1979)?

17. In wacky 1980 comedy hit *Airplane!* instead of watching their monitors, flight controllers are seen playing which Atari VCS sports game?

18. Which title for the Atari VCS was the first official license of an arcade game?

19. What company was the first third-party software producer for the Atari VCS? Also, name any two of their first four games for the system.

20. How did Atari reward game programmer Rob Furlop for developing the wildly successful VCS port of *Missile Command* (1981)?

21. What game for the Atari VCS was the first to use bank switching, a technique that increased available ROM space from 4 KB to 8 KB?

22. Which two-dimensional, side-scrolling shooter was originally envisioned as a version of *Space Invaders* rotated 90 degrees?

23. When, and why, did Atari change the name of the Atari VCS to the Atari 2600?

24. How much RAM did the Atari 2600 have?

GUEST STAR: Dominik Diamond

TV and radio presenter best known for hosting *GamesMaster* (1992–1998), the first show in the UK dedicated to videogames and gamers.

25. What Atari 2600 game had a T-shaped plunger handle and is so rare a copy sold in 2012 for $33,000?

2600. What was the name of *Berzerk*'s (1982) Big Bad, a bouncing smiley face who couldn't be killed?

27. How many hits does it take to completely destroy a mushroom in *Centipede* (1982)?

28. What was the best-selling Atari 2600 game of all time?

29. What would appear when you reached the roof of every skyscraper in *Crazy Climber* (1982)?

30. What was the name of the five-part miniature comicbook, written by Gerry Conway and Roy Thomas, that in 1982 was included in the boxes for Atari 2600 cartridges *Berzerk*, *Defender*, *Galaxian*, *Phoenix* and *Star Raiders*?

31. Mutated houseflies defend their world against an alien attacker in which Atari 2600 game named after Atari CEO Ray Kassar?

32. *Beat 'Em & Eat 'Em*, *Bachelor Party*, *Jawbreaker* and *Custer's Revenge*: Which one of these 1982 third-party releases for the Atari 2600 is the odd one out?

33. What is generally considered to be the very worst Atari 2600 game in the console's history, arguably the worst videogame of all time, a cautionary tale about studio interference and the dangers of rushed development?

34. When *Pitfall* was first released in 1982, players scoring over 20,000 points could win a prize from Activision by sending the developers a photo of themselves and their score on TV. What were they sent in return?

35. Released by Activision in 1982, what vertically-scrolling shooter was the first videogame banned for minors in West Germany by the Federal Department for Writings Harmful to Young Persons?

36. How was the player represented in *Haunted House* (1982), one of the earliest examples of a survival horror videogame?

37. What were the names of the three released *Swordquest* games and the unreleased fourth adventure?

38. What was the in-house name for the Atari VCS while it was in development?

39. What was the first space-related game for the Atari VCS?

40. What was the first licensed *Star Wars* videogame, a scrolling shooter for the 2600 described by science fiction author Harlan Ellison as a "time-wasting" and "shamelessly exploitative little toy" with "the potential to emerge as the most virulent electronic botulism of all"?

41. When was the Atari 2600 finally released in Japan, and what was it called?

42. What game saw an eccentric hopping hero menaced by Slick, Sam, Ugg, Wrongway and Coily the snake?

43. What controversial horror game saw players chasing and murdering trespassers while avoiding such obstacles as wheelchairs and cow skulls?

44. What was the name of the 1983 game created by Atari exclusively for Coca-Cola to give to their top 125 sales executives?

45. What colours were the knights, and what creatures did they ride, in early co-op classic *Joust* (1983)?

46. How was 1983 US release *Taz* retooled and retitled for Europe?

47. The last official release for the 2600 in North America, what 1989 sci-fi adventure game was inspired by NES game-changer *The Legend of Zelda* (1987)?

48. What was the last official release for the Atari 2600?

49. When was the Atari 2600 formally discontinued?

50. How many Atari 2600 consoles were estimated to have been sold over the system's lifetime?

Answers on page 208

RETROFUTURISTIC: FIFTIES' SCI-FI CINEMA

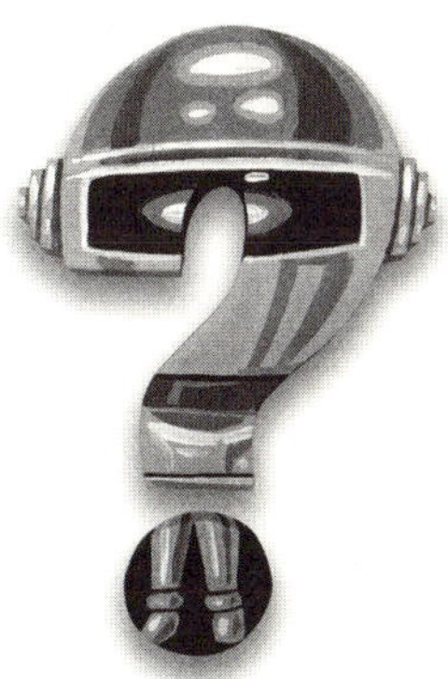

"Greetings my friends! We are all interested in the future, for that is where you and I are going to spend the rest of our lives!"

A lifetime ago, some 70 years, the Fifties happened. On the surface, God, mom, apple pie and Archie Comics. Lurking beneath though, EC Comics, Reds under the bed and atomic unknowns. And through it all, Hollywood, feeding on the zeitgeist and regurgitating all manner of wild amusements.

Imbued with the button-down values and saddled with the fearful concerns of the age they were made, yet likewise full of wonder and hope, 1950s' science-fiction movies countered meagre budgets and technical shortfalls with pluck, gumption and giant leaps of imagination.

Long before man got even a toe into space, Hollywood took us to the Moon, and beyond that, Mars, to square off against all manner of kooky, spooky alien invaders. It was a colourful age of ray guns and robots, of shiny flying saucers and radioactive mutations so terrifying that medical professionals were often required to mop the fevered brows of startled cinemagoers.

You watch those vintage movies, those cracked, outlandish classics, and they remind you how, as a kid, you dreamed of rocketing into space. Even today, given the chance, wouldn't you drop everything to explore infinity, and beyond? Our heads are already in the clouds. How much more would it take to nudge them past the exosphere?

You know what? I'm doing it. I'm packing my bags for Space Camp. I'm going to realise my astronaut dreams and live out my rocketship fantasies. Sure, I might not be the ideal candidate, and yes, I'll probably fall short of every measurable standard, and now that I think about it, I realise I probably lack the mental discipline, emotional control, scientific acumen, mathematic ability, raw courage, quick-wittedness, physical fitness and bendy dexterity required to advance through the space programme, but…Oh. Yeah… No. You know what? Maybe I'll just watch a bunch of old science fiction films instead.

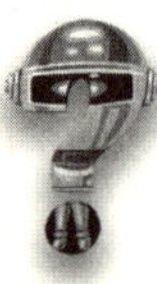

1. Where did "It" come from?

2. What trio of colours radiate from the Martians' electronic eye in *The War of the Worlds* (1953)?

3. What's the name of Captain Nemo's (James Mason) mighty vessel in the father of all steampunk sci-fi movies, *20,000 Leagues Under the Sea* (1954)?

4. What are the first signs of Scott Carey's (Grant Williams) dwindling stature in *The Incredible Shrinking Man* (1957)?

5. June 1956, in London's *Evening Standard* newspaper: "Shakespeare takes a journey into space" read the headline of Alan Brien's film review for which stellar sci-fi adventure?

6. "Please doctor, I've got to ask this," says Scotty (Douglas Spencer). "It sounds like, well, just as though you're describing some form of super carrot." What classic film gave birth to this immortal line?

7. To what event in *The Day the Earth Stood Still* (1951) does the title refer?

8. What's wrong with the title of George Pal's *When Worlds Collide* (1951)?

9. "Keep your eyes a little wide and blank. Show no interest or excitement..." When Miles (Kevin McCarthy) and Becky (Dana Wynter) hit the street, posing as Pod People, how does Becky immediately blow their cover, in *Invasion of the Body Snatchers* (1956)?

GUEST STAR: Neil Brand

Dramatist, composer and author, presenter of the BBC series' *Sound of Cinema: The Music that Made the Movies* (2013), *Sound of Song* (2015), *Sound of Musicals* (2017) and *Sound of Movie Musicals* (2018).

10. Bernard Herrmann famously used two theremins for *The Day the Earth Stood Still* (1951), but what was the concert instrument he also amplified electronically for the score?

11. What nourishes the rampaging extra-terrestrial vegetable man (James Arness) in *The Thing from Another World* (1951)?

12. Which visionary artist, dubbed the "Father of Modern Space Art", created special-effects art for George Pal's *Destination Moon* (1950), *When Worlds Collide* (1951), *The War of the Worlds* (1953) and *Conquest of Space* (1955)?

13. According to actor Ross Martin, why did the funeral sequence in *The Colossus of New York* (1958) have to be reshot?

14. Incorporating greater advances than hitherto known in the field of electronics, what's the name of the communication device that Cal (Rex Reason) and Joe (Robert Nichols) build in *This Island Earth* (1955)? Also, what's the secret purpose of the challenge?

15. What was designer Paul Blaisdell's nickname for the bizarre Venusian monster he fashioned for Roger Corman's *It Conquered the World* (1956)?

16. How were the effects guys able to simulate giant drops of water in *The Incredible Shrinking Man* (1957)?

17. In *Forbidden Planet* (1956), in the underground Krell laboratory, what is Morbius (Walter Pidgeon) able to conjure with the plastic educator?

18. What's the jaunty sea shanty sung by Ned Land (Kirk Douglas) in Disney's *20,000 Leagues Under the Sea* (1954)?

19. "When an armed and threatening power lands uninvited in our capitol," reasons General Edmunds (Grandon Rhodes) in *Earth vs. the Flying Saucers* (1956), "we don't meet him with..." What?

20. Years before making his name as a legendary filmmaker, who had a small role in *Invasion of the Body Snatchers* (1956) as Charlie the meter reader, also working on the movie as a dialogue coach?

21. Emblazoned across the movie poster for *It! The Terror from Beyond Space* (1958) was the eye-catching phrase, "$50,000 Guaranteed!" On closer inspection, how was one to earn this generous bounty?

22. According to Mac (Robert Nichols) in *The Thing from Another World* (1951), "The Air Force has discontinued investigating and evaluating reported flying saucers on the basis that there is no evidence", and that "reports of unidentified flying objects are the result of..." What three things?

23. Regarding the Martians, "Their senses could be quite different from ours," speculates Dr Forrester in *The War of the Worlds* (1953). "They may, for instance, be able to smell..." What?

24. What's unusual about the single-passenger Douglas DC3 plane that collects Cal (Rex Reason) to fly him to Exeter (Jeff Morrow), in *This Island Earth* (1955)?

GUEST STAR: Don Coscarelli

Writer/director of *Phantasm I–IV* (1979–1998), *The Beastmaster* (1982), *Bubba Ho Tep* (2002), *John Dies at the End* (2012) and lots more.

25. Which low-budget British creature invasion film was released in the States as *Enemy From Space* (1957)?

26. In *The Incredible Shrinking Man* (1957), what causes poor Scott Carey (Grant Williams) to shrink incredibly?

27. Why does Robby the Robot rarely partake of Altair IV's high oxygen content?

28. Long before the release of George Pal's *Destination Moon* (1950), a massive publicity campaign ensured the public were mad keen to see it. Taking advantage of the sudden national interest in space travel, indy producer Robert L. Lippert shot a low-budget sci-fi adventure in just 18 days and sneaked it into cinemas more than three weeks before the release of *Destination Moon*. What was the name of his cheeky film?

29. In *The Day the Earth Stood Still* (1951), what alien command does Klaatu (Michael Rennie) teach Helen (Patricia Neal), and why?

30. When Ned (Kirk Douglas) and Conseil (Peter Lorre) are pursued to the submarine by cannibals in *20,000 Leagues Under the Sea* (1954), how does Nemo (James Mason) repel them?

31. In *Invasion of the Body Snatchers* (1956), what does the pod person who replaces Dan Kauffman (Larry Gates) insist that life is so much simpler without?

32. The first score for a mainstream film performed entirely by electronic instruments, Louis and Bebe Barron's soundtrack for *Forbidden Planet* (1956) confused and upset the Musician's Union. As the Barrons didn't belong to the union, they were blocked from being credited as composers on the movie. How were they credited instead?

33. It creeps...It crawls...It strikes without warning! What is it?

34. Shot in four days on a shoestring budget, *Robot Monster* (1953) told the angry tale of Ro-Man Extension XJ-2 (George Barrows), an evil robot from the Moon with a dream of killing all humans. Although notable for its Elmer Bernstein score, and unexpectedly decent 3-D photography, it is perhaps best known for its thrown-together robot costume consisting of what two elements?

35. What does the last wire photo out of Paris depict in *The War of the Worlds* (1953)?

36. In *The Incredible Shrinking Man* (1957), what happens the moment after Louise (Randy Stuart) tells her insecure husband Scott (Grant Williams), "As long as you've got this wedding ring on, you've got me"?

37. Originally published in the October 1940 issue of *Astounding Science Fiction*, what was the name of the short story, written by Harry Bates, that *The Day the Earth Stood Still* (1951) was based on? Also, what was the original name of Klaatu's robot, named Gort in the movie?

38. Who is the only member of Nemo's (James Mason) original crew to survive till the end of *20,000 Leagues Under the Sea* (1954)?

39. The tunnel where Miles (Kevin McCarthy) and Becky (Dana Wynter) hide from the Pod People in *Invasion of the Body Snatchers* (1956) was shot in Griffith Park's Bronson Cave, a popular filmmaking location in Los Angeles due to its remote look but easy access. What do locals call the cave, and why?

GUEST STAR: Jeremy Dyson

Esteemed member of The League of Gentlemen and co-writer/co-director of *Ghost Stories* (2017).

40. There is a strong link between *Forbidden Planet* (1956) and absurd comedy in the form of Leslie Nielsen who plays Commander Adams in the former and would go on to essay numerous roles for the Zucker/Abrahams/Zucker partnership later in his career. But what is the connection between *Forbidden Planet* and absurd British TV comedy show *The League of Gentlemen* (1999–2017)?

41. What is Plan 9 in Ed Wood's hilariously loony *Plan 9 from Outer Space* (1959)?

42. Why do the Metaluna Mutants in *This Island Earth* (1955) wear trousers?

43. The sound effects accompanying the Martians' heat and death rays in *The War of the Worlds* (1953) were heard again, years later, in what classic sci-fi series?

44. What are the aliens' intentions in *It Came from Outer Space* (1953)?

45. In *The Day the Earth Stood Still* (1951), when Klaatu (Michael Rennie) requires cash to take Bobby (Billy Gray) to the movies, what does he offer to give the lad in exchange for his $2?

46. *They Come from Another World, Better Off Dead, Sleep No More, Evil in the Night* and *World in Danger* were rejected title suggestions for which 1956 sci-fi thriller?

47. While zooming to Metaluna in *This Island Earth* (1955), how does Cal (Rex Reason) describe the feeling of being squeezed into the snug conversion tube?

48. Following a close encounter with an enormous alien, an alcoholic heiress (Allison Hayes) grows incredibly in *Attack of the 50 Foot Woman* (1958). What motivates her wild rampage?

49. Who was the American realist artist responsible for creating the iconic movie posters for *This Island Earth* (1955), *The Incredible Shrinking Man* (1957), *Attack of the 50 Foot Woman* (1958) and scores more besides?

50. How is the murderous Martian stowaway (Ray "Crash" Corrigan) finally defeated in *It! The Terror from Beyond Space* (1958)?

Answers on page 216

CROSSING OVER INTO *THE TWILIGHT ZONE*

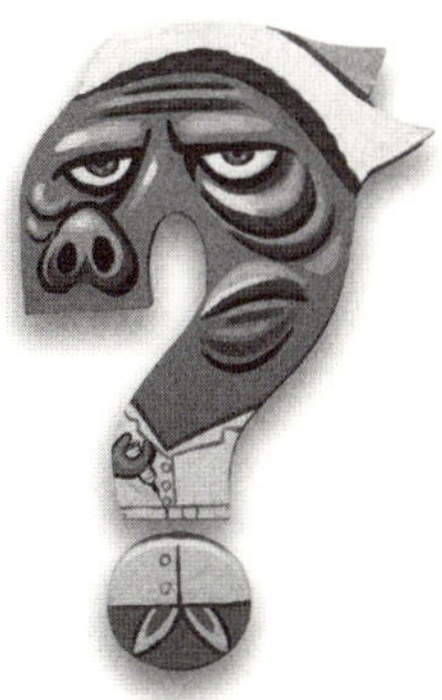

Forty-odd years ago, when re-runs of *The Twilight Zone* finally materialised on British TV – though it was treated with tremendous disrespect by the broadcaster, always screened late at night and at different times, with episodes often dropped to make room for tedious live sporting events – I was grateful for the opportunity to finally see those legendary half-hours and fill scores of raggedy old VHS tapes with their magic.

Back in those dark but adventurous days, before satellites, cables and the Internet delivered everything on a silver platter, the show and its secrets were really only available to those of us obsessed with it: sleep-deprived nerds compelled to travel through another dimension. A dimension not only of sight and sound, but also of mind. As vast as space and timeless as infinity, it was the middle ground between light and shadow. Between science and superstition. It was the dimension of imagination and we threw ourselves into it with absolute faith that writer, showrunner and host Rod Serling would somehow shepherd us safely through even the most turbulent terrain.

Running for five seasons, from 1959 to 1964 on the CBS network, *The Twilight Zone* was an uncommonly literate, provocative, creative and compelling anthology show that won multiple awards and, more significantly, the hearts and minds of generations of fans from then till now.

As different as each new episode was from the last, there was much that tied them together: The opening narration and bookend appearances from master of ceremonies Serling. The clever plots that grabbed like a vice and the everyman characters who could so easily have been us. And the music, of course. Those wonderful, eerie, scene-setting scores from such renowned composers as Jerry Goldsmith and Bernard Herrmann.

From light and mischievous to stormy and unsettling, from sci-fi to spooky, from socially relevant to far-out fantastic, though the series covered more ground than most other shows combined, still each one felt distinctively...Twilight Zoney. Endlessly imitated but never surpassed, it remains at the top of its game and now it's time to find out if you are at the top of yours...

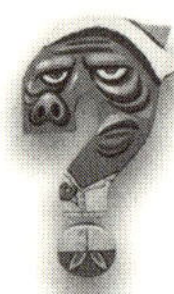

1. Rod Serling uttered his signature phrase "Submitted for your approval" an epic 94 times over *The Twilight Zone*'s 156-episode run. True or false?

2. What was the title of *The Twilight Zone*'s pilot episode, and who was the star?

3. Who is the Howling Man?

4. Who played Mr Death in "Nothing in the Dark" (S03E16)?

5. What's the first book we see Mr Bemis (Burgess Meredith) reading in all-time classic episode "Time Enough at Last" (S01E08)?

6. What's the name of the mysterious travelling salesman who gives drunken former gunslinger Al Denton (Dan Duryea) a second chance in "Mr. Denton on Doomsday" (S01E03)?

7. Rod Serling's initial deal with CBS stipulated that he write 80% of *The Twilight Zone*'s first season scripts himself. To make up the difference, Serling invited the show's viewers to send in manuscripts for consideration. Within five days of his request, Serling's staff received approximately 14,000 submissions. Of the 500 they read, how many did they end up using?

8. With nuclear war imminent, scientists Will Sturka (Fritz Weaver) and Jerry Riden (Joe Maross) plan to steal a spaceship and blast off with their families to which relatively safe planet?

9. What is Lt William "Fitz" Fitzgerald's (William Reynolds) regrettable ability in WWII tale "The Purple Testament" (S01E19)?

GUEST STAR: Marc Scott Zicree

Author of *The Twilight Zone Companion*, writer/director of *Star Trek New Voyages: Phase II* (2004–present), *Space Command* (2016–present) and much more!

10. How many lead actors from the original *Star Trek* (1966–1969) are in *The Twilight Zone*?

11. "The tools of conquest do not necessarily come with bombs and explosions and fallout. There are weapons that are simply thoughts, attitudes, prejudices – to be found only in the minds of men." Which first season episode includes this line in Rod Serling's closing narration?

12. Why doesn't Professor Sam Kittridge (Edgar Stehli) want his daughter to marry Walter Jameson (Kevin McCarthy)?

13. What does the sign say in the room prepared for astronaut Sam Conrad (Roddy McDowall) by his Martian captors?

14. A familiar face to *Twilight Zone* fans, Jack Klugman starred in which four classic episodes of the show?

15. What is Henry Temple's (Steven Perry) big, tall wish?

16. Where and when does harassed, exhausted New York executive Gart Williams (James Daly) decide he'd rather live?

17. What disconcerting fact eludes fretful, forgetful Marsha White (Anne Francis) until the bitter end of "The After Hours" (S01E34)?

18. Which season one episode of *The Twilight Zone* marked Rod Serling's first on-screen appearance? Also, how does the show's main character react after Serling describes the story as "ridiculous nonsense"?

19. What did *The Twilight Zone* win an Emmy for in 1960?

20. What's the first reply that Don Carter (William Shatner) gets from the Mystic Seer fortune teller machine in "Nick of Time" (S02E07)?

21. What is Arthur Castle (Luther Adler) left with, by the end of "The Man in the Bottle" (S02E02), as a result of the genie's (Joseph Ruskin) intervention?

22. How does Lew Bookman (Ed Wynn) initially cheat Death (Murray Hamilton) in "One for the Angels" (S01E02)?

23. Which episode of *The Twilight Zone* cast different actresses to play masked and unmasked versions of the same character?

24. Who wrote *The Twilight Zone*'s familiar guitar-and-bongo theme that ran from the second season onwards? Also, whose eerie season one theme did it replace?

GUEST STAR: Ron Fogelman

Producer of *Twilight Zone: The Stage Production*

25. What's the connection between *The Twilight Zone* and the black triangle stickers found above certain airplane windows?

26. What is the final line delivered by actress Agnes Moorhead in "The Invaders" (S02E15)?

27. "A vacuum-cleaner salesman whose volume of business is roughly that of a valet at a hobo convention", Mr Dingle (Burgess Meredith) first catches the eye of a two-headed Martian (Douglas Spencer and Michael Fox), then a pair of Venusians (Donald Losby and Greg Irvin), who each give him what special powers?

28. In "Long Distance Call" (S02E22), who does five-year-old Billy Bayles (Billy Mumy) chat with on his toy telephone?

29. How do the two aliens differ physically from humans in S02E28's "Will the Real Martian Please Stand Up"?

30. Why does Dr Stockton (Larry Gates) suddenly find himself at odds with his friends and neighbours?

31. How should one respond if Anthony (Billy Mumy) wishes a loved one into the cornfield?

32. Who were the "Five Characters in Search of an Exit" (S03E14)?

33. Who was Rod Serling's original choice of narrator?

34. "I'd never known a critic, but it was my idea of what a critic was like." Which character, from what episode, is writer Earl Hamner describing?

35. What is "To Serve Man"?

36. Which Serling-penned episode of *The Twilight Zone* was inspired by a sequence in British chiller *Dead of Night* (1945) and by a 1957 episode of *Alfred Hitchcock Presents*, "The Glass Eye" (S03E01)?

37. *Twilight Zone* writers Charles Beaumont and Richard Matheson both considered fantasy author Ray Bradbury a mentor. Rod Serling himself was a fan, often dropping Bradbury references into the show. How fortunate, then, that Bradbury was eager to contribute. How many of his scripts were ultimately produced, and what were the show titles?

38. Which significant change to *The Twilight Zone*'s format was forced upon the show by CBS for its relatively short fourth season?

39. "What you have just witnessed could be the end of a particularly terrifying nightmare. It isn't – it's the beginning. Although Alan Talbot doesn't know it, he's about to enter a strange new world, too incredible to be real, too real to be a dream. It's called The Twilight Zone." Which episode of *The Twilight Zone*'s fourth season opens with this narration?

GUEST STAR: Phil Nobile Jr

Editor-in-Chief, *Fangoria:* The World's Best Horror and Cult Film Magazine since 1979.

40. One episode of *The Twilight Zone* is an Oscar-winner. How is that possible?

41. What do the three astronauts (Jack Klugman, Ross Martin and Fredrick Beir) aboard Spaceship E-89 discover when they land on the 13th Planet of Star System 51 in the year 1997?

42. Which episode of *The Twilight Zone* sees Satan (Burgess Meredith) publishing a local newspaper with such outrageous but true headlines as "MAYOR'S WIFE GIVES BIRTH TO BABY

HIPPOPOTAMUS" and "BANK PRESIDENT'S WIFE CLAIMS DIVORCE – EXPLAINS CAUGHT HUSBAND TRIFLING WITH THREE MERMAIDS IN A BATHTUB"?

43. Described by Serling in his introduction as "a would-be writer who, if talent came 25 cents a pound, would be worth less than car fare", Julius Moomer (Jack Weston) inadvertently conjures up which legendary writer, in what amusing episode of *The Twilight Zone*?

44. During the opening narration for seasons four and five of the show, what visuals accompany Serling's phrases, "A dimension of sound" and "A dimension of mind"?

45. Which three episodes of *The Twilight Zone* starred sci-fi icon Robby the Robot?

46. Who directed the classic *Twilight Zone* episode, "Nightmare at 20,000 Feet" (S05E03)?

47. Voiced by June Foray, what does Tina say to Annabelle (Mary LaRoche) at the end of "Living Doll" (S05E06)?

48. Pioneering filmmaker and actress Ida Lupino was the only person during *The Twilight Zone*'s five-season run to star in one episode and direct another. What were those two episodes?

49. How many of *The Twilight Zone*'s 156 episodes were written by Rod Serling over the show's five-year run?

A. 56
B. 77
C. 92
D. 113

50. After CBS cancelled *The Twilight Zone* in 1964, ABC President Tom Moore seemed keen to pick it up. As CBS owned the rights to the title *Twilight Zone*, what did Moore suggest as an alternative?

Answers on page 226

WALT'S WONDERFUL WORLD OF DISNEY

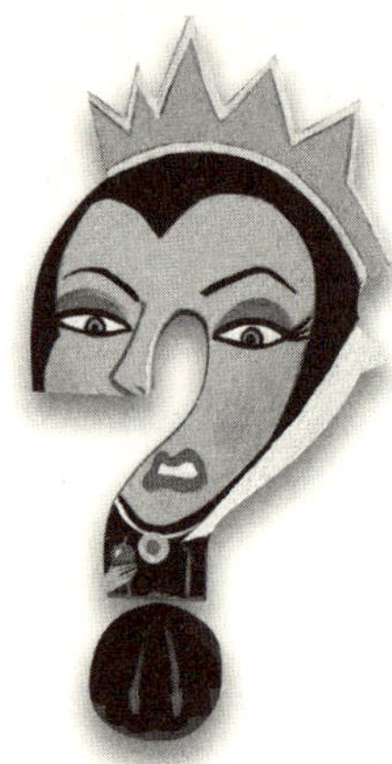

Even those who don't consider themselves Disney aficionados have to concede that when they were small, at least, the House of Mouse elicited from them the warmest, fuzziest feelings. Also, intermittent dread and heartbreak, but you have to take the rough with the smooth, of course, and the sooner you kids learn that, the better.

For many of us, our first cinema experience was a Disney film, most likely *Bambi* or some other artful classic that on the surface, at least, was like a kindly, nurturing, protective aunt or uncle.

But lurking just beneath that shiny surface...

Consider, if you will, Aunt Sarah in *Lady and the Tramp.* By all accounts, a trusty, selfless sort. Harmless, really. But the moment Jim Dear and Darling's backs are turned, Sarah's cats trash the house, she cruelly muzzles Lady, leaves the baby in the clutches of a demonic rat and insists the dogcatcher immediately come and destroy Tramp.

Now, that's the sort of darkness that prepares you for the real world.

So first we watch Walt Disney's films as children. Then again, with our children. And provided we don't croak, one final time, with our grandkids. I'm not usually one to use a phrase like "woven into the fabric of our lives", but, darn it all, that's Disney in a nutshell.

They've just always been around. They always will be. Everyone gets to experience them because that's the law. But whether or not you were paying attention remains to be seen in this Golden Age puzzler...

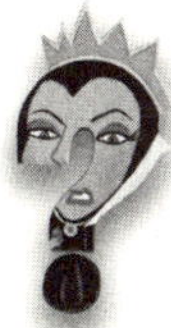

1. Where do the seven dwarfs keep the key to their jewel vault?

2. What three nationalities of marionettes does Pinocchio (Dickie Jones) sing and dance with during Stromboli's puppet show?

3. Featured in *Fantasia*'s (1940) "Night on Bald Mountain" sequence, the demon Chernabog was based upon which iconic horror movie star's facial expressions, mannerisms and dramatic poses?

4. What do the warning signs say on the front of Mrs Jumbo's makeshift cage in *Dumbo* (1940)?

5. During which season is Bambi's mother brutally gunned down?

6. Now, Sala-gadoola means menchicka-boolaroo, but the thing-a-ma-bob that does the job is?

7. What can one celebrate 364 days a year?

8. According to Peter Pan's (Bobby Driscoll) instructions, how would one fly to Never Land from London's Big Ben?

9. What breed of dog is Lady (Barbara Luddy)?

10. Princess Aurora (Mary Costa) hides out in the forest under which assumed name?

11. America's first animated feature, *Snow White and the Seven Dwarfs* (1937) was the greatest gamble of Walt Disney's career. Had it failed at the box office, there'd be no Walt Disney Productions, and the general consensus around Hollywood was that it was a fool's errand. Prior to its release, then, what did industry sceptics call the movie?

12. According to *Pinocchio*'s (1940) Jiminy Cricket (Cliff Edwards), how does one make their dreams come true?

13. Which Disney classic was described by olden-days film critic Otis Ferguson as "one of the strange and beautiful things that have happened in the world"?

14. What do *Dumbo*'s (1941) Mr Stork, *Bambi*'s (1942) Adult Flower and *Alice in Wonderland*'s (1951) Cheshire Cat all have in common?

GUEST STAR: Carrie Henn

Newt in *Aliens* (1986)!

15. In the 1950 classic *Cinderella*, how many times does Cinderella (Ilene Woods) lose her shoe: once, twice or three times?

16. Walt Disney holds the record for winning the most Academy Awards. Including his honorary Oscars, what's the magic number?

17. What does Peter Pan (Bobby Driscoll) break into the Darling household to recover?

18. What does Tramp (Larry Roberts) call Lady's (Barbara Luddy) part of town?

19. What precious resource was shared by 1959 releases *Plan 9 from Outer Space* and *Sleeping Beauty*?

20. What does Adult Flower (Sterling Holloway) name his pungent offspring?

21. What evidence does the Queen (Lucille La Verne) demand the Huntsman return to her as proof of his dark deed?

22. By what name is *Pinocchio*'s (1940) Jiminy Cricket (Cliff Edwards) known in Carlo Collodi's original 1883 novel, and how does he die in the book?

23. Though unnamed in *The Sorcerer's Apprentice*, what did Disney's animators dub Mickey's magical master?

24. According to the scornful crows in *Dumbo* (1940), though they've not yet seen an elephant fly, what sort of flies have they previously observed?

25. What is Bambi's first word?

26. By what name were legendary animators Les Clark, Marc Davis, Ollie Johnson, Milt Kahl, Ward Kimball, Eric Larson, John Lounsbery, Wolfgang Reitherman and Frank Thomas collectively known? Also, what was the first feature they all collaborated on?

27. What could a rabbit possibly be late for?

28. According to the Josh Billings quote that opens *Lady and the Tramp* (1955), what's the one thing that money can't buy?

29. Which Disney villain is dispatched by the Mighty Sword of Truth?

GUEST STAR: Dave Bossert

Artist, filmmaker, writer and Disney historian. Contributing animator to *Who Framed Roger Rabbit?* (1988) and *The Nightmare Before Christmas* (1993). Author of *Oswald the Lucky Rabbit: The Search for the Lost Disney Cartoons* (2017) and *Kem Weber: Mid-Century Furniture Designs for the Disney Studios* (2018).

30. *Cinderella* (1950) represents a stylistic transition from the more European-influenced book illustration look of *Snow White and the Seven Dwarfs* (1937) and *Pinocchio* (1940) to the more graphic design look of animation in the 1950s. What artist's style was most influential on *Cinderella*?

31. What wood is Pinocchio (Dickie Jones) made of?

32. For introducing him to Felix Salten's 1923 novel *Bambi: A Life in the Woods*, Walt Disney planned to thank animator Maurice Day by holding *Bambi*'s (1942) world premiere in his home town of Damariscotta, Maine, USA. That plan had to be scrapped, however, after Maine officials officially objected to Disney's plan for what reason?

33. What does Alice (Kathryn Beaumont) think Wonderland's flowers could learn a few things about?

34. Marilyn Monroe was the real-life model for Tinker Bell: True or false?

35. What was Disney's first widescreen animated feature?

36. Which one of the seven dwarfs wears glasses?

37. During *Fantasia*'s (1940) *Rite of Spring* sequence, which two dinosaurs fight to the death? Also, which of them emerges victorious?

38. Dopey, Gideon, Mrs Dumbo, Lucifer and Tinker Bell: Who's the odd one out?

39. According to Cinderella (Ilene Woods), what is a dream?

40. Which character in *Alice in Wonderland* (1951) recites lines from Lewis Carroll's epic nonsense poem "Jabberwocky"?

41. Where would two dogs in love best go for the best-a spaghetti in-a town?

42. Who are the three good fairies and what colour outfits do they wear?

43. What was the first Disney feature – actually the first film in cinema history – to release a soundtrack album?

44. Who teaches grown-up Bambi (John Sutherland), Thumper (Sam Edwards) and Flower (Sterling Holloway) about the birds and the bees? Also, who's the first of the trio to get "twitter-pated"?

45. In the *Star Trek* (1966–1969) episode "Shore Leave" (S01E12), Dr McCoy (DeForest Kelley) stumbles across live-action versions of which two characters from Disney's *Alice in Wonderland* (1951)?

46. As a lad, Walt Disney played which character – later immortalised in one of his movies – in a school play?

47. What does the word maleficent mean?

48. Give a bad boy enough rope and what will he make of himself?

49. What's the first mythological species that appears in *Fantasia*'s (1940) *Pastoral Symphony* sequence?

50. While playing croquet in *Alice in Wonderland* (1951), what do Alice (Kathryn Beaumont) and the Queen of Hearts (Verna Felton) use instead of traditional mallets and balls?

Answers on page 236

STEPHEN KING: *CARRIE* TO *CHRISTINE*

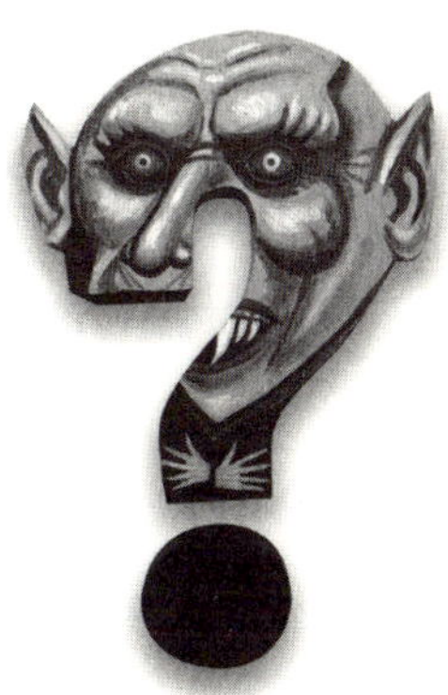

I was ten when I stopped opening my bedroom window at night.

Ten when Ralphie Glick came scratching at the glass, the dense fog swirling around him as he slowly floated there, hushed and pallid, in his yellow pyjamas. He was smiling, but it wasn't a friendly smile. It was evil, and sickly, and creepy music was playing in the background...

Trembling, I lurched towards the television and, fumbling for the off switch, sent Ralphie on his way. And when the scary second half of *Salem's Lot* aired in England, the TV in my house remained, resolutely, off.

A few years later, I mustered the courage to watch both parts of Tobe Hooper's haunting mini-series, and though honestly it still terrified me, the difference between wussy ten-year-old me and bolder twelve-year-old me was that I'd realised by then that I loved being scared. Horror was, indeed, my drug, and Stephen King – Satan bless him – my pusher.

Embarking on a thrilling period of desensitisation, I consumed every fright I could find, in movies, novels, comics, the lot. It's a hunger that never subsides. And King cranks out nightmares like no one else, as prolific as he is twisted, the dark, mischievous architect of the haunted house that opens for business every night when I close my eyes.

And look, there's Ralphie, standing out front in his pyjamas, handing out tickets.

Still grinning.

Still pale.

Still thirsty.

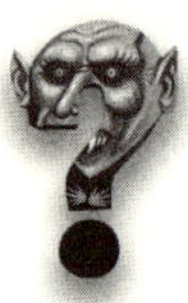

1. What was Stephen King's first published novel?

2. "Almost everyone thought the man and the boy were father and son." Which Stephen King novel opens with this line?

3. A stickler for authenticity, Sissy Spacek insisted that it be her hand, rather than a stunt double's, shooting out the grave in the shocking final moments of Brian De Palma's *Carrie* (1976): True or false?

4. What does all work and no play make Jack?

5. Convicted in 1948 for the double murder of his wife and her lover, where in Maine is banker Andy Dufresne sent to serve a double life sentence?

6. What's the first Stephen King novel set in his signature fictional town of Castle Rock, Maine?

7. What was the first novel credited to Stephen King's nom de plume, Richard Bachman?

8. What breed of dog is Cujo?

9. What's the name of the weaponised strain of influenza that kills 99.4% of the world's population in *The Stand* (pub. 1978)?

10. Written by King in the grand, ghastly tradition of EC horror comics of the 1950s, what are the titles of the five terrifying tales told in *Creepshow* (1982)?

11. The posters for which Stephen King feature adaptation included the tagline "How do you kill something that can't possibly be alive?"?

12. How did Carrie kill her crackpot mother in King's 1974 novel of the same name?

14. "There were fourteen steps exactly fourteen. But the top one was smaller, out of proportion, as if it had been added to avoid the evil number." To what phobia, suffered by King, does this line from *Salem's Lot* (pub. 1975) allude?

GUEST STAR: Dan Lloyd

Danny in *The Shining* (1980)!

15. For Stanley Kubrick's *The Shining*, in any snowy exterior scene with actors present, the snow was not, in fact, snow. There was so much of this anti-snow around that it ended up in all our coat pockets by the end of the day. Which of these four options served as our snow?

A. Sodium bicarbonate
B. Salt
C. Styrofoam
D. Rice

16. How does Cujo contract rabies?

17. What was the title of Stephen King's 1981 non-fiction exploration of horror fiction, a book in which he states that radio is a superior medium for horror than film and TV, as it requires more active use of the imagination?

18. Stephen King's performance in *Creepshow* (1982) was informed by which choice bit of acting advice from director George Romero?

19. How is Marty able to identify the werewolf terrorising the residents of Tarker's Mills, Maine, in Stephen King's novella *Cycle of the Werewolf* (1983)?

20. What poem does Johnny (Christopher Walken) read his class at the beginning of David Cronenberg's *The Dead Zone* (1983)?

21. What song plays during *Christine*'s (1983) opening scene, as the cars roll down the production line and the star of the show claims her first victim?

22. Having already scored two of Brian De Palma's movies – 1972's *Sisters* and 1976's *Obsession* – it's likely Bernard Herrmann would have scored 1976's *Carrie* too. Sadly, though, he passed away in 1975, before that was possible. Ultimately, the film was scored by Pino Donaggio, who, let's say, "paid homage" to Herrmann in what distinctive way?

23. Which film adaptation of one of his novels did Stephen King famously dislike, dismissing it as "cold" and "misogynistic"?

24. Which character died in King's novel *Cujo* (1983), but survived in the 1983 film adaptation?

25. What kind of car is Christine?

26. Who's that scratching at Mark Petrie's (Lance Kerwin) bedroom window?

27. "For a long time," said King, "ten years at least, I had wanted to write a fantasy epic like *The Lord of the Rings*, only with an

American setting." Set in a plague-decimated USA, what's the name of that oft-revised novel? Also, what location served as the book's Mordor, and which characters did King consider his Frodo and Sauron?

28. "By the time he graduated from college, John Smith had forgotten all about the bad fall he took on the ice that January day in 1953." Which Stephen King novel begins with this line?

29. Besides King's crazy performance as doomed, dumb Jordy Verrill in *Creepshow* (1982), which other member of the King household played a role in the film?

GUEST STAR: Steve Casino

Artist and toymaker. Painter of Nuts and Tic Tacs. Great and powerful Oz-like creator of *Vintage Geek* Question Marks.

30. What are Tad's (Danny Pintauro) two nick-names in *Cujo* (1983)?

31. In Kubrick's *The Shining* (1980), what does Ullman (Barry Nelson) tell Wendy (Shelley Duvall) the Overlook Hotel was built over?

32. As *Christine* (1983) wasn't violent enough to earn an "R" rating, and the last thing the producers wanted to release was a PG horror movie, what was their solution?

33. Which early film adaptation of one of his books does King prefer to his own original novel?

34. According to Stephen King's 1977 novel *The Shining*, which Overlook Hotel room is best avoided?

35. Though it wasn't the first of his novels to be published, what was the first novel ever written by Stephen King?

36. Which of King's early novels did the author reveal he "barely remembers writing at all"?

37. For whom does The Gunslinger gun?

38. Plume's comicbook adaptation of *Creepshow* (1982) marked Stephen King's first collaboration with which master monster illustrator?

39. In Kubrick's *The Shining* (1980), what does Jack (Jack Nicholson) say he'd give his goddamned soul for?

40. While shooting *Cujo* (1983), actress Dee Wallace was bitten by one of the canines in the cast: True or false?

41. Carrie is responsible for all of the deaths in King's 1974 novel, with which exception?

42. "Children of the Corn", "Graveyard Shift", "The Mangler" and "The Lawnmower Man" lurk among the twenty tales gathered in Stephen King's first collection of short stories. What was its title?

43. What is Danny Torrance's (Danny Lloyd) nickname in Stanley Kubrick's *The Shining* (1980)? Also, what's the name of the little boy who lives in his mouth?

44. In *Creepshow* (1982), what was effects wiz Tom Savini's nickname for the ferocious, bitey creature in the crate?

45. Which Stephen King feature adaptation was described in its print ads as a terrifying blend of *American Graffiti* (1973) and *Psycho* (1960)?

46. Introduced in the novel *Firestarter* (pub. 1980), and featured in several Stephen King projects since, what's the name of the fictional, top-secret US government agency specialising in largely evil scientific research?

47. In Cronenberg's *The Dead Zone* (1983), what vision terrifies Johnny (Christopher Walken) when he shakes hands with vile senatorial candidate Greg Stillson (Martin Sheen)?

48. What's the name of Ellie Creed's cat, back from the grave but still "a little dead" in *Pet Sematary* (pub. 1983)?

49. King had originally planned for his pseudonym to be Guy Pillsbury – his maternal grandfather's name. When this secret was accidentally spilled, and King had to come up with a last-minute replacement, Richard Bachman was born. How did the author arrive at this name?

50. In *Creepshow* (1982), what does grating Nathan Grantham (Jon Lormer) demand?

51. "His single-minded purpose. His unending fury." Which Stephen King novel ends with these lines?

Answers on page 244

Ray Harryhausen's Creature Features

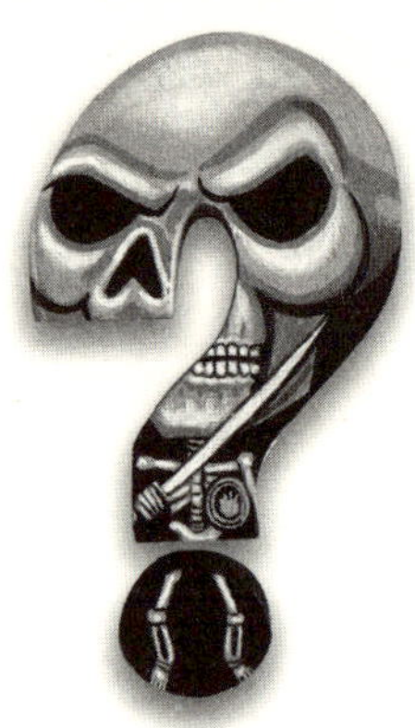

Ray Harryhausen was the first filmmaker I was ever aware of. When I was very small, and barely able to distinguish between real life and the fantasies I'd get lost in on screen, the last thing I thought about were the folks behind the scenes. Ray, though, was something special – an artist and a technician, a magician, really, or the next best thing, who breathed patient, artful life into the creatures inhabiting many of our favourite films.

In an age before computer effects made everything almost instantly possible, Ray gave us all our first peeks of the impossible. Of roaring, stomping prehistoric beasts. Of exotic, hypnotic mythical creatures. Telling wonderful tales of long ago and far away, he was the star of the movies he made, and his name on a poster was all it took it took to send us to the cinema in droves.

I was 19 when I first met him. It was 1988 and I hadn't been working long as a journalist. Ray was promoting something or other and I was invited to meet him for a chat and a tour of his West London home. Until that moment, I had no idea he lived in England. What a revelation! A few days later, there I was, sharing tea, biscuits and stories with a legend, surrounded by art and props from the films that formed me. It was such an exciting afternoon, even today, 30 years later, I've still not calmed down.

Stop-motion model animation was his game, of course. Working largely alone with models he designed and built himself, Ray would snap a beast, move it a bit, shoot it again, and so on, hundreds of thousands of times. That's a mad simplification, of course, but you're not here for the science bit, are you? That, I'm sure, you already know. What we're here to discover is how much else you know about Ray's wondrous creature features. And find out we shall...

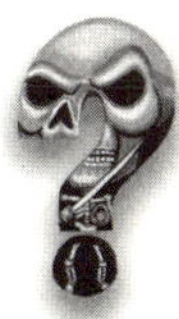

1. What film inspired Ray Harryhausen to become a stop-motion animator?

2. What is Mr Joseph Young's favourite tune?

3. *The Beast from 20,000 Fathoms* (1953) inspired which Japanese monster movie? Also, what was Ray's opinion of the film?

4. How did Ray Harryhausen famously cut costs on *It Came from Beneath the Sea* (1955)?

5. In *Jason and the Argonauts* (1963), who are the Children of the Hydra's Teeth?

6. What incantation does Sokurah the Magician (Torin Thatcher) recite to summon the Genie (Richard Eyer) from his lamp in *The 7th Voyage of Sinbad* (1958)?

7. After the castaways overpower the giant crab in *Mysterious Island* (1961), what do they do with it?

8. In *20 Million Miles to Earth* (1957), when the army attempts to lure the Ymir into an electric net, what do they use for bait?

9. What does Professor Cavor (Lionel Jeffries) name his gravity-defying metallic paste in *First Men in the Moon* (1964)?

10. "Travel back through time and space to the edge of man's beginnings...Discover a savage world whose only law was lust!" This juicy tagline adorned the posters for which movie?

11. "I had to do everything because I couldn't find another kindred soul," said Ray of his arduous and time-consuming creative process. "Now you see 80 people listed doing the same things I was doing by myself." Though Harryhausen famously animated the majority of his projects solo, everyone needs help sometimes. George Lofgren, a taxidermist, co-created many of Ray's furry critters. Willis Cook, an occasional assistant, built some of his miniature sets. But what vital roles did Ray's parents play in the making of his movies?

12. What's in the sack brought back from The Forbidden Valley at the beginning of *The Valley of Gwangi* (1969)? Also, what does T.J. (Gila Golan) name it?

13. In *The Golden Voyage of Sinbad* (1973), what does Margiana (Caroline Munro) have tattooed on the palm of her right hand?

14. In *Sinbad and the Eye of the Tiger* (1977), the bronze colossus Minaton was both a stop-motion creation and a man in a suit. Which 7'3"-tall performer made his uncredited movie debut in the role?

15. In *Clash of the Titans* (1981), what's the only safe way to view Medusa?

16. Ray's movie-making idol since *King Kong* (1933), who worked with Harryhausen on his first feature, *Mighty Joe Young* (1949)?

17. What's the name of the generic-sounding secret base, far north of the Arctic Circle, that's featured at the very beginning of *The Beast from 20,000 Fathoms* (1953)?

18. What was Ray Harryhausen's first colour feature?

19. Who was the one-sandalled man?

20. In whose name does Professor Cavor (Lionel Jeffries) claim the Moon, in *First Men in the Moon* (1964)?

21. Where does Sinbad (John Phillip Law) find the third golden tablet in *The Golden Voyage of Sinbad* (1973)?

22. Malcolm McDowell, Michael York, Richard Chamberlain and Arnold Schwarzenegger were all considered for which role in what movie?

23. What triggers Joe's nightclub rampage in *Mighty Joe Young* (1949)?

24. "If you can load it, I can fire it..." Which up-and-coming actor played military sharpshooter Corp. Stone in *The Beast from 20,000 Fathoms* (1953)?

GUEST STAR: Joel Hodgson

Creator, co-writer and star of *Mystery Science Theater 3000* (1988–1999) and *Mystery Science Theater 3000: The Return* (2017–present).

25. Was Ray Harryhausen British? Because he sure sounded like it.

26. What was the promotional term coined by producer Charles H. Schneer to distinguish Harryhausen's model animation technique from mere cartoon animation?

27. When the castaways discover a chest washed ashore in *Mysterious Island* (1961), what suitable novel do they discover inside?

28. How does Jason (Todd Armstrong) defeat Talos in *Jason and the Argonauts* (1963)?

29. What are the names of the two tribes featured in *One Million Years B.C.* (1966)?

30. What actor, best known for playing the Doctor in *Doctor Who*, appeared in which two Ray Harryhausen movies?

31. What breaks the steaming surface of the cauldron when the Stygian Witches (Flora Robson, Anna Manahan and Freda Jackson) meet Perseus (Harry Hamlin) in *Clash of the Titans* (1981)?

32. "Nobody paid any attention to us. Nobody said, 'Why did you do this?' and 'Why did you do that?' We just did it, and when the picture was finished, they saw it. We had full control, artistic control without any interference. That was worth the price of making a 'B' picture, as opposed to an 'A' picture." Which close collaborator of Ray Harryhausen said this, and how many films did they make together?

33. After the producers of *Monster from the Sea* bought the rights to Ray Bradbury's short story "The Beast from 20,000 Fathoms" (pub. 1951) – principally so they could use his superior title for their creature feature – Bradbury later renamed the story when including it in his 1953 anthology *The Golden Apples of the Sun*. What was his new name for it?

34. Which actor, who played Capt. Patrick Hendry in *The Thing from Another World* (1951) and was often cast as stoic military types, later played Col. Jack Evans in *The Beast from 20,000 Fathoms* (1953) and Cmdr. Pete Mathews in *It Came from Beneath the Sea* (1955)?

35. What guards the entrance to Sokurah's fortress in *The 7th Voyage of Sinbad* (1958)?

36. Which three Harryhausen films were directed by Nathan Juran?

37. What's Loana (Raquel Welch) teaching Tumak's (John Richardson) tribe when she's attacked and carried off by a Pteranodon?

38. In which two movies, and with which two creatures, do battles with elephants occur?

39. What's the final line, spoken in unison by Sinbad (John Phillip Law) and the Grand Vizier of Marabia (Douglas Wilmer), in *The Golden Voyage of Sinbad* (1973)?

40. Which of Ray Harryhausen's movies features Petra's iconic Treasury (Al-Khazneh), a striking 1st-century temple carved from a sandstone rock face that also appeared in Hergé's *The Adventures of Tintin: The Red Sea Sharks* (1958) and Steven Spielberg's *Indiana Jones and the Last Crusade* (1989)?

41. What do Calibos (Neil McCarthy) in *Clash of the Titans* (1981) and the Id Monster from *Forbidden Planet* (1956) have in common?

42. Where is Ray's star situated on Hollywood Boulevard's Walk of Fame?

43. Besides the usual fatalities associated with sea creature invasion – being eaten, squished or drowned, crushed by toppling masonry or trapped in exploding vehicles – what additional aspect of the Rhedosaurus' assault on New York proves deadly in *The Beast from 20,000 Fathoms* (1953)?

44. In *20 Million Miles to Earth* (1957), when McIntosh (Thomas Browne Henry) tells Signore Contino (Jan Arvan) that Calder's (William Hopper) just returned from an expedition to Venus, Contino laughs and corrects him how?

45. Although initially Ray Harryhausen was eager for either Miklós Rózsa or Max Steiner to score *The 7th Voyage of Sinbad* (1958), producer Charles H. Schneer persuaded him to go another way. Who did they ultimately hire, and since it went so very well, which additional Harryhausen films did he end up scoring?

46. How long did it take Ray to animate the legendary skeleton scene from *Jason and the Argonauts* (1963)?

47. What are Professor Cavor's (Lionel Jeffries) thoughts regarding the Selenites' practice of putting their chemical workers to sleep until they're needed again?

48. When Zenobia (Margaret Whiting) turns from a seagull back to a full-sized human being in *Sinbad and the Eye of the Tiger* (1977), as there wasn't enough magic potion left to effect a full transformation, what souvenir of her shape-shifting adventure remains?

49. What was Ray's final feature?

50. When Ray Harryhausen received his honorary Oscar – The Gordon E. Sawyer Award – at the Academy's Science and Technical Ceremony in 1992, host Tom Hanks remarked, "Some people say *Citizen Kane* (1941) or *Casablanca* (1942) is the greatest movie ever made. I say…" What film did he name?

Answers on page 254

STAR TREK: THE ORIGINAL SERIES

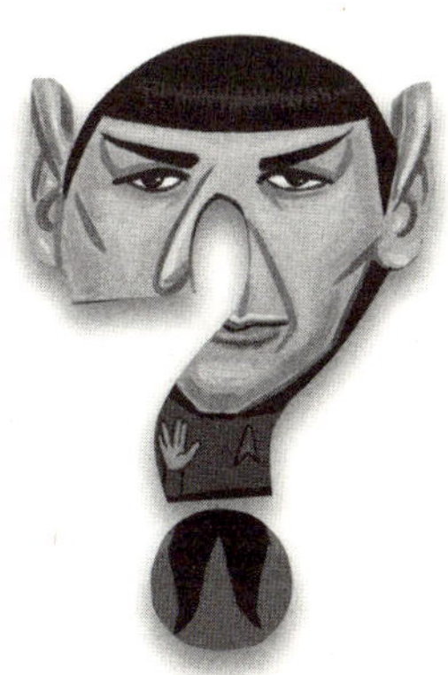

Our story begins in 1964. Pitching a series to NBC is Gene Roddenberry, a decorated WWII bomber pilot and former cop turned TV writer and producer. Describing his show to the western-loving executives as "*Wagon Train* to the stars", the programme was to be set "somewhere in the future" on the USS *Yorktown*. It was the seed from which a mighty series, and subsequent franchise, grew.

With $630,000 to spend, Roddenberry introduced the brave crew of the re-christened USS *Enterprise* in a pilot entitled *The Cage*, starring Jeffrey Hunter as Captain Christopher Pike, with Leonard Nimoy as an uncharacteristically cheery Mr Spock, and the future Mrs Roddenberry, Majel Barrett, as executive officer Number One.

NBC hated it. Complaining that the show was too cerebral, the studio execs were also uncomfortable with a woman ranking so highly aboard the *Enterprise*. They passed on the series, and for a while at least, *Star Trek* seemed dead as a dodo.

In an incredible twist the equal of anything featured on the show, NBC decided to give the series another chance, commissioning a second pilot that they insisted be more exciting. They also wanted Barrett out, and Nimoy too. Sticking to his guns on Nimoy, claiming he was far too important to the series to axe, Roddenberry relented by re-casting Barrett as the lovelorn Nurse Chapel, also beefing up the action with all manner of cosmic rough and tumble.

Passing on the do-over, actor Jeffrey Hunter was quickly replaced by William Shatner as James T. Kirk, with science officer Spock, the featured alien of the series, standing beside him as second-in-command. He may have been from outer space, but at least, agreed the stone-age network executives, he wasn't a woman.

When *Star Trek* finally premiered on September 8, 1966, the show was a critical success that won the instant devotion of throngs of sci-fi-starved nerds who responded with tremendous enthusiasm to the show's progressive approach, optimistic outlook and tight ensemble cast.

Regardless, *Star Trek*'s ratings were never strong and it would have been cancelled after its first season, and then again after its second, if not for fierce fan campaigns. By the end of the third though, there was no saving it, and in June 1969, the show was no more.

For the purpose of this quiz, that's where the story ends, but for the record, of course, we know better. Just a month after the show was cancelled, Neil Armstrong walked on the Moon, at which point everyone was suddenly obsessed with space exploration. As a result, the series was quickly syndicated, fast developing from a cult gem into the all-out phenomenon we know and love today.

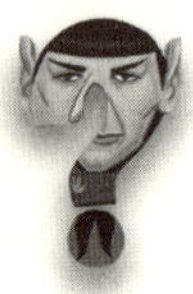

1. What is the registry number of the USS *Enterprise*?

2. Including the original pilot, how many episodes of *Star Trek* were produced?

3. What does the "T" in James T. Kirk (William Shatner) stand for?

4. What colour is Spock's (Leonard Nimoy) blood?

5. Who convinced Nichelle Nichols not to quit playing Uhura, insisting she was an essential role model for black women in America?

6. How do you stop Tribbles from reproducing?

7. What is the show's legendary opening monologue?

8. What three colours of uniform are worn by Command, Sciences and Operations?

9. What was the message burnt into the ground by the Horta in "The Devil in the Dark" (S01E25)?

GUEST STAR: George Takei

Sulu!

10. In "The Naked Time" (S01E04), Sulu stalks the corridors of the *Enterprise* with a fencing foil. What weapon was proposed for Sulu in the initial script written by John D.F. Black?

11. What was the first episode of the show to feature all seven main cast members?

12. Which one of these three eccentric mutterings was never uttered by cantankerous Dr McCoy (DeForest Kelley)?

A – "I'm a doctor, not a bricklayer!"
B – "I'm a doctor, not a proctor!"
C – "I'm a doctor, not an escalator!"

13. What was the name of the book that caused widespread cultural contamination in "A Piece of the Action" (S02E17)?

14. What was Gene Roddenberry's nickname?

15. What rare crystals power the *Enterprise*'s warp core?

16. In which episode did Kirk (William Shatner) romance a doomed, Great Depression-era missionary (Joan Collins)?

17. Joining the cast in its second year to increase youth appeal, Chekov's (Walter Koenig) look and attitude were inspired by which singer/actor?

18. Which alien race invented cloaking technology?

19. Who wrote *Star Trek*'s theme tune?

20. Gene Roddenberry originally wrote lyrics for *Star Trek*'s theme tune: True or false?

21. Many tubes in the hallways of the Enterprise are marked "GNDN". What does this stand for?

22. Why were Spock's (Leonard Nimoy) pointed ears and eyebrows airbrushed out of early publicity pictures for the series?

23. Which species of aliens force Kirk (William Shatner) and Uhura (Nichelle Nichols) to kiss?

24. Who founded Desilu Productions, the company that produced the first season-and-a-half of *Star Trek*?

GUEST STAR: Julie Nimoy

Leonard Nimoy's daughter and co-director/co-producer of *Remembering Leonard: His Life, Legacy and Battle with COPD* (2017).

25. Which instrument did Mr Spock (Leonard Nimoy) play in "Charlie X" (S01E02)?

26. "Beam me up, Scotty." During the run of the show, how many times did Kirk (William Shatner) utter this immortal catch-phrase: never, 12 times, or 62 times?

27. Every seven years, Vulcans experience ponn farr, where they're stricken with a blood fever, become violent and finally die unless they do either one of which two things?

28. Which two main cast characters didn't have first names in the series?

29. How was writer and script editor Dorothy Fontana credited on the show, and why?

30. According to Chekov (Walter Koenig) in "The Trouble with Tribbles" (S02E15), who invented Scotch?

31. What are the slanting crawlways that lead up to the warp-drive nacelles called? Also, who were they named after?

32. Which member of *Star Trek*'s main cast also voiced Providers 2 and 3 in "The Gamesters of Triskelion" (S02E16), a radio announcer in "A Piece of the Action" (S02E17), Sargon in "Return to Tomorrow" (S02E20), Commodore Enwright in "The Ultimate Computer" (S02E24) and a NASA technician in "Assignment: Earth" (S02E26)?

33. Rather than knock out evil Kirk (William Shatner) with the butt of Spock's phaser in "The Enemy Within" (S02E05), Leonard Nimoy devised which fascinating alternative?

34. Created by writer Gene L. Coon, the Klingons first appeared in which episode of the show? Also, who played the Klingon Kor?

35. Which actors' names appeared in the opening credits of *Star Trek*'s first season?

36. Why wouldn't you ever want to see a Medusan?

37. With what message does Trelane, the all-powerful and eccentric Squire of Gothos played by William Campbell, first greet the Enterprise?

38. Which member of *Star Trek*'s cast claims never to have seen a single episode of the show?

39. Who is the only non-crew character in *Star Trek* to be featured in more than one episode? Also, who played him, and what were the names of the episodes he appeared in?

GUEST STAR: James Callis

Gaius Baltar in *Battlestar Galactica* (2003–2009), Tom in the *Bridget Jones* trilogy (2001–2016) and the voice of Alucard in *Castlevania* (2017–2018).

40. What did Leonard Nimoy originally want to change about his character?

41. What is the name of the ancient sleeper ship containing 72 genetically engineered passengers in suspended animation? Also, who was their leader?

42. Which intimate Vulcan technique was first featured in the episode "Dagger of the Mind" (S01E09)?

43. Which notorious season three episode was described by William Shatner as one of the show's worst, calling the episode's plot a "tribute" to NBC executives who slashed the show's budget and placed it in a bad time slot?

44. Which member of the cast was nominated for an acting Emmy for each of the show's three seasons? Also, how many Emmys did the series eventually win?

45. Which two-part episode of the show used footage originally shot for the series' unscreened pilot, "The Cage"?

46. Why is Kirk (William Shatner) offended when Commodore Wesley (Barry Russo) calls him Captain Dunsel in "The Ultimate Computer" (S02E24)?

47. Where would you find the ISS *Enterprise*?

48. An RCA advert in 1967 cited *Star Trek* as the best reason to buy which luxury item?

49. How do the Melkotians sentence Kirk (William Shatner) and his landing crew to die in "Spectre of the Gun" (S03E06)?

50. What saves Spock (Leonard Nimoy) from being permanently blinded by an intense beam of light in "Operation: Annihilate!" (S01E29)?

Answers on page 264

If It Bleeds, We Can Kill It: Eighties' Action Classics

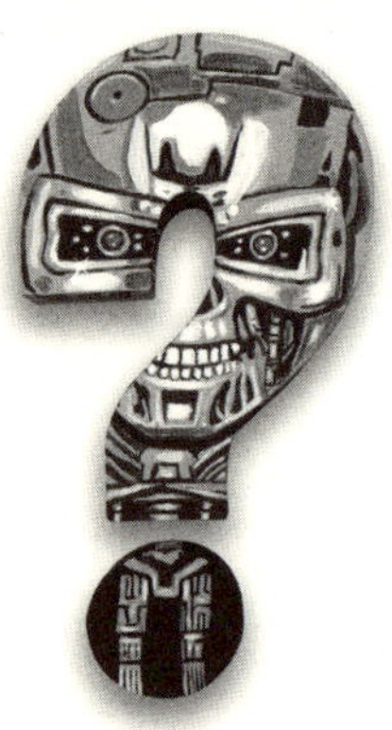

Eighties' action heroes scratched a significant itch, back in the day. A proper grown-up might argue that's because justice was in short supply in the real world, so of course it was satisfying seeing bad guys pay for their crimes at the cinema. Also, with the threat of nuclear extinction looming large in all our lives, at least in our fantasies, we could rely on our heroes to save us. The truth though, for most action fans of yore, is that we were vicious little bastards who got off on destruction, violence, blood and boobs.

Before everything was done on computers, Arnie, Sly, Jackie Chan and the rest were the special effects we flocked to see. Years earlier, our parents thrilled to the urbane, balletic grace of Fred Astaire and Gene Kelly. Likewise, our heroes took our breath away, only our guys didn't so much trip the light fantastic as they did blow off faces and kick asses back to the Stone Age.

The way I see it, action's Golden Age began in the early Seventies, with Clint Eastwood's landmark cop thriller *Dirty Harry* (1971), Bruce Lee's martial arts milestone *Enter the Dragon* (1973) and Roger Moore's initial Bond romp, *Live and Let Die* (1973). Inspired by these influential classics, action movies achieved their ultimate evolution in the Eighties with *Terminator* (1984), *RoboCop* (1987), *Die Hard* (1988) and the like. These films didn't just feature action. They were driven by it. Defined by it. Revelled in the stark, brutal chaos of it.

Fantastic action features were the lucky by-product of a harsh and ugly decade. Though everything seemed so uncertain back then, on the big screen at least, life remained simple: no matter the question, violence was always the answer.

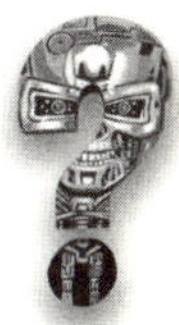

1. According to the hero of *Rambo: First Blood Part II* (1985), what does one have to do in order to survive war?

2. What is best in life?

3. What might Arjen Rudd (Joss Ackland), South African Minister for Diplomatic Affairs, say if you pointed a gun at him?

4. Which action classic features the characters The Toadie (Max Phipps), The Humungus (Kjell Nilsson), The Gyro Captain (Bruce Spence) and The Feral Kid (Emil Minty)?

5. Who's all out of bubblegum? What's the only thing he wants to do besides chew?

6. A daydreaming romantic novelist lives out her fantasies when a treasure map arrives in the post, leading her to Colombia on the trail of a priceless emerald, in which lively 1984 adventure?

7. Jon Voight and Eric Roberts earned Oscar nominations for playing fugitive stowaways on what sort of vehicle?

8. According to the 1987 movie of the same name, what's the highest-rated show in 2019?

9. "Crime is a Disease. Meet the Cure." Who's the cure? What's the movie?

GUEST STAR: Sam J. Jones

Flash Gordon (Quarterback, New York Jets) in *Flash Gordon* (1980) and Sam Jones in the *Ted* films (2012 & 2015).

10. During production on *Flash Gordon*, Brian Blessed's Hawkman wings were so large that he couldn't sit on a chair. Instead, a special perch was constructed for him, and whenever he leaned on it, the cast and crew would whistle bird sounds to tease him. True or false?

11. Which classic western was remade as sci-fi adventure *Battle Beyond the Stars* (1980)? Also, which actor starred in both?

12. Who played The Beastmaster? Who were his closest animal friends?

13. According to 1985's *Code of Silence*, what will Eddie Cusack (Chuck Norris) do if he wants your opinion?

14. What does the acronym JAFO stand for in 'copter classic *Blue Thunder* (1983)? How was it sanitised for the short-lived TV spin-off the following year?

15. What did henchman Jimmy (Marshall Teague) used to do to guys like Dalton (Patrick Swayze) in prison? How does Dalton respond to this information?

16. Who are "They"? Where are they? When do they mostly come out?

17. According to his *Commando* (1985) back-story, why was Bennett (Vernon Wells) booted out of Matrix's (Arnold Schwarzenegger) army unit?

18. When a representative of the Teamsters Union contacted director Michael Winner to swearily enquire how he'd had the gall to shoot *Death Wish III* (1985) in New York without hiring a single Teamster, how did the exploitation filmmaker calm them down?

19. What's better than a shower and a hot cup of coffee after a tiring flight?

20. Who served for one term as mayor of Carmel-by-the-Sea, California? What was his first official act?

21. How many people does Rambo (Sylvester Stallone) kill in *First Blood* (1982)?

22. How long do cranky homicide detective Jack Cates and fast-talking convict Reggie Hammond have to catch cop killers on the loose in San Francisco?

23. When quizzed on the matter by Princess Jehnna (Olivia d'Abo), what is the one thing that drunk Conan (Arnold Schwarzenegger) admits can hurt him, in *Conan the Destroyer* (1984)?

24. In which movie do Kurt Sloane (Jean-Claude Van Damme) and "Tiger" Tong Po (Michel Qissi) "fight the old way, hands wrapped in hemp and resin, dipped in broken glass"?

GUEST STAR: Lea Thompson

Star of *Red Dawn* (1984), *Back to the Future I–III* (1985-1990), *SpaceCamp* (1986) and *Howard the Duck* (1986).

25. Which two *Red Dawn* stars were former professional ballet dancers?

26. Which Aikido master broke Sean Connery's wrist while teaching him martial arts during the production of 1983's *Never Say Never Again*?

27. John Woo dedicated *The Killer* (1989) to which one of his filmmaking heroes?

28. Who's too old for this shit? How old is he when we first meet him?

29. Which legendary action movie producer parodied his own fast-talking, booming, in-your-face image by playing the aggravated director at the beginning of 1988's *Who Framed Roger Rabbit*?

30. Who once remarked of his *Lone Wolf McQuade* (1983) co-star that "David Carradine is about as good a martial artist as I am an actor"?

31. What are RoboCop's three Prime Directives and secret Fourth Directive?

32. What ability does Remo Williams (Fred Ward) share with Superman? Also what does he have in common with James Bond?

33. Who teaches troubled Seattle youth Jason Stillwell (Kurt McKinney) martial arts in 1986's *No Retreat, No Surrender*?

34. What does Jesse Ventura not have time for?

35. Who flew the Gullfire over Leningrad?

36. What, according to Mark Kaminski (Arnold Schwarzenegger) in *Raw Deal* (1986), should you never do while drinking?

37. Which one of these four frantic sequels has the highest body count: *Mad Max 2: The Road Warrior* (1981), *Rambo: First Blood Part II* (1985), *A Better Tomorrow II* (1987) or *Lethal Weapon 2* (1989)?

38. What 1984 sci-fi thriller predicted the Internet, social media, tablet PCs, voice-activated computers, wireless headsets, video mail, camera drones, biometric security and domestic robots? Which visionary filmmaker wrote and directed it?

39. Which action superstar originally worked as a gym teacher and dorm bouncer at a Swiss boarding school for girls, and as a lion cage cleaner at the Central Park Zoo?

GUEST STAR: Clancy Brown

Star of *Highlander* (1986), *The Shawshank Redemption* (1994), *Starship Troopers* (1997) and the voice of Mr Krabs in *SpongeBob SquarePants* (1999–present).

40. How many people won Oscars after working on *Highlander*, can you name them, and how many total Oscars did they win?

41. Which legendary action movie star was once described by the Guinness Book of World Records as "the most perfectly developed man in the history of the world"?

42. What does a guy have to do to sleep with Red Sonja?

43. Californian character actor Brion James plays Requin, a wild-eyed, pony-tailed henchman with a cockney accent even Dick Van Dyke wouldn't stoop to – favourite phrases include "I'll cut your bloody froat" and "You ain't werf a toss" – in what crazy team-up classic?

44. What is Tso (Conan Lee) and Fai's (Gordon Liu) weapon of choice for their climactic battle in 1988's *Tiger on the Beat*?

45. Which martial arts master cites Charlie Chaplin, Buster Keaton and Harold Lloyd as his greatest influences?

46. Which 1989 blockbuster did Sylvester Stallone claim led to the decline of muscle-bound action entertainment, stating, "It was the beginning of a new era. The visuals took over. The special effects became more important than the single person. I wish I had thought of Velcro muscles myself. I didn't have to go to the gym all those years, all those hours wedded to the iron game, as we call it."

47. The Chinese characters in the main title screen for which lively 1986 actioner literally translate to "Evil Spirits Make a Big Scene in Little Spiritual State"?

48. Who ran the often notorious Cannon Group production company throughout the Eighties? What was their nickname?

49. "The Dancing's Over. Now it gets dirty." Which film's UK quad poster bore this shameless tagline?

GUEST STAR: Gale Anne Hurd

Producer of *The Terminator* (1984), *Aliens* (1986), *Armageddon* (1998) and Executive Producer of TV's *The Walking Dead* (2010 to present).

50. What was the name of the nightclub in *The Terminator* where The Terminator first targets Sarah Connor?

Answers on page 271

2000 AD: THE FIRST 500 THRILL-POWERED PROGS

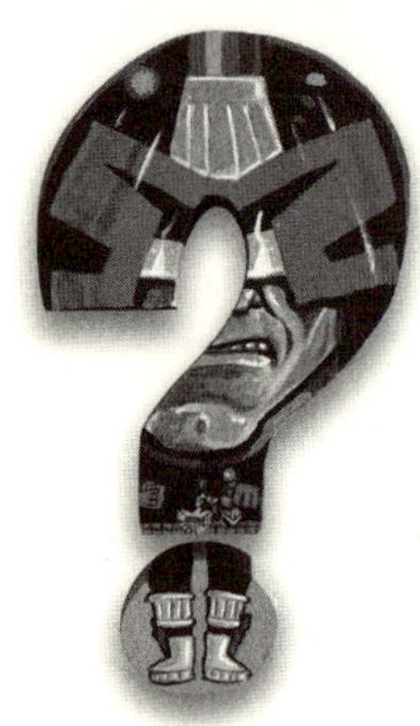

Borag Thungg, Earthlets!

Travel with me, if you will, back in time. The Dateline: 05 Mar 77. You see that cheeky-looking North London lad, walking home from the newsagents? That's me. Seven years old, with a pocket full of sherbet lemons, blissfully unaware that in just ten years' time my hair will start thinning.

The moment I get home I find a quiet place to sit and gaze at the day's essential purchase: Programme 2 of the Galaxy's Greatest Comic, *2000 AD*. Since the first issue dropped a week earlier, it's all my friends and I have been talking about. We'd always considered Saturdays special – no school, and all that. Now, though, they were sacred.

Initially created to capitalise on the growing excitement for *Star Wars*, which was still, sadly, several months away, *2000 AD* was a swift kick in the conkers to everything we'd seen before. Neither polite, light, soft nor safe, it wasn't the sort of comic that, if they'd taken the time to inspect it, our parents would approve of. It was mad, anarchic, violent, explosive, giddy, gorgeous and quite the most fantastic fun that comics could be.

The only thing that could make them more appealing would be free gifts and, oh look, they had those too! Naturally, I immediately pasted Prog 2's stickers all over my body before running around in slow motion, fighting Bigfoot and the like. Though I wish I still had those stickers, how could I resist the opportunity, back then, to become...Biotronic? How, indeed, could I resist anything about *2000 AD*?

Splundig vur thrigg, and good luck!

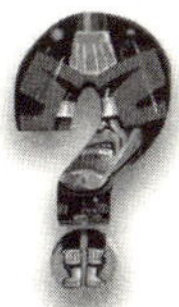

1. "It sums up the facelessness of justice – justice has no soul. So it isn't necessary for readers to see his face, and I don't want you to." Who is John Wagner describing here?

2. Bastich, Drokk, Grud, Sneck, Stomm: which is the odd one out?

3. What does the acronym M.A.C.H. stand for?

4. What's the term for Mega-City One citizens who attempt to cross the Cursed Earth for a fresh start in the New Territories?

5. What free gifts came with the first and third Progs in 1977?

6. What trio of Harry Harrison novels were adapted for *2000 AD* by Kelvin Gosnell and Carlos Ezquerra?

7. What comedy sci-fi series created by John Wagner, Alan Grant and Massimo Belardinelli included the 1982 adventures "Lugjack" (#244, 1982), "The Great Mush Rush" (#251, 1982) and "Stoop Coop Soup" (#288, 1982)?

8. Who are the four Dark Judges, and in which story do they first appear together?

9. Who is *2000 AD*'s fictional editor and from where does he hail?

10. Which treasured 1950s comicbook character was resurrected for the launch of *2000 AD* in 1977?

11. The ABC Warriors are a squad of war 'bots designed to withstand which three varieties of warfare?

12. Where does Kano keep a secret he refuses to share?

13. What's the sport – described as "Football, Boxing, Kung Fu and Basketball rolled into one!" – featured in "Harlem Heroes" (#1, 1977)?

14. What stories did *2000 AD* inherit from struggling sister comics *Starlord* and *Tornado*?

GUEST STAR: Pat Mills

The Godfather of British Comics: Editor of *2000 AD* from Progs 1 to 16 (1977), co-creator of *Flesh* (#1, 1977), *ABC Warriors* (#119, 1979), *Nemesis the Warlock* (#167, 1980) and *Sláine* (#330, 1983).

15. What was the name of the art editor who laid out most of the early Progs and was thus responsible for its unique look?

16. January 1, 1999: Bombed in the morning and defeated by teatime, Britain is defeated by what force, during which conflict, in what series?

17. "It's only three pages long, written and drawn by Kevin O'Neill showing some really unsettling artwork. I read this when

I was very young and couldn't help feeling concern for the kid that Tharg psychologically damages. If he's alive today I hope he's okay," wrote artist Henry Flint of which short tale from Prog 24 (1977)?

18. Where did she go? What did she do?

19. What was the first Judge Dredd story to exceed twenty episodes?

20. Who were the four original members of the Angel Gang, introduced and promptly killed off in "The Judge Child" (#156, 1980)?

21. During the Scrawl War documented in John Wagner, Alan Grant and Ron Smith's "Unamerican Graffiti" (#206, 1981), Chopper is provoked into defacing which enormous relocated landmark?

22. What is Waldo Dobbs' alias, and what do those initials stand for?

23. Who was named "Character Most Worthy of Own Title" in the British Section of the 1984 Eagle Awards?

24. What range of Mega-City One confectionery was known as the sweet that was too good to eat?

25. How much did Prog 1 (1977) cost in UK Earth Money, and also, on Mercury?

26. A short-lived series by Alan Hebden and César López Vera, "Death Planet" (#62, 1978) featured what important first for *2000 AD*?

27. To illustrate his line of thinking, and inspire artist Carlos Ezquerra, John Wagner handed him an advert featuring what character, from which movie, suggesting he use it as a guideline when designing the look of Judge Dredd?

28. "NO! Please let me drown before the GIANT SCORPIONS get to me!" Accompanied by similarly sensational art, this legendary cover line from Prog 93 (1978) promoted what gory tale in the pages within?

29. How is The Jam's Paul Weller connected with Nemesis the Warlock, a fire-breathing demonic alien sworn to defeat the fanatical Torquemada, Grand Master of the Terran Empire?

GUEST STAR: Matt Smith

2000 AD's longest-serving editor, Matt has been Tharg the Mighty's right-hand droid since 2002. Reader of the Galaxy's Greatest Comic since 1985.

30. What frozen – and canned – vegetable figure-head made an appearance in Judge Dredd to much controversy?

31. What's the name of the extra-dimensional agency dedicated to the maintenance and repair of breaks and distortions across the multiverse? Also, what is most unusual about its agents?

32. 5 Men plus 1 Droid plus 1 Alien plus 1 Panther equals what?

33. What was the first Judge Dredd story ever created? Also, what was the first Judge Dredd story ever published?

34. A former S.A.S. officer who's blasted into the future by a mighty nuclear boom, the adventures of Nick Stone and his Yujee chums – cat girl Liana, wolf man Gruff, bull man T-Bone and dog man Billy the Pup – are detailed in which eye-popping series?

35. Who are Sam Slade's two robotic sidekicks?

36. Prior to "The Apocalypse War" (#245, 1982), by John Wagner, Alan Grant and Carlos Ezquerra, approximately how many people were unemployed in Mega-City One?

37. The last of Nu Earth's Genetic Infantrymen, Rogue Trooper pursues the despicable Traitor General with help from three fallen comrades whose consciousnesses are stored on biochips implanted in his equipment. What are their names and which items do they inhabit?

38. Who is the only bear on the CIA Death List?

39. What does Birmingham schoolgirl Roxie prefer to call Interpreter Zhcchz, of the Tau Ceti Imperium, after he crash lands on Earth and she takes him in?

40. What was Judge Dredd's first extended storyline, and which long-running character did it introduce?

41. Based on the body-distorting battle frenzy of the Irish hero Cú Chulainn, what is the power that transforms Sláine into a terrifying and prodigiously powerful warrior?

42. Johnny Alpha's mutated eyes give him which two key abilities?

43. Who killed Halo Jones' flatmate Brinna, and why?

44. What do "Borag Thungg" and "Splundig vur thrigg" mean?

45. Who is the only member of the ABC Warriors to lead the team besides Hammerstein? Also, what is the name of his signature weapon, and what does it enable him to do?

46. What are the six basic settings available to wielders of the Lawgiver MK I?

47. Following his vengeful attack on the Trans Time Base, where does the Nothosaurus known as Big Hungry end up in Geoffrey Miller and Massimo Belardinelli's "Flesh: Book II" (#86, 1978)?

48. Your skin and surface muscular tissue have become transparent. You are the first man to see inside his own body. To see his own bones, heart, lungs and liver! You are unique. You are…?

49. Created by John Wagner and Brian Bolland, how does Psi-Judge Anderson save Mega-City One in her debut adventure, "Judge Death" (#149, 1980)?

50. Released on the short-lived Zarjazz record label in February 1985, what was the name of the Judge Dredd tribute single by The Fink Brothers?

Answers on page 278

UNIVERSAL MONSTERS UNLEASHED!

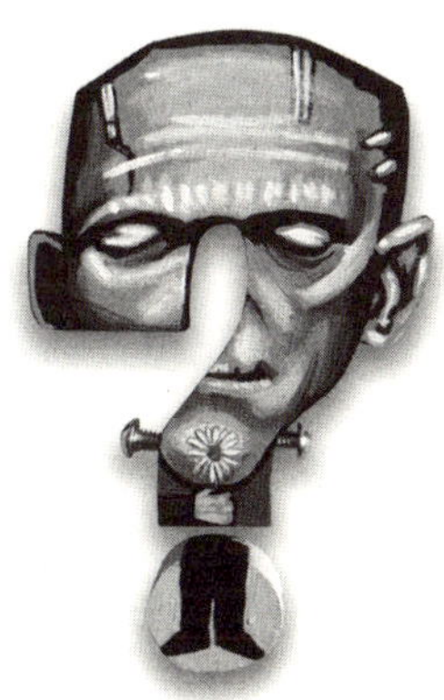

A good night's sleep is no friend to the nerd. Don't succumb to its pillowy embrace. Though the physical and psychological benefits of being well rested are, indeed, tremendous, so too are the rewards gained from staying up too late. Can you imagine how much TV you'd miss if you went to bed at a sensible hour? How many comicbooks you'd never know? How few videogames you'd conquer? Exactly.

When I was small, and had no say regarding when I'd clock in for my nightly slice of death, staying up late was my favourite treat – one that was usually accompanied by a movie. Though today, I love the access we have to everything, instantly, wherever and whenever we want it, what the digital age has taken from us is the specialness of scheduled programming with no second chances. Back then, if you snoozed, you losed. And the last thing I ever wanted to snooze through was a late-night double bill of Universal Monster Movies.

Sat on the sofa in my dressing gown with the lights down low and my eyes wide as the night sky, I was mesmerised by those vintage chillers, powerless to resist as they filled my living room with misty, dreamlike, bump-in-the-night terrors. Though they wanted to suck my blood, scoop out my brain, feast on my flesh or drag me down to Davy Jones' Locker, somehow I'd always survive. To me, they weren't just movies. They were life-affirming experiences. And if that's not worth losing sleep for, I don't know what is.

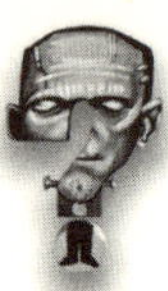

1. What was Lon Chaney's well-earned nickname?

2. When Bela Lugosi died in 1956, aged 73, at his request he was buried in the cape he wore in 1931's *Dracula*: True or false?

3. Commonly mistaken for bolts, what items actually protrude from The Monster's (Boris Karloff) neck in *Frankenstein* (1931)?

4. Who is the only actor to portray all four of Universal's major monsters: Dracula, Frankenstein's Monster, The Mummy and The Wolf Man?

5. What side effect of the drug monocane is Dr Jack Griffin (Claude Rains) unaware of when he uses it to create his invisibility formula?

6. Eager to drink to his new partnership with Henry Frankenstein (Colin Clive), Doctor Pretorius (Ernest Thesiger) pours them each a gin and makes what memorable toast?

7. Described by *New York Times* film critic Frank S. Nugent as a "charming bit of lycanthropy", what was the world's first feature-length werewolf movie?

8. The poster for which Universal creature feature included the suggestive tagline, "She gives you that weird feeling!"?

9. In *The Wolf Man* (1941), while flirting with Gwen (Evelyn Ankers) in her antique shop, what curious item does Larry Talbot (Lon Chaney Jr) purchase for the princely sum of £3?

10. What was the first Universal horror movie featuring more than one of the studio's classic monsters?

11. What's the name of the boat in *Creature from the Black Lagoon* (1954)?

12. Which iconic monster make-up involved the application of fish skin to the actor's nose, and egg membrane to his eyeballs?

13. What is the life?

14. Who was known as "The Uncanny", and what was his real name?

GUEST STAR: Xander Berkeley

Star of *Candyman* (1992), *Gattaca* (1997), *24* (2001–2010), *Taken* (2008), *The Spectacular Spider-Man* (2008–2009), *Kick-Ass* (2010) and *The Walking Dead* (2010–present).

15. Who designed the iconic make-up and prosthetics used in Universal's *Frankenstein* (1931), *The Mummy* (1932) and *The Wolf Man* (1941)?

16. For what sacrilege was Imhotep (Boris Karloff) condemned to the Nameless Death, in *The Mummy* (1932)?

17. After seeing *The Invisible Man* (1933), who told director James Whale that while he liked the picture, he had one grave fault to find with it: it had taken the novel's brilliant scientist and changed him into a lunatic – a liberty he could not condone?

18. What inspired Elsa Lanchester's piercing hiss as the Monster's frightened, scornful bride in 1935's *The Bride of Frankenstein*?

19. What's the name of the striking, iconic rock formation, in northern Los Angeles, that doubled for Tibet in *Werewolves of London* (1935) and was most famously featured in the classic *Star Trek* episode "Arena" (S01E18), where Captain Kirk (William Shatner) battles the fearsome Gorn?

20. Which Universal frightener marked the launch of Lon Chaney Jr's prolific career as a horror movie star?

21. "Even a man who is pure in heart, And says his prayers by night...

22. What is the only Oscar-winning Universal horror film?

23. "The LAUGHS Are MONSTERous", and "It's SCARE-EWY", teased the trailer for which hit horror comedy?

24. Which Universal monster movie did acclaimed art-house filmmaker Ingmar Bergman screen for himself every year as a birthday treat?

25. Whose premature demise led to Bela Lugosi winning the title role in *Dracula* (1931)?

26. Though it sneaked past the censor during the film's initial run, which line of dialogue from *Frankenstein* (1931) was later deemed blasphemous and replaced with a loud clap of thunder when the film was re-released in the late 1930s?

27. Though no direct sequels to *The Mummy* (1932) were ever produced, Universal released a quartet of chillers in the 1940s that told terrifying tales of a different Mummy, Kharis, first played by Tom Tyler, then three times in a row by Lon Chaney Jr. What were the titles of those four fearsome films?

28. What varieties of homunculi does Doctor Pretorius (Ernest Thesiger) reveal to Henry (Colin Clive) in *Bride of Frankenstein* (1935)?

29. What phrase does Baron Wolf von Frankenstein (Basil Rathbone) find scrawled in chalk on his father's sarcophagus in *Son of Frankenstein* (1939)?

GUEST STAR: Tony Todd

Star of *Night of the Living Dead* (1990), *Candyman* (1992), *Candyman: Farewell to the Flesh* (1995), *Final Destination* (2000), *Star Trek: The Next Generation* (1987–1994), *24* (2001–2010), *Chuck* (2007–2012) and much, much more!

30. Who played Universal's terrifying Gill-man in *Creature from the Black Lagoon* (1954) and its two sequels, *Revenge of the Creature* (1955) and *The Creature Walks Among Us* (1956)?

31. Which classic chiller endured multiple reshoots after the test audience at its initial preview judged it too horrific for release, causing up to 60% of the original film to be scrapped?

32. What film was shot at night, at the same time and on the same sets as *Dracula* (1931)?

33. Insisting he'd been a star in his native Hungary, and had not moved to America to be a "scarecrow", Bela Lugosi rejected which iconic role?

34. Years before co-writing the screenplay for *The Mummy* (1932), John L. Balderston covered which momentous Egyptian event for the *New York World* newspaper?

35. What's the only time in *The Invisible Man* (1933) that Claude Rains is visible?

36. What three staples of classic werewolf lore were invented for 1935's *Werewolf of London*?

37. Count Alucard, Baron Latos and Dr Lahos are all names assumed in different movies by which fiendish character?

38. Clint Eastwood made his first screen appearance, as lab technician Jennings, in which Universal monster movie?

39. "My mind drifted off, and I thought, 'If one vampire is scary, what if the whole world is full of vampires?'" Which author was inspired by *Dracula* (1931) to write what masterpiece of horror fiction?

40. What's the name of Henry's hunchback assistant in *Frankenstein* (1931)?

41. What was Boris Karloff's tragic final line as The Monster in *The Bride of Frankenstein* (1935)?

42. In *Son of Frankenstein* (1939), what crime was Ygor (Bela Lugosi) hung for, only to survive and swear vengeance on the jurors who sent him to the gallows?

43. What Universal classic was known as *El Hombre Lobo* in Argentina and *O lykanthropos* (*ο λυκανθρωπος*) in Greek?

44. How many times did Bela Lugosi play Count Dracula?

45. Which Universal monster was known to The Munsters as Uncle Gilbert, appearing in the episode "Love Comes to Mockingbird Heights" (S01E31)?

46. Eager to avoid even a whiff of homoeroticism, Universal nixed a sequence in *Dracula* (1931) where The Count (Bela Lugosi) has Renfield (Dwight Frye) for dinner. To clarify the studio's position, a memo was sent to director Tod Browning. What did it say?

47. How is the esteemed author of *Frankenstein; or, The Modern Prometheus* (1818) credited at the beginning of Universal's celebrated 1931 adaptation?

48. What did Boris Karloff describe as "the most trying ordeal I ever endured"?

49. The great spell by which Isis raised Osiris from the dead is inscribed on which cursed artefact?

50. "Certainly, I was typed. But what is typing? It is a trademark, a means by which the public recognises you. Actors work all their lives to achieve that. I got mine with just one picture. It was a blessing." Whose wise words were these, and what film was he talking about?

Answers on page 287

HANNA-BARBERA: THE GENERAL MOTORS OF ANIMATION

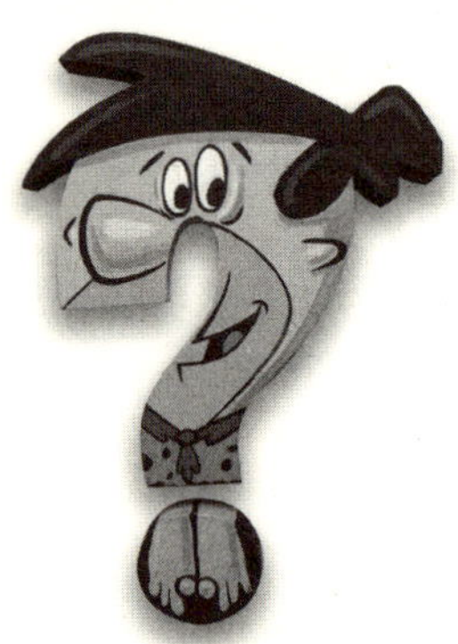

From 1940 until 1957, animation legends William Hanna and Joseph Barbera – Bill and Joe to us – produced 114 flawlessly executed and shinily beautiful Tom and Jerry shorts for Metro-Goldwyn-Mayer. Winning seven Academy Awards for their painstaking efforts, not to mention untold legions of lifelong fans, they were ultimately rewarded for their diligence and craft with unemployment. Once the bean counters at MGM realised that re-releasing old Tom and Jerry cartoons was no less profitable than distributing new ones, they promptly closed the studio's animation wing and Bill and Joe were suddenly out on their ears.

With help from their director pal George Sidney, who in 1945 had enlisted Jerry Mouse to dance alongside Gene Kelly in *Anchors Aweigh*, Bill and Joe immediately took charge of their own destinies by forming Hanna-Barbera Productions in 1957. Producing cartoons exclusively for the small screen, they quickly dominated the market, and by the Sixties were responsible for 80% of all children's programming, cranking out up to six hours of entertainment every single week.

Contrary to their extravagant Tom and Jerry style, Bill and Joe worked fast and cheap for TV, pioneering a technique that came to be known as Limited Animation. Using "fewer drawings", explained Hanna, it "required less inking and painting, less camera work, less of everything, in fact, except background art". Less focused on action than snappy dialogue, often scenes required just a character's mouth and eyes to be animated, and in close-up too, which meant even less to draw.

Regardless of these drastically cut corners, and Hanna-Barbera's willingness to recycle show ideas, plots, characters and dialogue for series after series, for more than three decades the company's cartoons charmed audiences worldwide, earning record-breaking ratings and a respectable eight Emmys.

In addition to their live-action and feature-length efforts, Hanna-Barbera produced more than 3,000 animated half-hours for television. They were the shows we'd rush home from school to watch every afternoon. The cartoons we'd wake up early to see every Saturday morning – surely the most sacred TV time of the week. How close did you pay attention, though? It's time to find out...

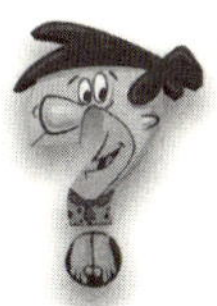

1. They would have gotten away with it too, if it weren't for what?

2. What was Hanna-Barbera's first original animated television series?

3. What's the song that Huckleberry Hound was so fond of singing, badly but with great enthusiasm?

4. When visiting Jellystone Park, what must you keep your eye on at all times?

5. What's playing at the Drive-In Movie featured in *The Flintstones*' opening titles?

6. Whose alter ego was El Kabong, a Zorro type who'd bash bad guys with his guitar?

7. At a charity speaking engagement in London, shortly before his death in 1997, voice actor Don Messick performed many of his most popular Hanna-Barbera characters, yet neglected to perform arguably his most famous, claiming that giving up smoking had robbed him of the rasp he needed to do the voice justice. Which character was he talking about?

8. What are the names of the cats in T.C.'s gang?

9. What was Touché Turtle's catchphrase?

GUEST STAR: James Arnold Taylor

Veteran voice actor best known for playing Obi-Wan Kenobi in *Star Wars: The Clone Wars* (2008–2019) and Johnny in *Johnny Test* (2005–2014), as well as videogame heroes Tidus (*Final Fantasy*) and Ratchet (*Ratchet & Clank*).

10. Besides Yogi, what do Boo-Boo Bear and Mr Ranger have in common?

11. What was the first Hanna-Barbera show to win an Emmy?

12. Wally Gator, Yogi Bear, Captain Caveman, Elroy Jetson and Huckleberry Hound: who's the odd one out?

13. What was Hanna-Barbera's first prime-time animated series?

14. What company employs George Jetson to press a button for an hour a day, two days a week?

15. What was Hanna-Barbera's first action show, an adventure serial with the working title *The Saga of Chip Baloo*?

16. How, in 1957, did Bill Hanna and Joe Barbera decide who'd come first in their new company name?

17. Which one of the vintage comedy legends featured in animated spin-offs *Laurel and Hardy* (1966) and *The Abbott and Costello Cartoon Show* (1967–1968) lived long enough to voice his own character?

18. Which three heroes formed Beatlesque superteam *The Impossibles*?

19. Of the four fleecy, anthropomorphised animal musicians who formed bubblegum rock quartet The Banana Splits, what was unique about Snorky? Also, what species was he, and what instrument did he play?

20. What are the names of the Flintstones' pets?

21. In the Top Cat episode "Top Cat Falls in Love" (S01E07), what does T.C. do to spend time with Miss LaRue (Jean Vander Pyl), a pretty cat nurse he has a crush on?

22. Which Hanna-Barbera production was the first TV show broadcast in colour on ABC-TV?

23. Which long-running Eighties' 'toon was based on a comic strip by Belgian cartoonist Pierre "Peyo" Culliford?

24. Who never won a single Wacky Race and what was their atrocious auto?

GUEST STAR: Brad Meltzer

Best-selling novelist, non-fiction writer and comic-book author best known in nerd circles for DC's classic *Identity Crisis.*

25. What were the three team names in the Laff-a-Lympics?

26. What vintage sitcom inspired Hanna-Barbera's *Top Cat* (1961–1962). Also, which actor appeared in both shows?

27. Who is the adopted son of Dr Benton Quest?

28. What were Clyde, Dum Dum, Pockets, Snoozy, Softy, Yak Yak and Zippy collectively known as, and which two shows did they feature in?

29. What inspired CBS's head of daytime programming, Fred Silverman, to christen Hanna-Barbera's Greatest Dane, Scooby-Doo?

30. In the first episode of which series does Melody Valentine (Jackie Joseph/Cherie Moor) adopt Bleep, a fluffy, pink-limbed alien who makes bleep sounds only she can understand, and generates invisible sound waves from its mouth and eyes?

31. Who's got style, a groovy style, and a car that just won't stop?

32. Why did the BBC rename *Top Cat* a month into the show's 1962 UK TV debut, and what did they call it instead?

33. What was unusual about the tandem motorbike ridden by the Hair Bear Bunch?

34. Superman, Wonder Woman, Aquaman, Batman and Robin assembled in 1973 to form which team for Hanna-Barbera?

35. Barney Rubble was voiced by Mel Blanc for all but five episodes of *The Flintstones* (1960–1966). Who covered for him while he was absent, and what was the extraordinary story behind his sooner-than-expected return to work?

36. How old is Captain Cavemen?

37. Who voiced Frankenstein Jr, Meteor Man and Godzilla for Hanna-Barbera?

38. "The problem with the show was simply this: When they start telling you in Standards and Practices, 'Don't shoot any flame at anybody, don't step on any buildings or cars,' then pretty soon, they've taken away all the stuff he represents." What show is Joe Barbera describing here?

39. What are the full names of those four meddling teens and their cowardly Great Dane?

GUEST STAR: Eric Lewald

Showrunner and writer on *The X-Men* (1992–1997); Writer and story editor on *Beetlejuice* (1989–1991) and *RoboCop: Alpha Commando* (1998–1999).

40. In the mid-1980s, Hanna-Barbera had their own hit transforming-vehicles action series that was NOT called Transformers. What was its full name and who were its lead hero and villain?

41. Which classic 'toon antagonist was known as Sharshabeel in Arabic, Drakoumel in Greek and Lão Gà Mên in Vietnamese?

42. The appearance of which recurring character, during the final season of *The Flintstones* (1960–1966), is considered by many fans to be the series' shark-jumping moment?

43. Who did Dastardly and Muttley spend weeks on end fruitlessly trying to nab, jab, tab and/or grab?

44. Larry, Curly and Moe with bionic powers, fighting crime in superhero show *The Robonic Stooges*. Was that really a thing?

45. Which super-powered sidekicks joined DC's finest in *The All-New Super Friends Hour*, and what were their abilities?

46. Where does mild-mannered janitor Penrod "Penry" Pooch transform into his fan-riffic alter-ego?

47. Which troubled superstar gave Joe Barbera an autographed photo of himself with the inscription, "To my hero of yesterday, today, and tomorrow, with many thanks for all the many cartoon friends you gave me as a child. They were all I had."

48. Who was born in St Bernard's Memorial Hospital to Scooby's sister, Ruby-Doo?

49. Which three *Happy Days* (1974–1984) castmates reunited for time-travelling spin-off 'toon *The Fonz and the Happy Days Gang* (1980–1982)?

50. What phrase would Bez the Beast (Henry Corden) have to incant if he wanted to shapeshift into, say, an elephant, in *Arabian Knights* (1968–1969)?

Answers on page 298

STEVEN SPIELBERG: *JAWS* TO *JURASSIC PARK*

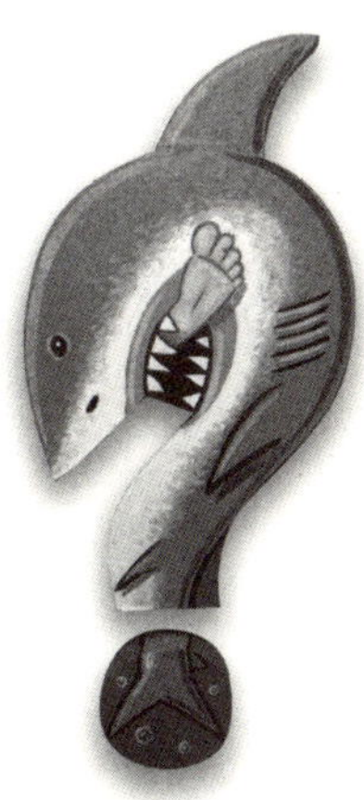

I remember when my three big brothers came home from the cinema after seeing *Jaws* in 1975. They were all raving about it. As I was just six at the time, it wasn't something I was allowed to go and see with them. They did, however, bring me a souvenir badge, which I still have, and treasure.

Years later, my brother Russell took me to see the movie at the National Film Theatre, on London's South Bank. Though I'd seen it on TV several times by then, when Ben Gardner's bloated, mangled head popped into view, I still jumped out of my skin. Everyone did.

I'd just turned 15 when *Indiana Jones and the Temple of Doom* rollercoastered into cinemas. It was 1984 and my mum took me to see it, opening weekend, at the Empire Leicester Square. I was so excited to be there, my enthusiasm could have powered the Death Star. Literally millions of voices could have cried out in terror, and been suddenly silenced, from the devastating power of my flushed cheeks alone.

After the movie, which astounded me with its continuous thrills, the thought occurred that no future cinema-going experience could possibly compete. That entertainment had peaked for me. I was so happy, I was almost sad.

That's how much I adored Steven Spielberg's films.

I was so cross when he made *The Color Purple*, his first overtly grown-up feature, in 1985. "Why would he waste his time," I wailed, "directing a film that any one of a hundred Hollywood types could crank out?" The movies he made his name with, the films my friends and I felt were made just for us...Those were everything. And no one could make them like Spielberg. No one could come even close. Why, then, would he want to move on?

But move on he did, and so did we, and obviously he's made many wonderful, grown-up films since then, but for the purposes of this chapter, I'm focusing on the movies of his that made people crazy, they loved them so much.

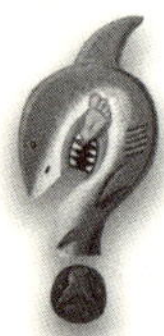

1. You yell shark and what?

2. Shaving cream, mud, sand, clay, mashed potato: what's the odd one out?

3. *1941* (1979) opens with a parody of which classic monster movie?

4. What is packed in Top Secret Army Intelligence crate #9906753?

5. In *E.T. The Extra-Terrestrial* (1982), what does Elliott (Henry Thomas) use to lure E.T. back to his house?

6. What delicacies are served at the infamous feast of Pankot Palace in *Indiana Jones and the Temple of Doom* (1984)?

7. What scares Professor Henry Walton Jones Sr (Sean Connery)?

8. What is the first dinosaur that Hammond's (Richard Attenborough) visitors see in *Jurassic Park* (1993)?

9. The first film to make over $100 million at the box office, *Jaws* (1975) was crowned the highest-grossing film of all time, holding the title until which film snatched it away?

10. "I wanted the aliens to look like aliens," said Steven Spielberg of *Close Encounters of the Third Kind*'s (1977) design process. "I did not want the aliens to look like people in costumes." To that end, what was Spielberg's first, frankly crazy, idea for portraying visitors from outer space?

11. Where are Claude (Murray Hamilton) and Herbie (Eddie Deezen) stationed on watch in *1941* (1979)?

12. What does the student in Indy's classroom have written on her eyelids in *Raiders of the Lost Ark* (1981)?

13. When are the first three Indiana Jones movies set?

14. How did Henry (Sean Connery) know Ilsa (Alison Doody) was a Nazi in *Indiana Jones and the Last Crusade* (1989)?

GUEST STAR: Jerry Ordway

Co-creator of *All-Star Squadron* (1981–1987), *Infinity, Inc.* (1984–1988), inker on *Crisis on Infinite Earths* (1985–1986), writer and artist on *The Power of Shazam!* (1994) and stacks of Superman titles too.

15. What's the connection between Nick Fury and Indiana Jones?

16. Which John Williams score did Spielberg insist was "clearly responsible for half the success of that movie"?

17. What are close encounters of the first, second and third kinds?

18. "Can't it just beam up?"

19. Before conspiring with the Nazis in *Indiana Jones and the Last Crusade* (1989), actors Julian Glover (who played Walter Donovan) and Michael Sheard (who played Adolf Hitler) served which other evil army?

20. What is Alan Grant's (Sam Neill) first line in *Jurassic Park* (1993)?

21. Which Spielberg movie holds the record for longest theatrical run?

22. What, according to Hammond (Richard Attenborough), does Malcolm (Jeff Goldblum) suffer from?

23. What does Hooper (Richard Dreyfuss) pull out of the tiger shark that he cuts open in *Jaws* (1975)?

24. When Roy (Richard Dreyfuss) boards the Mothership at the end of *Close Encounters of the Third Kind* (1977), John Williams' soaring score references what Oscar-winning song from which vintage Disney classic?

25. Where do Loomis (Tim Matheson) and Donna (Nancy Allen) crash land in *1941* (1979)?

26. How does Indy (Harrison Ford) respond to Marion's (Karen Allen) observation that he's not the man she knew ten years ago?

27. What does E.T. dress as to sneak out of the house during All Hallows' Eve?

28. Which three characters in *Indiana Jones and the Temple of Doom* (1984) were named after the filmmaker's dogs?

29. What make of gun does Donovan (Julian Glover) shoot Henry (Sean Connery) with in *Indiana Jones and the Last Crusade* (1989)?

GUEST STAR: Ed Solomon

Co-writer of *Bill & Ted's Excellent Adventure* (1989), *Bill & Ted's Bogus Journey* (1991), *Men in Black* (1997), *Charlie's Angels* (2000) and *Now You See Me* (2013).

30. What was the on-set nickname of the shark in *Jaws* (1975)?

31. What's the first toy that activates in Barry's (Cary Guffey) bedroom when the aliens visit his house?

32. According to Jack Nicholson, what did Stanley Kubrick say to Steven Spielberg about *1941* (1979)?

33. Who was famously offered the role of Indiana Jones in *Raiders of the Lost Ark* (1981), but forced to turn it down due to a prior commitment?

34. What song does famous American female vocalist Willie Scott (Kate Capshaw) sing, mostly in Mandarin, during *Indiana Jones and the Temple of Doom*'s (1984) sparkling opening credits?

35. What do Quint (Robert Shaw) and Hooper (Richard Dreyfuss) toast to, in *Jaws* (1975)?

36. Following a demonstration in which Dennis Muren proved that full-body dinosaur effects for *Jurassic Park* (1993) could be achieved digitally, what did creature designer and go motion pioneer Phil Tippett whisper to Steven Spielberg?

37. Why did wee Cary Guffey, who played adorable Barry Guiler in *Close Encounters of the Third Kind* (1977), find the scene where he exits the Mothership embarrassing to shoot?

38. When it seemed Spielberg's career might be a casualty of the relative failure of *1941* (1979), John Belushi took to wearing a t-shirt bearing what hilariously spiteful message?

39. Whose signature stunt inspired the memorable moment in *Raiders of the Lost Ark* (1981) where Indy (played by stuntman Terry Leonard, doubling for Harrison Ford) drops from the front of a German transport truck and is dragged underneath, between the wheels?

40. In *Jurassic Park* (1993), what is the girl on Nedry's (Wayne Knight) computer wallpaper wearing?

41. What are E.T.'s final words to Gertie (Drew Barrymore), Michael (Robert MacNaughton) and Elliott (Henry Thomas) in *E.T. The Extra-Terrestrial* (1982)?

42. Besides Harrison Ford, who's the only actor to appear in each of the first three Indiana Jones films?

43. What do you call a blind dinosaur's dog?

44. What's the name of Quint's (Robert Shaw) boat in *Jaws* (1975)?

45. Which celebrated fantasy author declared that *Close Encounters of the Third Kind* (1977) was the greatest science fiction film ever made?

46. What film does General Stilwell (Robert Stack) insist on seeing in *1941* (1979)?

47. What happens to Belloq (Paul Freeman), Toht (Ronald Lacey) and Dietrich's (Wolf Kahler) heads during the climactic Ark-opening sequence in *Raiders of the Lost Ark* (1981)?

48. "X never, ever…"?

49. Which of Spielberg's monster movies has a higher human body count: *Jaws* (1975) or *Jurassic Park* (1993)?

50. In *Raiders of the Lost Ark* (1981), who does Major Eaton (William Hootkins) insist will be researching the unspeakable power of the new-found Ark?

Answers on page 307

BATMAN: THE ANIMATED SERIES

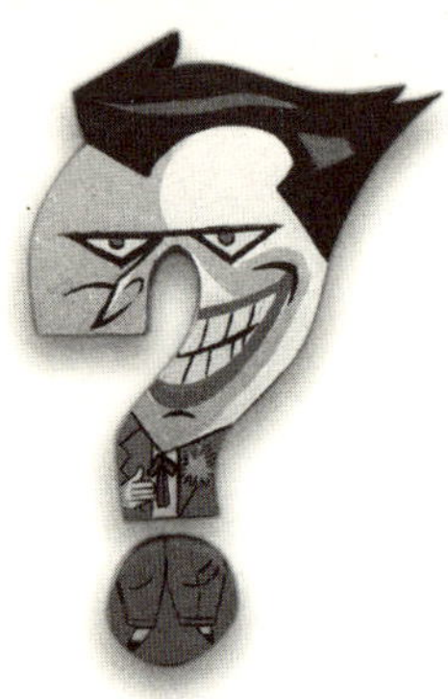

Superpowers are cool and all, but as a rule, they're not earned. More quirks of birth, or random collisions of time, place and circumstance. Often alien in origin, other times gifts from gods or demons, then there's mad science tech, of course, and let's not forget biological mutations, as there's always some experimental compound or toxic goo sitting around, waiting to be spilled and mixed or zapped by lightning. All of which makes instant heroes. Just add a costume and a can-do attitude, and POW! You've got yourself a super-type.

Batman, though, is better than that. While yes, it helps to have billions in the bank, and a tragic back-story certainly keeps one motivated, what ultimately powers the Caped Crusader is his remarkable will. To be the smartest. The shrewdest. The most insightful. To be the fittest. The fastest. The strongest. To train harder and longer than anyone else. To be Sherlock Holmes, Harry Houdini and Bruce Lee, all in one. To never compromise. Never back down. And never give up.

That is why, whenever anyone asks me, "Who do you think would win in a fight between Batman and..." I cut them short. It matters not, who else they name. The answer is, and always will be, Batman, because Batman's earned his victories. Created by Bob Kane and Bill Finger in 1939, he is us, only better. The ultimate version of what we could be, if only we were prepared to sacrifice everything – family, security, happiness, the lot – in pursuit of justice.

Speaking of ultimate versions, here's where we get to *Batman: The Animated Series*. Drawing, for the show's initial 1992 to 1995 run, upon half a century of Batman history, the series took the best of everything that came before, the choicest cuts of plot, design, characterisation and tone from screen as well as print, lovingly distilling them into the greatest, most perfect superhero cartoon ever made. Respectful, but not slavishly so, it also knew what to throw out, what to refresh, what to reinvent entirely, and beyond that, what new elements could be added that would sit beside the old in perfect harmony.

Beyond simply doing justice to Batman and his rich, eccentric comicbook world, *The Animated Series* crafted its definitive depiction. It's so damn good, it feels like Batman made it himself.

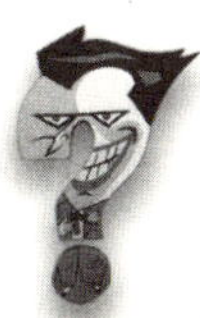

1. Although "On Leather Wings" (S01E02) was the first produced episode of *Batman: The Animated Series*, what was the first episode that actually aired?

2. What does The Joker (Mark Hamill) ask of Charlie (Ed Begley Jr) in "Joker's Favor" (S01E07)?

3. What colour are Pamela Isley's eyes?

4. What links The Bookworm, from *Batman* (1966–1968), to The Mad Hatter, from *Batman: The Animated Series*?

5. What has kept Ra's Al Ghul (David Warner) alive for 600 years?

6. In "Harley and Ivy" (S01E47), after Poison Ivy (Diane Pershing) boasts that "No man can take us prisoner", who, then, does?

7. Eager to understand how he'd earned the role of The Joker, Mark Hamill approached casting director Andrea Romano. "I asked [her], 'How did I get it? How did you know you wanted me?'" What did she tell him?

8. In "The Cat and the Claw Part I" (S01E01), when Catwoman (Adrienne Barbeau) says to Batman, "You can't deny there's something between us," how does he respond?

9. Who was Bruce Wayne's boyhood TV hero?

GUEST STAR: Paul Dini

Co-creator of Harley Quinn. Emmy Award-winning writer of *Tiny Toon Adventures* (1990–1992), *Batman: The Animated Series* (1992–1995), *The New Batman/ Superman Adventures* (1997–2000) and *Batman Beyond* (1999–2001). Co-writer (with Bruce Timm) of Eisner and Harvey Award-winner *The Batman Adventures: Mad Love* (February 1994).

10. How did sadistic Arkham guard Lyle Bolton (a.k.a. Lock Up, voiced by Bruce Weitz) torture Scarface (George Dzundza)?

11. Using dark paper instead of white to lay down their moody art deco backgrounds, artists Eric Radomski and Ted Blackman refined a style dubbed what, by storyboard artist Bruce Timm?

12. *Batman: The Animated Series* features a much older Robin than in the comicbooks. Voiced by Loren Lester, Dick Grayson's about 20 years old in the cartoon. This was partly because the creators of the show didn't want him around all the time, a constant sidekick who'd "diminish Batman's role", says Paul Dini, "as a brooding, solitary hero". However, there was another key reason why Robin couldn't be a kid in the series. Any idea what that was?

13. Which actress and former classmate of writer Paul Dini inspired the creation of Harley Quinn, originally intended as a one-time character in "Joker's Favor" (S01E07), but now a staple of Batman's comicbook and live-action universe as well?

14. In "Pretty Poison" (S01E09), District Attorney Harvey Dent (Richard Moll) is sentenced to death by Poison Ivy (Diane Pershing) for committing what terrible crime?

15. During the casting process for *Batman: The Animated Series*, which actor originally set his sights on playing The Joker, Jim Gordon or Harvey Bullock?

16. How much is the contract that crime boss Rupert Thorne (John Vernon) puts on Two-Face in "Two-Face Part II" (S01E18)?

17. While masquerading as Jekko the Clown, who does The Joker (Mark Hamill) identify as his mentor?

18. "Setting the look and tone for all that was to come," says Paul Dini, the dramatic, two-minute 'toon that sold the studio on *Batman: The Animated Series* saw the Caped Crusader interrupt a daring rooftop heist. How was that specific scene later repurposed for the series?

19. What is the name of the ancient, forbidden martial art detailed in "Day of the Samurai" (S01E55) that is so efficient and terrible, a mere touch can render a man unconscious, or cripple him, or even kill him?

20. Which staple of the Batcave's décor features in Two-Face's "Almost Got 'Im" (S01E35) tale?

21. Created by Alex Toth for Hanna-Barbera in 1966, which superhero's iconic suit design was appropriated by Bruce Timm for Batman?

22. How many roles did Kevin Conroy voice in his personal favourite episode of *Batman: The Animated Series*, "Perchance to Dream" (S01E26)?

23. Who presides over Arkham's kangaroo court of Batman, where the Caped Crusader (Kevin Conroy) stands accused of turning the assembled "freaks and monsters" to lives of crime?

24. What's Baby-Doll's (Alison La Placa) catchphrase, originally uttered with great frequency in her dreadful sitcom *Love That Baby*?

GUEST STAR: Patrick Savage

Composer and violinist who wrote the soundtrack for 2009's *The Human Centipede* (with Holeg Spies) and played on the scores of the *Lord of the Rings* trilogy (2001-2003), *Harry Potter and the Half-Blood Prince* (2009), *Guardians of the Galaxy Vol. 2* (2017) and *Jurassic World: Fallen Kingdom* (2018).

25. Pioneering composer Shirley Walker's much-loved score for *Batman: The Animated Series* was crafted to seamlessly incorporate Danny Elfman's 1989 Batman movie theme. Which earlier DC TV show, also with an Elfman theme, did Walker likewise score?

26. Which episode of *Batman: The Animated Series* won a Primetime Emmy for Outstanding Animated Program (one hour or less)?

27. What's the name of the hit game Edward Nygma (John Glover) created for Competitron?

28. Rather than record each role separately, which is the norm for voice-over work, the cast of *Batman: The Animated Series* recorded their work as an ensemble, all of them sitting in the same room, at the same time, performing together. One of the actors, though, was permitted to stand. Which one, and why?

29. After the first season of *Batman: The Animated Series*, what key change did Fox Kids demand be made to the show?

30. What are the full, real names of the villains Roxy Rocket (Charity James), The Clock King (Alan Rachins), Baby-Doll (Alison LaPlaca) and The Ventriloquist (George Dzunda)?

31. Before Richard Moll won the part, which iconic Hollywood Oscar-winner was approached to play Two-Face?

32. How does The Joker escape Arkham Asylum in "Christmas with the Joker" (S01E38)?

33. Which supervillain, introduced as Mr Zero in Batman #121 (February 1959), was dramatically reinterpreted for *Batman: The Animated Series*, transforming him from a gimmicky mad scientist into a far more complex and tragic character whose "frigid exterior [hid] a doomed love and vindictive fury"?

34. Before Harvey Dent's (Richard Moll) explosive transformation in "Two-Face Part 1" (S01E17), writer/producer Alan Burnett broke new ground for the character by establishing he already had a dual personality. What does Harvey's shrink call his dark, hidden half?

35. What's Harley's (Arleen Sorkin) nickname for The Joker (Mark Hamill)?

36. Until the series was rebranded *The Adventures of Batman & Robin*, what was unusual about the show's original title sequence?

37. Which member of *Batman: The Animated Series*' voice cast was its biggest comicbook geek, destined from birth to join the cast, it seems, as the name of Gotham's gloriously gothic asylum is literally hidden within his name?

38. At what point in "Perchance to Dream" (S01E26) are Bruce Wayne's suspicions that's he's dreaming confirmed?

39. Under what lame pseudonym did a young Bruce Wayne (Kevin Conroy) learn escape artistry from Zatara the Magician (Vincent Schiavelli)?

GUEST STAR: Stefan Blitz

Editor of Forces of Geek (www.forcesofgeek.com).

40. Who originally voiced The Joker, though none of his recordings were used?

41. Disfigured in an accident, over-the-hill actor Matt Hagen (Ron Perlman) becomes addicted to what experimental compound that, though initially it restores his youthful good looks, eventually transforms him into lumpen shapeshifter Clayface?

42. Hailed by Paul Dini as "a high point of each episode", what element from *Batman: The Animated Series* was largely the domain of Eric Radomski, described by the artist as a way to "create great drama in a very subtle fashion" and capture the overall feel of every show?

43. Who originally voiced Alfred Pennyworth, leaving after just three episodes to honour a stage commitment?

44. With what unusual vehicle does Lloyd Ventrix (Michael Gross) attempt to squish Batman (Kevin Conroy) in "See No Evil" (S01E56)?

45. How much does The Joker (Mark Hamill) bid for the atom bomb up for auction in "Harlequinade" (S02E10)?

46. What's most notable about DC's *The Batman Adventures* #12 ("Batgirl: Day One", September 1993)?

47. Which cracking two-part episode of *Batman: The Animated Series* was a direct adaptation of "Daughter of the Demon" (Batman #232, June 1971) and "The Demon Lives Again" (Batman #244, September 1972), both by writer Denny O'Neil and artist Neal Adams?

48. What's the first line spoken in "The Clock King" (S01E14)?

49. What's the name of Catwoman's (Adrienne Barbeau) favourite cat?

50. In "The Man Who Killed Batman" (S01E49), what tune does Harley (Arleen Sorkin) play on her kazoo while Sid the Squid's (Matt Frewer) coffin rolls down the conveyor belt, into the acid?

Answers on page 315

The Answers

James Bond: The Roger Moore Years

1. Q. What does the sign say on the gate of Kananga's crocodile farm?

   A. "TRESPASSERS WILL BE EATEN" (*Live and Let Die*, 1973).

2. Q. Hugo Drax's Viennese laboratory is opened by playing which famous 5-note movie theme on a touchtone keypad?

   A. *Close Encounters of the Third Kind*, by John Williams. Steven Spielberg later used Monty Norman's Bond Theme in *The Goonies* (1985).

3. Q. Which actor who played one of Moore's Bond villains was related to Ian Fleming?

   A. Christopher Lee, who played Francisco Scaramanga in *The Man with the Golden Gun* (1974), was Fleming's step-cousin.

4. Q. "Bond! What do you think you're doing?"

   A. "Keeping the British end up, sir!" (*The Spy Who Loved Me*, 1977).

5. Q. What card represents Bond (Roger Moore) in Solitaire's (Jane Seymour) tarot deck?

   A. The Fool.

6. Q. Which long-time Bond villain finally receives his comeuppance in *For Your Eyes Only* (1981)? Also, how does Bond despatch him?

A. Though officially billed as "Man in Wheelchair" for legal reasons, it's clearly Ernst Stavro Blofeld, hooked by Bond on a 'copter's landing gear and dropped, to his doom, down an industrial chimney.

007. **Q.** The sheep's eyeball enthusiastically gobbled by Louis Jourdan in *Octopussy* (1983) was the real thing: True or false?

A. False: it was made from marzipan.

8. **Q.** Which Eighties action star made his acting debut in *A View to a Kill* (1985) – cast at the last minute by director John Glen to play a henchman while he happened to be on set, visiting girlfriend Grace Jones?

A. Dolph Lundgren.

9. **Q.** Moore was the youngest actor to debut as James Bond: True or false?

A. False: he was the oldest. In the novel *Moonraker*, Ian Fleming wrote that at 45 Bond would be "automatically taken off the OO list and given a staff job at Headquarters". Regardless, Moore made his Bond debut at 45, in *Live and Let Die* (1973). Connery, by contrast, was 32 when he made *Dr No* (1962), George Lazenby was 30 when he made *On Her Majesty's Secret Service* (1969), Timothy Dalton was 41 when he made *The Living Daylights* (1987), Pierce Brosnan was 42 when he made *Goldeneye* (1995) and Daniel Craig was 38 when he made *Casino Royale* (2006). Moore was also the oldest ever Bond, having played him at 57 in *A View to a Kill* (1985).

10. **Q.** What is Jaws' sole line of dialogue?

A. Richard Kiel (Jaws) delivered just one line of dialogue during his two Bond appearances, toasting his new girlfriend Dolly (Blanche Ravalec), at the very end of *Moonraker* (1979), with a simple, "Well, here's to us."

11. Q. After Bond seduces double agent Rosie Carver (Gloria Hendry), then pulls a gun on her, demanding information, she pleads, "But you couldn't. You wouldn't. Not after what we've just done?" How does Bond respond?

A. "Well I certainly wouldn't have killed you before" (*Live and Let Die*, 1973).

12. Q. Which director helmed more of Moore's Bonds than any other?

A. Guy Hamilton (*Live and Let Die, The Man with the Golden Gun*) and Lewis Gilbert (*The Spy Who Loved Me, Moonraker*) drew with two each, but John Glen directed the most, with three (*For Your Eyes Only, Octopussy, A View to a Kill*).

13. Q. Prior to shooting *The Man with the Golden Gun* (1974), where in Los Angeles did Hervé "Nick Nack" Villechaize reside?

A. In his car. The actor was pretty much broke when cast in the role.

14. Q. As a result of his failing eyesight, cinematographer Claude Renoir was unable to see to the end of the supertanker set in *The Spy Who Loved Me* (1977). Who was secretly enlisted by designer Ken Adam to supervise the lighting in Renoir's place?

A. Stanley Kubrick, who suggested using floodlights. Adam, of course, was Kubrick's production designer on *Dr. Strangelove* (1964) and *Barry Lyndon* (1975). A second Kubrick link for *The Spy Who Loved Me* (1977) is that Jaws' metal dentures were designed by Kubrick's stepdaughter, Katharina Kubrick.

15. GUEST STAR Mark Millar

Q. Which Bond movie was promised next in the closing credits of *The Spy Who Loved Me* (1977)?

A. James Bond promised to return in *For Your Eyes Only*, but the canny producers opted for *Moonraker* (1979) instead after the massive success of *Star Wars* in 1977. *For Your Eyes Only* was thus delayed until 1981.

16. Q. Early on in *For Your Eyes Only* (1981), the movie establishes a more serious, less gadgety tone by making which grand gesture?

A. By blowing up Bond's beautiful Lotus Turbo Esprit. The car Bond uses in its place, the Citroen 2CV, was Moore's favourite to drive in the series.

17. Q. While posing as a snake charmer, how does MI6 agent Vijay (Vijay Amritraj) attract Bond's attention in *Octopussy* (1983)?

A. By playing the Bond theme on his pungi!

18. Q. Which one of Moore's Bond movies was known as *Moving Target* in Italy, *Dangerously Yours* in France and *Murder in the Eyes* in Israel?

A. *A View to a Kill* (1985).

19. Q. Who played Bond's CIA chum Felix Leiter in *Live and Let Die* (1973), and how many times did the character return during Moore's tenure as Bond?

A. David Hedison played Felix in Moore's first Bond film, but neither he nor the character returned for any additional Roger adventures. It wasn't until Timothy Dalton's *Licence to Kill* (1989) that we saw Hedison return as Leiter, at which point he was promptly fed to a shark and spent most of the movie in a coma.

20. Q. Which fellow Bond star first met Moore at the Royal Academy of Dramatic Arts in the mid-Forties, sharing a class with him in 1944?

A. Lois Maxwell (Miss Moneypenny).

21. Q. Which one of his Bond films did Moore like best? Also, which was his least favourite?

A. Of his seven Bonds, Moore's personal favourite was *The Spy Who Loved Me* (1977), while his least favourite – and that's putting it mildly – was *A View to a Kill* (1985).

22. Q. With which four shiny elements did Scaramanga (Christopher Lee) construct his signature golden gun?

A. Designed by Oscar-winning effects wiz John Stears, Scaramanga's golden gun was assembled from a cigarette case, a ballpoint pen, a cufflink and a lighter, with a bullet hidden in Scaramanga's belt (*The Man with the Golden Gun*, 1974).

23. Q. What is the one movie in which Moore got to drive Bond's iconic 1964 silver birch Aston Martin DB5?

A. *The Cannonball Run*, a 1981 action comedy in which he parodied his slick Bond image.

24. Q. Of which Bond actress would Roger Moore only comment, "My mother once said if you have nothing good to say about someone, say nothing at all!"?

A. Grace Jones, who played May Day in *A View to a Kill* (1985).

25. Q. When asked why he accepted the role of Bond, given his distaste for guns and violence, master of self-deprecation Moore revealed that as a young actor at RADA, he'd been approached by a famous English writer, director, actor and wit, who gave him the following advice: "Young man, with your devastating good looks and your disastrous lack of talent, you should take any job ever offered you. In the event that you're offered two jobs simultaneously, take the one that offers the most money." This, said Moore, is why he played Bond. But who was it that gave him this advice?

A. Noël Coward.

26. Q. Which of Moore's Bond girls was born Joyce Penelope Wilhelmina Frankenberg and, in the Eighties, dubbed Queen of the Miniseries?

A. Jane Seymour, who named herself after Henry VIII's third wife.

27. Q. Moore suffered from which unusual phobia?

A. Ironically for an actor known for his action roles, Moore suffered from hoplophobia, which is a fear of firearms. "Two years after National Service you had to go back for a two-week refresher course," he once told me. "I had a bit of an accident when I did mine. A gun blew up in my hands, which deafened me for a few days, and caused me to blink before I squeezed the trigger of any gun." Even a prop gun. "Anything that went bang would make me blink." Which can't have been easy, what with Bond's trusty Walther PPK brandished in every other scene. "I used an old Gary Cooper trick, which was to clench my eyes." That explains Bond's steely stare. "Yes, though I call that look, 'Please don't let me blink!'"

28. Q. How, famously, did Roger Moore describe his acting range?

A. "My acting range?" Moore said with a smirk. "Left eyebrow raised, right eyebrow raised."

29. Q. Besides the Log Cabin Girl (Sue Vanner), who else needs James?

A. England (*The Spy Who Loved Me*, 1977).

30. GUEST STAR Sanjeev Bhaskar

Q. Which is the only Bond film to feature the singer of the title song in the opening credits?

A. *For Your Eyes Only* (1981), featuring Sheena Easton.

31. Q. Q (Desmond Llewelyn) appears as a field agent for the first time in which Roger Moore Bond film?

A. *Octopussy* (1983).

32. Q. Who composed the score for *Live and Let Die* (1973)?

A. Former Beatles producer George Martin.

33. Q. What year did Roger Moore first play James Bond?

A. 1964, in a comedy sketch with Millicent Martin in her short-lived show, *Mainly Millicent*.

34. Q. Which of Moore's Bonds holds the record for the most-watched film ever broadcast on British television?

A. *Live and Let Die* (1973) attracted a record-breaking 23.5 million viewers when it was shown on ITV on January 20, 1980.

35. **Q.** The first stunt ever calculated by computer modelling, the 360° corkscrew car jump in *The Man with the Golden Gun* (1974), was performed by uncredited British stuntman Loren "Bumps" Willard as eight cameras simultaneously captured the action. How many takes, though, did it take to get it right?

A. Just one, earning Bumps a large bonus from the film's grateful producers.

36. **Q.** Swedish actress Maud Adams appeared in which three Roger Moore Bond films?

A. Adams played Scaramanga's ill-fated mistress, Andrea Anders, in *The Man with the Golden Gun* (1974); also the title character in *Octopussy* (1983); and while visiting Roger on the set of *A View to a Kill* (1985), she clocked up a third appearance with an uncredited cameo as "Woman in Fisherman's Wharf Crowd".

37. **Q.** Moore's Bond contract provided him with an unlimited supply of which brand of Cuban cigar?

A. Montecristos: The bill for each film usually ran to thousands of pounds.

38. **Q.** James Bond appeared in a trio of features in 1983. What were they, and who played him in each film?

A. Moore played Bond in official series entry *Octopussy.* Sean Connery played Bond in unofficial effort *Never Say Never Again.* George Lazenby, meanwhile, delivered a cheeky cameo as "JB" in lively TV movie *The Return of the Man from U.N.C.L.E.: The Fifteen Years Later Affair.*

39. **Q.** Which of Moore's Bonds has the lowest body count?

A. *The Man with the Golden Gun* (1974) has only six fatalities, the lowest in the history of the entire franchise. In fact,

007 only kills one person in the entire movie: Scaramanga (Christopher Lee)!

40. Q. Having worked previously with Moore in *Sherlock Holmes in New York* (1976) and *The Sea Wolves* (1980), which actor took a role in *A View to a Kill* (1985), not because he liked the Bond films, but to work with his old mate Sir Roger again?

A. Patrick Macnee, best known as Steed in TV's *The Avengers* (1961–1969), played Sir Godfrey Tibbett in *A View to a Kill* (1985), though he'd never made a secret of the fact that he preferred Ian Fleming's books, and was in fact friends with the author. Ultimately, *A View to a Kill* was Moore and Macnee's final film together.

41. Q. Which one of Moore's Bond girls was a doctor? Also, what was her qualification and who played her?

A. Dr Holly Goodhead, played by Lois Chiles, was a Doctor of Astrophysics in *Moonraker* (1979).

42. Q. How was Bond's bayou boat chase originally described in the screenplay for *Live and Let Die* (1973)?

A. Scene 156 – The most terrific boat chase you've ever seen.

43. Q. Originally created to house the epic supertanker set for *The Spy Who Loved Me* (1977), Pinewood Studio's colossal 007 Stage was destroyed by a fire in 1984 during the production of which movie?

A. Ridley Scott's *Legend* (1985). It was rebuilt in less than four months and christened The Albert R. Broccoli 007 Stage. It later burned down again, shortly after filming wrapped on *Casino Royale* (2006).

44. Q. Which one of Moore's Bond films featured Bernard Lee's final appearance as M?

A. *Moonraker* (1979). Lee died in 1981, while *For Your Eyes Only* was still in pre-production.

45. Q. Which item of clothing had to be custom-made for *The Man with the Golden Gun* (1974), at an apparent cost of $10,000?

A. Hervé Villechaize's white gloves.

46. Q. After starring together in *The Spy Who Loved Me* (1977), Barbara Bach and Richard Kiel appeared alongside one another in which two additional movies?

A. *Force 10 from Navarone* (1978) and *The Humanoid* (1979).

47. Q. Desmond Llewellyn appeared in all but one of Moore's Bond films as the irascible Q. Which one did he miss?

A. *Live and Let Die* (1973).

48. Q. Which three Moore 007 movies feature fighting sequences aboard trains? Also, who did Bond battle in each of them?

A. 007 tangled with Tee Hee (Julius W. Harris) in *Live and Let Die* (1973); with Jaws (Richard Kiel) in *The Spy Who Loved Me* (1977); and Kamal Khan (Louis Jourdan), Gobinda (Kabir Bedi) and Grischka (aka Twin Two, played by Anthony Meyer) in *Octopussy* (1983).

49. Q. Which of Moore's Bonds is the only film in the franchise to feature two boat chases?

A. The only James Bond movie, to date, to include two boat chases is *Moonraker* (1979): the "Bondola" gondola chase in Venice, and Q's hydrofoil boat chase, set in South America but shot in Florida.

50. Q. What were the three functions of Bond's Rolex Submariner in *Live and Let Die* (1973)?

A. Modified by art director Syd Cain, Bond's Rolex could create a hyper-intensified magnetic field, strong enough to deflect bullets and unzip dresses; it also had a serrated bezel that worked like a tiny circular saw; plus it told the time!

The Simpsons: The First Ten Years

1. Q. Matt Groening named the five core members of Springfield's first family after his own relatives. True or false?

A. False: though Homer and Marge are Groening's parents' names, and his younger sisters are named Lisa and Maggie, Bart is an anagram of Brat.

2. Q. What were Bart (Nancy Cartwright), Lisa (Yeardley Smith) and Maggie's first words?

A. Bart's first word/phrase was "Ay, caramba!" Lisa's first word was "Bart". Voiced by Elizabeth Taylor, Maggie's first word was "Daddy" ("Lisa's First Word", S04E10).

3. Q. Homer (Dan Castellaneta) was destined to lead which secret society? Also barred from joining which subsequent secret society?

A. The Stonecutters; The Ancient, Mystic Society of No Homers ("Homer the Great", S06E12).

4. Q. What did Kirk Van Houten (Hank Azaria) sing to try to woo his wife back?

A. "Can I borrow a feeling?" He did not succeed ("A Milhouse Divided", S08E06).

5. Q. What was the name of Abraham Simpson's (Dan Castellaneta) army unit?

A. The Flying Hellfish (Raging Abe Simpson and His Grumbling Grandson in "The Curse of the Flying Hellfish", S07E22).

6. Q. What is Radioactive Man's catchphrase?

A. "Up and Atom!" ("Radioactive Man", S07E02).

7. Q. How, in 1992, was *The Simpsons* credited with saving the life of an 8-year-old boy?

A. 10-year-old Chris Bencze saved his younger brother Alex's life after learning the Heimlich manoeuvre from a *Simpsons* episode in which Homer (Dan Castellaneta) chokes on a donut ("Homer at the Bat", S03E17).

8. Q. Name four of the Seven Duffs.

A. Sleazy, Queasy, Surly, Edgy, Tipsy, Dizzy and Remorseful ("Selma's Choice", S04E13).

9. Q. Who shot Mr Burns (Harry Shearer)?

A. Maggie Simpson ("Who Shot Mr. Burns? Part 2", S07E01).

10. GUEST STAR Yeardley Smith

Q. What is Lisa Simpson's middle name and who is she named after?

A. Lisa's middle name is Marie. She was named after Elvis' daughter, Lisa Marie Presley.

11. Q. Who is Maggie's arch-enemy?

A. Gerald Samson, a.k.a. Baby Gerald, a.k.a. The Monobrow Baby, a.k.a. The Unibrow Baby.

12. Q. What's the address of the Simpsons' residence?

A. 742 Evergreen Terrace.

13. Q. What is Homer's (Dan Castellaneta) official job title at the nuclear power plant?

A. Safety Inspector.

14. Q. What is Krusty the Clown's (Dan Castellaneta) real name?

A. Herschel Shmoikel Pinchas Yerucham Krustofsky – though I'll accept Herschel Krustofsky.

15. Q. Who did Bart (Nancy Cartwright) sell his soul to, and for how much?

A. Bart sold his soul to Milhouse (Pamela Hayden) for $5 ("Bart Sells His Soul", S07E04).

16. Q. Which word, invented by *The Simpsons* and first featured in "Lisa the Iconoclast" (S07E16), was added to the Merriam-Webster dictionary in 2018?

A. Embiggen – a transitive verb meaning, to make bigger or more expansive. “A noble spirit embiggens the smallest man.”

17. **Q.** What did Mr Burns (Harry Shearer) steal from the US government in 1945?

A. A trillion dollar bill (“The Trouble with Trillions”, S09E20).

18. **Q.** Who is Homer (Dan Castellaneta) mistaken for after getting lost in the woods in “The Call of the Simpsons” (S01E07)?

A. Bigfoot. After being taken to a lab for testing, Homer is allowed to return home after the scientists conclude that he is “either a below-average human being or a brilliant beast”.

19. **Q.** What’s the one thing Homer (Dan Castellaneta) can offer Marge that no one else can?

A. Complete and utter dependence (“Secrets of a Successful Marriage”, S05E022).

20. **Q.** How did Matt Groening work his initials into Homer’s (Dan Castellaneta) design?

A. Homer’s hair forms an “M” and his ears are shaped like “G”s.

21. **Q.** How old are Homer (Dan Castellaneta), Marge (Julie Kavner), Bart (Nancy Cartwright), Lisa (Yeardley Smith) and Maggie?

A. Homer is 36, Marge is 34, Bart is 10, Lisa is 8 and Maggie is 1…Forever!

22. **Q.** What is Homer’s (Dan Castellaneta) favourite donut filling?

A. Purple.

23. **Q.** Name any two Kent Brockman (Harry Shearer) shows.

A. *Springfield Action News*, *Eye on Springfield*, *Smartline* and *My Two Cents*.

24. Q. Who, in 1990, remarked that *The Simpsons* single "Do the Bartman" was a slap in the face to rappers everywhere?

A. Vanilla Ice.

25. GUEST STAR Josh Weinstein

Q. What episode in the first eight seasons has the most ad-libbed lines from any actor?

A. "You Only Move Twice" (S08E02). Easily 50% of Albert Brooks' lines in the episode as Hank Scorpio were ad-libbed (as were Homer's responses by Dan Castellaneta). That episode was painstakingly pieced together from over two hours of recorded material. The tape of that recording session is a Simpsons Holy Grail of mine – you could make an entirely new episode out of it (or a much expanded Director's Cut).

26. Q. What's Patty and Selma's (both voiced by Julie Kavner) favourite brand of cigarette?

A. Lady Laramie 100s.

27. Q. What is Reverend Lovejoy's (Harry Shearer) hobby?

A. He's a toy train enthusiast.

28. Q. What's the name of Flanders' (Harry Shearer) stupid shop?

A. The Leftorium ("When Flanders Failed", S03E03).

29. Q. Who voiced both Lionel Hutz and Troy McClure?

A. Phil Hartman.

30. Q. What does it mean, to "Pull a Homer"?

A. To succeed through dumb luck ("Homer Defined", S03E05).

31. Q. What did Mr Burns (Harry Shearer) call his autobiography?

A. *Will There Ever Be A Rainbow?* ("Blood Feud", S02E22).

32. Q. How and why does Homer (Dan Castellaneta) get himself declared disabled?

A. He gorges himself with food until he weighs more than 300lbs so that he can work from home ("King-Size Homer", S07E07).

33. Q. What was the name of Homer's (Dan Castellaneta) bowling team, and who were the founding members?

A. Homer, Apu (Hank Azaria), Moe (Hank Azaria) and Otto (Harry Shearer) were the original Pin Pals, though Otto was later replaced by Mr Burns (Harry Shearer) ("Team Homer", S07E12).

34. Q. Which member of *The Simpsons* cast voices the most characters in the show?

A. Dan Castellaneta, who voices more than twenty characters, including Homer, Abe, Barney, Krusty, Sideshow Mel, Groundskeeper Willie, Mayor Quimby and Hans Moleman.

35. Q. What's the secret ingredient of a Flaming Moe (formerly a Flaming Homer)?

A. Krusty's Non-Narkotic Kough Syrup for Kids ("Flaming Moe's", S03E10).

36. Q. What does Smithers (Harry Shearer) collect?

A. Malibu Stacy dolls and accessories.

37. Q. What's the name of Springfield's baseball team?

A. The Springfield Isotopes.

38. Q. What does Springfield have in common with Ogdenville, Brockway and North Haverbrook?

A. They were all scammed by Lyle Lanley (Phil Hartman) into buying defective monorail systems ("Marge vs. the Monorail", S04E12).

39. Q. How does the phrase "D'oh!" appear in *Simpsons* scripts?

A. "Annoyed Grunt".

40. GUEST STAR Michael Price

Q. "Simpsons Roasting on an Open Fire" (S01E01) was the first episode of the series that aired in December of 1989, but it wasn't originally slated to be the premiere. What episode, which aired later in season one, was the original "pilot"?

A. "Some Enchanted Evening" (S01E13).

41. Q. What was the name of Homer's (Dan Castellaneta) barbershop quartet, and who else was in the group?

A. Homer, Apu (Hank Azaria), Principal Skinner (Harry Shearer) and Barney (Dan Castellaneta) were the fab four members of The Be Sharps ("Homer's Barbershop Quartet", S05E01).

42. Q. Where does Bart (Nancy Cartwright) find Mr Burns' (Harry Shearer) cherished teddy bear Bobo?

A. In a bag of Kwik-E-Mart ice ("Rosebud", S05E04).

43. Q. What is Homer's (Dan Castellaneta) middle initial, and what does it stand for?

A. The J in Homer J. Simpson stands for Jay and was a tribute to *The Rocky and Bullwinkle Show*'s Rocket J. Squirrel and Bullwinkle J. Moose, who themselves got their middle initial from series creator Jay Ward ("D'oh-in' in the Wind", S10E06).

44. Q. Krusty (Dan Castellaneta), although illiterate, subscribes to which magazine?

A. *Gigantic Asses* ("Homie the Clown", S06E15).

45. Q. What were the names of Bart's (Nancy Cartwright) elephant and Homer's (Dan Castellaneta) lobster?

A. Stampy and Mr Pinchy ("Bart Gets an Elephant", S05E17 & "Lisa Gets an 'A'", S10E07).

46. Q. Who composed *The Simpsons*' memorable theme tune?

A. Danny Elfman.

47. Q. Which *Simpsons* character is a parody of Arnold Schwarzenegger, and what's the name of his death-dealing alter ego?

A. Rainier Wolfcastle (Harry Shearer), star of the long-running McBain franchise.

48. Q. In the "Dial 'Z' for Zombies" segment of "Treehouse of Horror III" (S04E05), how does Homer (Dan Castellaneta) respond after Bart (Nancy Cartwright) exclaims, "Dad, you killed the zombie Flanders!"?

A. "He was a zombie?"

49. Q. "We wanted to do an episode where the thinking was, 'What if a real-life, normal person had to enter Homer's [Dan Castellaneta] universe and deal with him?'" Which episode, and what person, is *Simpsons* writer/producer Josh Weinstein referring to?

A. "Homer's Enemy" (S08E23), Frank Grimes (Hank Azaria).

50. Q. Where in Springfield might you find the latest issues of *Manboy*, *Batchick*, *Birdguy*, *Dog Kid*, *Lava Lady* and *The Human Bee*?

A. The Android's Dungeon & Baseball Card Shop.

George A. Romero: *Night*, *Dawn* and *Day*

1. Q. Whose grave are Johnny (Russell Streiner) and Barbra (Judith O'Dea) visiting in *Night of the Living Dead*?

A. They're going to visit their long-dead dad.

2. Q. "When there's no more room in Hell..."

A. "...the dead will walk the Earth". A great line of dialogue, sharply delivered by Peter (Ken Foree) in *Dawn of the Dead*, and also one hell of a poster tagline!

3. Q. What's the headline on the newspaper that blows up against the trashcans in *Day of the Dead*?

A. "THE DEAD WALK!"

4. Q. Who is first to die in *Night of the Living Dead*?

A. After tangling with the Cemetery Zombie (S. William Hinzman), Johnny (Russell Streiner) takes a lethal tumble, cracking his skull on a headstone.

5. Q. What happens to the zombie (Jim Krut) that sneaks up behind Roger (Scott H. Reiniger) while he's refuelling the chopper in *Dawn of the Dead*?

A. It gets rather closer than it should to the helicopter's spinning rotor blades and loses the top few inches of its head.

6. Q. What animal is seen on the steps of the First National Bank at the beginning of *Day of the Dead*?

A. An alligator. The "well-fed" zombie who steps out of the bank behind it was herpetologist Bill Love, who brought the beast to the set.

7. Q. What does Barbra (Judith O'Dea) lose before making it to the relative safety of the house in *Night of the Living Dead*?

A. Her shoes (also her brother, her car and her mind).

8. Q. When Peter (Ken Foree) and Roger (Scott H. Reiniger) first go shopping in *Dawn of the Dead*, which two items are at the top of Peter's list?

A. Lighter fluid and chocolate.

9. Q. What is Dr Logan's (Richard Liberty) nickname in *Day of the Dead*? Also, what is his mad dream?

A. Everyone calls him Frankenstein. As there are more zombies than bullets, rather than kill the creatures, his goal is to domesticate them.

10. GUEST STAR John A. Russo

Q. How many "Ben's Trucks" were used in *Night of the Living Dead*?

A. There were actually two almost identical trucks. The first one, which we bought for $50, would not run when we needed it to be driven to the gas pump for the escape attempt. But we got lucky as a man down the road owned an almost identical truck. We used it for the driving part, then destroyed the other one in the explosion.

11. Q. When the boys first head down into the mall in *Dawn of the Dead*, which iconic zombie heads up the stairs after Fran (Gaylen Ross)?

A. The Hare Krishna Zombie (Mike Christopher).

12. Q. Who's the only clean-shaven soldier in *Day of the Dead*?

A. Rhodes (Joe Pilato), who wants to at least look like a proper military man, though he behaves like a bully, a psycho and, ultimately, a coward.

13. Q. What's the first thing Barbara (Judith O'Dea) manages to say to Ben, in *Night of the Living Dead*?

A. "What's happening?"

14. Q. Where is Roger (Scott H. Reiniger) bitten when he's caught between the trucks, in *Dawn of the Dead*?

A. His left arm, followed by his left leg.

15. Q. According to Dr Logan's (Richard Liberty) calculations in *Day of the Dead*, what's the ratio of zombie to human survivor?

A. 400,000:1

16. Q. What, according to TV reports in *Night of the Living Dead*, is likely responsible for corpses reanimating around the globe?

A. High-level radiation from a detonated satellite that was returning to Earth from Venus. Though that's the leading theory in the movie, the filmmakers never clarified the cause as it's frankly irrelevant.

17. Q. Which film in Romero's Dead Trilogy was both the lowest grossing and the filmmaker's favourite?

A. *Day of the Dead.*

18. Q. What book does Dr Logan (Richard Liberty) give Bub in *Day of the Dead*?

A. *Salem's Lot* by Stephen King. The author and Romero were good friends who worked together on *Creepshow* (1982), a cracking horror anthology that King both wrote and appeared in. Romero also directed the 1993 feature adaptation of King's novel *The Dark Half*. Though it's perhaps anachronistic that a book published in the real world in 1975, would exist in a post-apocalyptic world that went to hell in 1968, the timeline of Romero's Dead Trilogy is riddled with contradictions so really the best way to approach them is with the same relaxed attitude to logic and detail that Romero clearly had.

19. Q. Though hired by Romero to create the make-up effects for *Night of the Living Dead*, why was Tom Savini ultimately unable to work on the movie?

A. Savini didn't work on *Night of the Living Dead* as he was called to duty by the US Army to serve in Vietnam just before filming began. "When I was in Vietnam I was a combat photographer," said Savini. "My job was to shoot images of damage to machines and to people. Through my lens, I saw some hideous [stuff]. Now, if I'm creating a gory effect and I don't get the same feeling as when I saw the real stuff, I'm not satisfied."

20. Q. What are the creatures called in *Night of the Living Dead*?

A. Ghouls and flesh-eaters. "It was a weird evolution," George Romero once told me. "At first I didn't think of them as zombies. I thought of them as flesh-eaters or ghouls and never called them zombies in the first film. Then people started to write about them as zombies, and all of a sudden they were the new zombies, but I didn't have anything to do with that."

21. Q. What does Bub (Howard Sherman) do to Rhodes (Joe Pilato) after shooting him and leaving him in the clutches of his zombie brethren, in *Day of the Dead*?

A. He salutes him.

22. Q. How many people are hiding out in the house in *Night of the Living Dead*?

A. Seven: Ben (Duane Jones), Barbra (Judith O'Dea), Harry (Karl Hardman), Helen (Marilyn Eastman), Tom (Keith Wayne), Judy (Judith Ridley) and Karen (Kyra Schon).

23. Q. After killing all the mall zombies in *Dawn of the Dead*, what do Stephen (David Emge) and Peter (Ken Foree) do with their rotting corpses?

A. They pile them up in one of the mall's walk-in freezers, beside the other meat. Yum!

24. Q. In *Day of the Dead*, what does Rhodes (Joe Pilato) scream at the zombie horde who rip him in half and feast on his entrails?

A. "Choke on 'em! Choke on 'em!" Apparently the line was a gutsy ad-lib by Pilato.

25. GUEST STAR Tom Savini

Q. Whose head was blown off at the beginning of *Dawn of the Dead* when the SWAT team shows up?

A. It was a fake head made from a cast of Gaylon Ross. I made it for the alternate ending where Fran kills herself by jumping up into the helicopter blades. We didn't do that so I put an Afro wig on it with dark make-up and blew the piss out of it with a shotgun.

26. Q. What's most important to Harry (Karl Hardman), according to his long-suffering wife Helen (Marilyn Eastman), in *Night of the Living Dead*?

A. "To be right", and for "everybody else to be wrong".

27. Q. Which actor's hobbling, stumbling zombie walk did Romero single out as his all-time favourite?

A. David Emge's in *Dawn of the Dead*. Seeing him stumble from the elevator near the end of the movie is a thing of twisted beauty. Emge's zombie moves were reportedly inspired by Lon Chaney Jr in Universal's vintage Mummy sequels.

28. Q. What does Harry (Karl Hardman) call the TV aerial in *Night of the Living Dead*?

A. Rabbit ears.

29. Q. How do Peter (Ken Foree) and Fran (Gaylen Ross) accidentally attract the attention of the motorcycle raiders in *Dawn of the Dead*?

A. When Peter gives Fran a flying lesson. Good job she learned how to fly the chopper though!

30. Q. What's the one thing that frightens Romero's zombies?

A. Fire.

31. Q. Who played the first creature that makes it into the house, only to be bashed in the head with a tyre iron by Ben (Duane Jones), in *Night of the Living Dead*?

A. Co-writer John A. Russo. Russo also played the ghoul who was set on fire in the Molotov cocktail sequence. "I said to George that we were going to look silly if none of the ghouls caught on fire from those exploding cocktails," he recalls, "so I volunteered to do the stunt. Real gasoline was used and we got three takes, and they are all in the movie – the three different angles. I risked my life but the other people there were all delighted that we were getting such a great stunt for our low-budget movie – and so was I!"

32. Q. As shooting didn't start till late most nights on *Dawn of the Dead*, made-up zombie extras often drank, sometimes heavily, at local bars. What alcohol-fuelled incident cost the production $7,000?

A. A zombie couple stole a golf cart and crashed it into a marble pillar inside the mall.

33. Q. Regarding the main casts only, which film in Romero's Dead Trilogy sees the most survivors at the end?

A. No one survives *Night of the Living Dead*. Peter (Ken Foree) and Fran (Gaylen Ross) fly off in the chopper at the end of *Dawn of the Dead*. But the winner with three survivors is *Day of the Dead*, which sees Sarah (Lori Cardille), John (Terry Alexander) and McDermott (Jarlath Conroy) all sunning themselves on the beach in the film's final moments.

34. Q. How do Tom (Keith Wayne) and Judy (Judith Ridley) die in *Night of the Living Dead*?

A. When the truck explodes during their botched escape attempt.

35. Q. What's the title of the polka, by British composer Herbert Chappell, that plays so dissonantly over *Dawn of the Dead*'s closing credits?

A. The Gonk.

36. Q. What did the filmmakers primarily use for blood in *Night of the Living Dead*?

A. Bosco Chocolate Syrup.

37. Q. What's the real-life name of the mall featured in *Dawn of the Dead*?

A. The movie was shot in Pennsylvania's Monroeville Mall, at night, while it was closed. Shooting would start around 10.30pm, but even though the mall wouldn't open again before 9am the following morning, the crew had to wrap up at 7am every day as that's when the music came on in the building, and no one knew how to switch it off.

38. Q. How does Sheriff McClelland (George Kosana) respond to being asked by the reporter (Bill "Chilly Billy" Cardille) if the creatures are slow-moving, in *Night of the Living Dead*?

A. "Yeah, they're dead. They're all messed up."

39. Q. From where in the mall, in *Dawn of the Dead*, does Stephen (David Emge) attempt to destroy the Starship *Enterprise*?

A. In the arcade! Though not officially a *Star Trek* game, Atari's *Starship 1* was an arcade shooter, released in 1977, featuring spacecraft that were strongly reminiscent of the *Enterprise* and Klingon Birds of Prey. Incidentally, *Starship 1* contains the first known example of a videogame Easter Egg, predating Warren Robinett's hidden *Adventure* credit by three years. To activate it, players had to feed the machine a coin while holding the "phasor" and start buttons down. This triggered a message that read "Hi Ron" – a reference to game designer Ron Milner – and rewarded the player with ten free games!

40. GUEST STAR Howard Berger

Q. What was Greg Nicotero's nickname in *Day of the Dead*?

A. Gut Boy, as he handled all the real guts and entrails used by the make-up department for killing humans and feeding zombies.

41. Q. How does Harry (Karl Hardman) die, in *Night of the Living Dead*?

A. He's shot by Ben (Duane Jones) for being an insufferable dick.

42. Q. Which noted US film critic wrote that *Dawn of the Dead* was "one of the best horror films ever made", adding that while it was undeniably "gruesome, sickening, disgusting, violent, brutal and appalling, nobody ever said art had to be in good taste"?

A. Roger Ebert of the *Chicago Sun-Times*, who gave the film four out of four stars.

43. Q. Who grabs Barbra and drags her outside when the creatures finally make it into the house, in *Night of the Living Dead*?

A. Zombie Johnny (Russell Streiner).

44. Q. How many times does Romero appear in his Dead Trilogy?

A. Four: In *Night of the Living Dead* he plays a journalist reporting on the troubles from Washington; In *Dawn of the Dead* he plays a director in the TV studio and, later on, the Santa-suit-wearing motorcycle raider. Finally, in *Day of the Dead*, when the bunker's overrun by flesh-eaters, he plays a cart-pushing, scarf-wearing zombie.

45. Q. What's Peter's (Ken Foree) nickname for Stephen (David Emge) in *Dawn of the Dead*?

A. Flyboy.

46. Q. What's the real-life name of the cemetery featured in *Night of the Living Dead*?

A. Romero shot the movie in Evans City Cemetery, Pennsylvania. Partly because it was remote and secluded, allowing them to work without attracting the attention of too many nosy bystanders. Ironically, thanks to the movie's notoriety, the cemetery is now a busy tourist attraction.

47. Q. What's unusual about the zombie kids who attack Peter in the airport hangar office, in *Dawn of the Dead*?

A. They're the only zombies in the Dead Trilogy who run rather than shuffle. The kids in this scene were played by Tom Savini's niece and nephew, Donna and Mike Savini.

48. Q. A huge fan of *Night of the Living Dead*, who helped Romero and producer Richard P. Rubinstein secure financing for *Dawn of the Dead* in exchange for international distribution rights?

A. Italian director Dario Argento, of *Deep Red* (1975), *Suspiria* (1977) and *Tenebrae* (1982) fame. Argento also invited Romero to write the movie in Rome, which he did, free from distraction, in three weeks. In addition, Argento collaborated with four-piece Italian band Goblin to produce much of the movie's music.

49. Q. What do *Dawn of the Dead*'s motorcycle raiders throw in the zombies' faces?

A. Custard pies! While writing the script for *Night of the Living Dead*, Romero and Russo debated how best to kill their flesh-eating creations. Marilyn Eastman, who played Helen in *Night of the Living Dead*, jokingly suggested they should throw pies in the monsters' faces! That surely was the inspiration for *Dawn of the Dead*'s wacky pie-throwing scene.

50. Q. Who's the only character in Romero's Dead Trilogy to use the word "zombies"?

A. "I didn't use the word zombie," explained Romero, "until *Dawn of the Dead*, when Peter [Ken Foree] says in the film, 'There's gonna be a thousand zombies in here'. I guess that's when I surrendered to the idea of the creatures being called zombies. But I don't care what they are. It's not important."

The Mighty Marvel Age of Comics

1. Q. Inspired by the success of DC's Justice League of America (*The Brave and the Bold* #28, March 1960), Marvel Comics publisher Martin Goodman directed editor Stan Lee to create their own superhero team. What was the result?

A. The Fantastic Four: "I went home and wrote a two-page outline and sent it to [Jack] Kirby. We talked about it, and he went home and drew it. We didn't know we were doing something historic. It was just another story." Far from being just another story, with vibrant art and characters whose fears, failings and real-life troubles gave them unparalleled relatability, *The Fantastic Four* #1 (November 1961) was Marvel's game-changer.

2. Q. When Namor the Sub-Mariner grumpily encounters an isolated tribe of Eskimos in *The Avengers* #4 (March 1964), what strange object are they praying to?

A. A petrified figure frozen in a cake of ice...Captain America!

3. Q. Thirties radio drama *Chandu the Magician* inspired the creation of which enchanting Marvel Comics' character?

A. Steve Ditko and Stan Lee's Doctor Strange. Created by Harry A. Earnshaw and Raymond R. Morgan, *Chandu the Magician* was originally broadcast from 1931 to 1936. Trained in mystical ways by an Indian yogi, American Frank Chandler goes forth "with his youth and strength to conquer the evil that threatens mankind" as Chandu, a magician whose powers include teleportation and astral projection.

4. Q. What message is inscribed in the side of Thor's hammer, Mjölnir?

A. "Whosoever holds this hammer, if he be worthy, shall possess the power of...THOR" (*Journey into Mystery* #83, August 1962).

5. Q. What's the official name of Professor X's mutant academy?

A. Xavier's School for Gifted Youngsters (*The X-Men*, September 1963).

6. Q. According to artist Don Heck, what did Jack Kirby used to call superheroes?

A. "The guys in long underwear."

7. Q. What does the acronym S.H.I.E.L.D. stand for?

A. Supreme Headquarters International Espionage Law-enforcement Division (*Strange Tales* #135, August 1965).

8. Q. The Incredible Hulk was inspired by which iconic Universal Monster and what chilling Victorian novel?

A. Jack Kirby's early art for The Incredible Hulk was based on Karloff's Monster in *Frankenstein* (1931). "I always felt the monster was really the good guy," said Stan Lee, who was additionally inspired by Robert Louis Stevenson's *Strange Case of Dr. Jekyll and Mr. Hyde* (1886) to explore the theme of literal duality (*The Incredible Hulk* #1, May 1962).

9. Q. What, in 1965, did Stan Lee name Marvel's brand new, "honest-to-gosh, far-out fan club in the mixed-up Marvel manner"?

A. The Merry Marvel Marching Society: It cost just a buck to join and was an instant hit. "Nobody ever expected it to be so big," said secretary, receptionist and fan liaison legend "Fabulous" Flo Steinberg. "There where thousands of letters and dollar bills flying all over the place. We were throwing them at each other!"

10. GUEST STAR Dan Slott

Q. Vulture, Lizard, Green Goblin, Gog, Kraven: which one of these characters has never been a member of the Sinister Six?

A. Green Goblin: though the Hobgoblin's been a member, and Norman Osborn once had a hand in assembling a "Sinister Twelve" while he was stuck in prison, the Green Goblin has never been an active member of any version of the

Sinister Six. Guess Norman's never really been much of a team player (*The Amazing Spider-Man Annual* #1, January 1964).

11. Q. Which comicbook series was born from a bet between Stan Lee and publisher Martin Goodman, after Goodman scoffed at Lee's bold claim that the new Marvel style could be applied to and benefit any genre of comic, even one with "a horrible title" and a dated WWII theme?

A. *Sgt. Fury and His Howling Commandos* (May 1963): It was a bet Stan won. Not only did the Lee/Kirby series last a healthy 167 issues, but also it introduced the enduringly popular Nick Fury.

12. Q. What's the first thing Mary Jane Watson ever says to Peter Parker?

A. "Face it Tiger...You just hit the jackpot!" (*Amazing Spider-Man* #42, November, 1966).

13. Q. What are the alliterative real names of Marvel supervillains Doctor Octopus, The Lizard, The Leader and The Absorbing Man?

A. Doctor Octopus is Otto Octavius (*The Amazing Spider-Man* #3, July 1963), The Lizard is Curtis "Curt" Connors (*The Amazing Spider-Man* #6, November 1963), The Leader is Samuel Sterns (*Tales to Astonish* #62, December 1964) and The Absorbing Man is Carl "Crusher" Creel (*Journey into Mystery #114,* March 1965).

14. Q. Rather than clarifying every last detail with exhaustive scripts and layouts, Stan Lee would either hand his artists a synopsis, or even just talk them through a story, then leave them to create its art. "I never restricted them or said they had to follow what I gave them to the letter," said Lee, who'd write the dialogue and captions at the very end of the process to suit the finished art. What did this innovative practice come to be called?

A. The Marvel Method: "I'd tailor the writing to the art," said Lee, who developed the process with artist Jack Kirby on *The Fantastic Four* #1 (November 1961) and never looked back. Not every artist adjusted. "Some said the hell with it and left," said penciller Don Heck. "Stan would call me up and give me the first couple of pages, then the last page. I'd say, 'What about the stuff in between?' And he'd say, 'Fill it in.'"

15. Q. Hulk is to Smash what Thing is to...?

A. Clobbering! (*The Fantastic Four*, November 1961).

16. Q. Those who've studied their cosmic history understand the Silver Surfer heralds the arrival of which planet-consuming cosmic entity?

A. Galactus (*Fantastic Four* #48, March 1966).

17. Q. *The Fantastic Four* #1 (November 1961), *The Incredible Hulk* #1 (May 1962), *The Amazing Spider-Man* #1 (March 1963) and *The X-Men* #1 (September 1963): Which is the odd one out?

A. *The Amazing Spider-Man* #1 (Mar 1963): While the other books all marked the first appearances of the characters they featured, Spider-Man actually debuted in *Amazing Fantasy* #15 (Aug 1962).

18. Q. Debuting in August 1967, what was Marvel's satirical "Comic Magazine for Non-Believers Who Hate Comic Magazines"?

A. Not Brand Echh.

19. Q. "The publisher said if we gave him more action and treated him like a normal superhero, sales would pick up," said Stan Lee. "I didn't want to change him, so I said, let's just drop the book." Which hero's comicbook did Lee cancel rather than change?

A. The Silver Surfer, whose initial solo title ran for 18 issues from August 1968 to September 1970.

20. Q. In *The Amazing Spider-Man* #1 (March 1963), why does Spidey break into the Fantastic Four's headquarters and then pick a fight?

A. To prove his skills then ask for a well-paying job as a fantastic fifth member of the group. "I figure I'm worth your top salary," he says. "Afraid you made a mistake," replies Sue. "We're a non-profit organization." Suffice to say, it is not the job interview of Peter's dreams.

21. Q. Who, in 1963, designed and first drew Iron Man's original, cumbersome suit of armour, and what artist streamlined it into a slick red and gold affair later that same year?

A. Jack Kirby was the first to draw Iron Man, for the cover of *Tales of Suspense* #39 (March 1963). Iron Man's leaner, shinier look, courtesy of Steve Ditko, debuted in *Tales of Suspense* #48 (December 1963).

22. Q. While freelancing for DC in the 1960s, what artist drew Marvel's *Tales to Astonish* and *Tales of Suspense* on the side, under the pseudonym Adam Austin, later joining Marvel full-time, under his real name, to work on Captain America, Dr. Strange and Daredevil?

A. Gene Colan (a.k.a. Gene "The Dean" Colan, "Gentleman" Gene Colan and "Genial" Gene Colan).

23. Q. What was Stan Lee's original title for The X-Men?

A. The Mutants: publisher Martin Goodman nixed the idea as he didn't believe readers would know what a mutant was. Lee's second choice was The X-Men, which he felt had a nice air of mystery to it. Professor X explains the origin of the group's name in *The X-Men* #1 (September 1963), telling newcomer Jean Grey that "I call my students...X-Men, for EX-tra power!"

24. Q. While holidaying in windy Norway, frail Doctor Don Blake flees in terror from invading aliens, stumbling into a cave where he discovers a gnarled wooden stick that he strikes against a boulder in frustration. What reaction does this provoke?

A. The stick transforms into a mighty hammer and Blake becomes Thor, Asgardian God of Thunder (*Journey into Mystery* #83, August 1962).

25. GUEST STAR Fabian Nicieza

Q. Who was the first African-American character to regularly appear in a Marvel Comic?

A. Gabe Jones debuted in *Sgt. Fury and his Howling Commandos* #1, published May 1963.

26. Q. "I think they're the greatest team in comics ever," said artist John Buscema of which legendary partnership?

A. Jack Kirby and Stan Lee: "They worked so well together," added Buscema. "It was unbelievable."

27. Q. Who is mankind's only hope against The Toad Men?

A. The Hulk! (*The Incredible Hulk* #2, July 1962).

28. Q. Which two superhero series debuted in September 1963, and what were their original line-ups?

A. *The Avengers* #1 featured Iron Man, Thor, Ant-Man, Wasp and the Hulk. *The X-Men* #1 saw Professor X joined by Angel, Beast, Cyclops, Iceman and Marvel Girl (Jean Grey). Both comicbooks were created by Stan Lee and Jack Kirby, so quite a big month for them, then!

29. Q. Complete these three crazy Dr. Strange incantations:

A) By the ***** ***** of Hoggoth!
B) By the ******** ***** of Watoomb!
C) By the **** ***** of Raggadorr!

A. A) Hoary Hosts; B) Wondrous Winds; C) Ruby Rings.

30. Q. What could readers hope to win if they spotted an error in a Marvel comic and wrote to tell Stan Lee about it?

A. A No-Prize! Eagle-eyed readers who noticed a mistake, or better yet, those who offered plausible explanations of previously identified errors, were from 1964 awarded a No-Prize, which amounted to literally nothing. In 1967, however, Lee began to generously mail empty envelopes to winners of the No-Prize, upon which the following message was printed: "Congratulations! This envelope contains a genuine Marvel Comics No-Prize which you have just won!" Ironically, these empty envelopes became highly coveted rewards.

31. Q. During their first encounter with Doctor Doom in *The Fantastic Four* #5 (July 1962), Doom holds The Invisible Girl hostage so the others will do his bidding. To secure Sue's safe return, what does he demand of Reed, Johnny and Ben?

A. That they use his time travel device to go centuries into the past and obtain for him Blackbeard's legendary treasure chest. And that's just the beginning of the story!

32. Q. What was the title of Henry Pym's debut adventure in *Tales to Astonish* #27 (January 1962)?

A. *The Man in the Ant Hill*: "It was about a guy who shrunk down and there were ants chasing him," said editor/plotter Stan Lee. "That sold so well, I thought making him into a superhero might be fun." Pym returned as Ant-Man in *Tales to Astonish* #35 (September 1962).

33. Q. "Slowly, the figure speaks...In a voice which is not a voice...Mouthing words which are more than words... Expressing thoughts no mortal has ever gleaned before!" What momentous Marvel meeting does this grand caption precede?

A. Doctor Strange's first encounter with Eternity in *Strange Tales #138* (November, 1965). Strange seeks additional power to defeat the threat of Baron Mordo and the Dreaded Dormammu, but Eternity sends him packing. "You already possess the means to defeat your foes! Power is not the only answer! Events have occurred which require a key...And WISDOM is that key!"

34. Q. What grand comicbook occasion did Stan Lee describe as "the world's most colossal collection of costumed characters, crazily cavorting and capering in continual combat!"?

A. The wedding of Mister Fantastic and The Invisible Girl in *Fantastic Four Annual* #3 (1965): Sue and Reed's big day is disrupted by 21 wedding-crashing villains. Good job an equal number of invited heroes are there to save the day!

35. Q. Who was the first supervillain faced by Spider-Man?

A. The Vulture (*The Amazing Spider-Man* #2, May 1963).

36. Q. Whose early adventures involved scuffles with the likes of The Absorbing Man, The Wrecker, The Destroyer, Lava Man, Radioactive Man, Mister Hyde, The Enchantress and The Grey Gargoyle?

A. The Mighty Thor!

37. Q. What is Daredevil's signature weapon and which key function was added by artist Wally Wood in *Daredevil* #7 (April 1965)?

A. Daredevil never leaves the office without his trusty Billy Club, a weapon made all the more useful by Wood's addition of a grappling hook.

38. Q. Jack Kirby's original concept art for Black Panther revealed that he and Stan Lee originally had a very different name in mind for the character. What was it?

A. Coal Tiger! Fortunately Jack and Stan came to their senses, and Black Panther made a striking debut in *Fantastic Four* #52 (July 1966).

39. Q. Who are The Fantastic Four and what are their superhero names?

A. Reed Richards is Mister Fantastic, Susan Storm is The Invisible Girl, Johnny Storm is The Human Torch and Ben Grimm is The Thing (*The Fantastic Four*, November 1961).

40. GUEST STAR Rob Bruce

Q. Before he turned green, The Incredible Hulk was originally what colour?

A. Grey: At the advent of the Marvel Comic Age, in May 1962, Stan Lee and Jack Kirby created the first Incredible

Hulk comic. Stan had originally intended for the Hulk to be grey, and he appears in his first story as such, but due to printing problems his colour was switched to green as it was easier to maintain a consistent tone of that colour.

41. Q. What was Stan Lee's real name?

A. Stanley Martin Lieber.

42. Q. Mister Fantastic, Spider-Man, Iron Man, Daredevil: who's the odd one out?

A. Mister Fantastic: while the others keep their identities secret, for fear of super-villainous reprisals against their loved ones, Reed Richards and his Fantastic Four teammates entertain a full disclosure policy with the public (*The Fantastic Four*, November 1961).

43. Q. Where in the world was Tony Stark injured, and by whom was he subsequently captured, triggering the creation of Iron Man, in his original origin tale?

A. While testing experimental weapons in Vietnam, Tony is injured by an exploding booby trap and taken prisoner by the Vietcong (*Tales of Suspense* #39, March 1963).

44. Q. What were Stan "The Man" Lee's nicknames for Jim Steranko, Jack Kirby and John Buscema?

A. "Jaunty" Jim Steranko, Jack "King" Kirby (also "Jolly" Jack Kirby and "Jumpin'" Jack Kirby) and "Jovial" John Buscema (also "Big" John Buscema). Stan himself was also occasionally known as "Smilin'" Stan Lee.

45. Q. How do The Fantastic Four acquire their powers?

A, They're exposed to cosmic rays during a test flight through outer space in an experimental rocket ship (*The Fantastic Four* #1, November 1961).

46. Q. Dormammu, Kingpin, Loki, Magneto: rearrange this alphabetical list of classic supervillains in order of their arrival in the Marvel Universe.

A. Loki came first, in *Journey into Mystery* #85 (October 1962), then Magneto in *X-Men* #1 (September 1963), Dormammu in *Strange Tales* #126 (November 1964) and finally The Kingpin in *The Amazing Spider-Man* #50 (July 1967).

47. **Q.** Best known for creating Golden Age antihero Namor the Sub-Mariner (*Marvel Comics* #1, October 1939), and co-creating Daredevil (*Daredevil* #1, April 1964) with Stan Lee, writer/artist "Wild" Bill Everett was a descendant of which iconoclastic English poet and artist?

A. Bill Everett, whose full name was William Blake Everett, was a descendant of revered, Romantic-era poet, artist and printmaker William Blake (1757–1827). The elder Blake's most notable works include *Songs of Innocence and of Experience* (1789), *The Marriage of Heaven and Hell* (composed between 1790 and 1793) and *Milton: A Poem in Two Books* (written and illustrated between 1804 and 1810).

48. **Q.** After fooling the Skrulls into cancelling their first invasion by showing them clippings of monsters from old Marvel comics and convincing them those horrors awaited them on Earth, how does Reed Richards deal with the three remaining Skrulls left stranded among the humans?

A. Begging for mercy, the Skrulls agree to shapeshift one final time into anything Reed suggests, so in the final panel of *The Fantastic Four* #2 (January 1962), we see they've transformed into cows, and, having been hypnotised by Reed into truly believing they're bovines, are left happily grazing in a field. "So ends the menace of the Skrulls!"

49. **Q.** Which three Marvel heroes might you bump into in Queens, Hell's Kitchen and Greenwich Village?

A. Spider-Man lives in Forest Hills, Queens; Daredevil lives and operates in Hell's Kitchen; and Doctor Strange's Sanctum Sanctorum is located at 177A Bleecker Street in Greenwich Village. New York being the centre of Marvel's real-life and fictional universe.

50. Q. After Peter Parker dumps his Spidey costume in the trash in angsty Stan Lee/John Romita Sr. tale *Spider-Man No More*, an excited kid charges with it into J. Jonah Jameson's office, expecting a reward from the beaming newsman. What is he offered?

A. A free copy of *The Daily Bugle*! (*The Amazing Spider-Man* #50, July 1967).

The Force Is Strong with These Three: *Star Wars/Empire/Jedi*

1. Q. What's the name of Lucasfilm's special effects division?

A. Industrial Light & Magic – ILM for short – was founded in 1975 when George Lucas began production on *Star Wars*.

2. Q. Name any three of the six bounty hunters hired by the Empire to hunt Luke, Han and Leia.

A. The six bounty hunters hired to pursue our heroes were Bossk (Alan Harris), Zuckuss (Cathy Munroe), Dengar (Maurice Bush), IG-88 (Paul Klein), 4-Lom (Chris Parsons) and, of course, Boba Fett (Jeremy Bulloch/Jason Wingreen) (*The Empire Strikes Back*).

3. Q. Name two lifeforms indigenous to Hoth.

A. Tauntauns and wampas (*The Empire Strikes Back*).

4. Q. To throw fans and press off the scent, *Return of the Jedi* was shot under what false title?

A. Blue Harvest: the fake film even had its own phoney tagline – "Horror Beyond Imagination".

5. Q. Right up until the first day of filming *Star Wars*, what was Luke Skywalker's (Mark Hamill) original surname?

A. Starkiller: apparently Lucas ditched the name as he feared Luke might be associated with Charles Manson.

6. Q. Which of Luke's (Mark Hamill) hands gets sliced off by Darth Vader?

A. Luke loses his right hand (*The Empire Strikes Back*).

7. Q. Where, on Tatooine, does the Sarlacc reside?

A. The Sarlacc lives in the wastes of Tatooine's Dune Sea, in the Great Pit of Carkoon (*Return of the Jedi*).

8. Q. How does Obi-Wan Kenobi describe Mos Eisley Spaceport to Luke?

A. "You will never find a more wretched hive of scum and villainy" (*Star Wars*).

9. Q. What does Yoda have in common with Miss Piggy and Albert Einstein?

A. Muppet legend Frank Oz operates and speaks for both Miss Piggy and Yoda. Yoda's eyes, meanwhile, were modelled on Einstein's by designer Stuart Freeborn.

10. GUEST STAR Mark Hamill

Q. What's the first thing Luke ever said to Leia?

A. "Huh? Oh, the uniform!" – This is in response to "Aren't you a little short for a Stormtrooper?" and a perfect trick question because most will reply: "I'm Luke Skywalker. I'm here to rescue you!"

11. Q. Who's taller – Peter Mayhew or David Prowse?

A. Mayhew, who, at 7'3", towers over Prowse, 6'6".

12. Q. Who says "I have a bad feeling about this" in *Star Wars*, *Empire* and *Jedi*?

A. Luke (Mark Hamill) and Han (Harrison Ford) both say it in *Star Wars*, Leia (Carrie Fisher) says it in *Empire* and C-3PO (Anthony Daniels) says it in *Jedi*.

13. Q. Which of George Lucas' filmmaker friends insisted on editing the text of *Star Wars*' iconic opening crawl?

A. Brian De Palma: Apparently the original text contained a deluge of complex *Star Wars* lore. De Palma described it as gibberish, saying it went on forever. “George,” he said, “you’re out of your mind! Let me sit down and write this for you.”

14. Q. Two of the asteroids in the asteroid sequence were a potato and a shoe: True or false?

A. True! (*The Empire Strikes Back*).

15. Q. What was the original title of *Return of the Jedi*, and why did George Lucas change it?

A. The original title was *Revenge of the Jedi*, which Lucas changed because a Jedi should be above such things.

16. Q. Dave Prowse’s heavy Bristol accent earned him what cruel but hilarious nickname from the crew and his fellow cast mates?

A. Darth Farmer.

17. Q. How did Peter Mayhew win the role of Chewbacca? Also, what was his profession prior to being cast?

A. The 7’3” Londoner won the role within ten seconds of meeting George Lucas. All he had to do was stand up! Mayhew had previously worked as a hospital orderly in Yorkshire and he actually returned to that job between the end of shooting *Star Wars* and its eventual, life-changing release.

18. Q. It took three actors to play Darth Vader in *Return of the Jedi*. Who were they, and what was their contribution?

A. David Prowse wore the suit, James Earl Jones did all the talking and Sebastian Shaw played the big man when he took off his mask near the end of the movie.

19. Q. What’s unusual about a Tatooine sunset?

A. Tatooine has two suns (*Star Wars*).

20. Q. Meco's disco version of John Williams' *Star Wars* score, matter-of-factly titled "Star Wars Theme and Cantina Band", is the third best-selling instrumental single of all time: True or false?

A. False: it's actually the top selling! It's the only instrumental single ever to reach Platinum status by the Recording Industry Association of America (RIAA), having sold more than two million units. The track featured on the album *Star Wars and Other Galactic Funk*, which outsold the original movie soundtrack and was also certified Platinum.

21. Q. How many times is Luke (Mark Hamill) upside down in *The Empire Strikes Back*?

A. Three times: In the Wampa cave on Hoth, on Dagobah during his training, and then hanging from Cloud City.

22. Q. What's the name of the *Star Wars* simulator ride that's been a staple at Disney parks since 1987?

A. Star Tours.

23. Q. Famously uncommunicative as a director, while shooting *Star Wars*, George Lucas guided his actors with which two stock phrases?

A. "George Lucas was wonderful to work with, but he never spoke really," said Carrie Fisher in 2015. "He just said 'Faster!' or 'More intense!'" Stricken by laryngitis for a spell, Lucas was handed a board with those directions painted on it, and his directing style remained unaffected.

24. Q. A, B, D, X, Y: Which is the odd one out?

A. The odd one out is D, because all the others are classes of rebel ship (A-Wing, B-Wing, X-Wing and Y-Wing).

25. GUEST STAR Bonnie Burton

Q. Which well-known actor from Eighties' TV sitcom *Cheers* made an appearance in *The Empire Strikes Back*?

A. John Ratzenberger – who played mailman Cliff Clavin in Cheers – has a brief appearance in *The Empire Strikes Back* as Major Derlin. He advises Han Solo not to go out into the dangerous snowstorm to look for Luke Skywalker. Luckily for Luke, Han doesn't listen to him.

26. Q. Fish-faced rebel hero Admiral Ackbar (Tim Rose/Erik Bauersfeld) is a member of which species?

A. The Mon Calamari (*Return of the Jedi*).

27. Q. Why was TK-421 (Stephen Bayley) not at his post?

A. Because he was lured into the *Millennium Falcon* and blasted by Han Solo (Harrison Ford) (*Star Wars*).

28. Q. The day Mark Hamill filmed the scene where Luke makes it out of his snowspeeder just before it's crushed by an Imperial Walker was particularly memorable for the actor for what two reasons?

A. His first son, Nathan, was born that morning, and later that day, during a stunt, he broke his thumb (*The Empire Strikes Back*).

29. Q. Besides Luke (Mark Hamill), only one other X-Wing pilot survives all three movies. Who's the character and the actor who played him?

A. Wedge Antilles is played by Denis Lawson.

30. Q. What's the first line spoken in *Star Wars*, and who delivers it?

A. C-3PO (Anthony Daniels) says "Did you hear that?"

31. Q. What's the name of Darth Vader's (David Prowse/James Earl Jones) flagship destroyer in *The Empire Strikes Back*?

A. *Executor*.

32. Q. Which two *Star Wars* cast members have won Academy Awards, and what for?

A. Alec Guinness won Best Actor in 1957 for *The Bridge on the River Kwai*, while James Earl Jones won a well-deserved Honorary Award in 2012.

33. Q. Although "It's a trap" is famously Admiral Ackbar's (Tim Rose/Erik Bauersfeld) signature line in *Return of the Jedi*, it was spoken by which other character in which earlier movie?

A. By Leia (Carrie Fisher), in *Empire*, when Luke (Mark Hamill) arrives on Bespin to try to save his friends.

34. Q. How many languages does C-3PO (Anthony Daniels) speak?

A. "I am fluent," boasts Threepio to anyone who'll listen, "in over six million forms of communication."

35. Q. Before landing the role of Lando Calrissian, Billy Dee Williams first auditioned for which role in *Star Wars*?

A. Han Solo.

36. Q. Which member of *Star Wars*' cast wore fluffy slippers while filming anything that didn't show his feet, and why?

A. Peter Cushing, as his boots were punishingly tight (*Star Wars*).

37. Q. Leia (Carrie Fisher) strangling Jabba (Larry Ward) in *Return of the Jedi* was a homage to which character's murder in what movie?

A. Luca Brasi's (Lenny Montana) killing in *The Godfather* (1972). George Lucas helped out as an assistant editor on that classic crime flick, directed by his good friend Francis Ford Coppola.

38. Q. What's the name of the holographic chess game played by Chewbacca (Peter Mayhew) and the droids aboard the *Millennium Falcon* in *Star Wars*?

A. Dejarik.

39. Q. Where's Cloud City and what's mined there?

A. Cloud City floats above the clouds of the planet Bespin, where it mines Tibanna gas (*The Empire Strikes Back*).

40. GUEST STAR Ben Palmer

Q. The recording of Alfred Newman's "20th Century Fox Fanfare" which opened *Star Wars* was borrowed from the soundtrack of which 1954 western?

A. *River of No Return*, starring Robert Mitchum and Marilyn Monroe.

41. Q. What are Darth Vader's (Sebastian Shaw) final words in *Return of the Jedi*?

A. Darth Vader's final words are "Tell your sister...you were right."

42. Q. "Staggering as spectacle and technically brilliant, exciting, very noisy and warm-hearted. The battle scenes at the end go on for five minutes too long, and some of the dialogue is excruciating and much of it is lost in noise, but it remains a vivid experience." Which member of *Star Wars*' cast described the film this way?

A. Alec Guinness.

43. Q. Who owned the *Millennium Falcon* before Han Solo?

A. Lando Calrissian (Billy Dee Williams), who lost it to Han in a card game.

44. Q. How far apart were the US and UK cinema releases of *Star Wars*?

A. *Star Wars* was released in the States on May 25, 1977, but didn't reach the UK until December 27, 1977. That's a staggering 216 days, or 30 weeks and 6 days, or 7 months and 2 days between the two releases. If you answered "Forever", that's also acceptable, as that's how long it felt. And really the December 27 UK release date only applied to those lucky enough to make it to the exclusive London screenings. The film didn't receive its general release until January 29, 1978, which is plain crazy.

45. Q. Who's a feisty little one?

A. R2-D2 (Kenny Baker)! Though he never learned to respect Jabba or his goons (*Return of the Jedi*).

46. Q. What does the TIE in TIE Fighter stand for?

A. TIE is an acronym for Twin Ion Engines.

47. Q. Who directed each of the three original movies?

A. George Lucas directed *Star Wars*, Irvin Kershner directed *The Empire Strikes Back* and Richard Marquand directed *Return of the Jedi*.

48. Q. George Lucas accepted a lower salary for making *Star Wars* in exchange for what two requests that, at the time, seemed like small potatoes to Fox executives eager to save money on a film they were convinced would fail?

A. First, that he retain all merchandising rights, and second, that he retain the rights to any sequels. In effect, Lucas traded $350,000 in 1977 for a personal fortune that, following the franchise's sale to Disney in 2012, exceeded $5 billion. As business decisions go, that's one of the best of all time!

49. Q. What was the name of the Official *Star Wars* Fan Club's newsletter?

A. *Bantha Tracks*: it was published quarterly from 1978 to 1987.

50. Q. Who shot first?

A. Greedo (Paul Blake/Maria De Aragon/Larry Ward). Obviously. Never suggest otherwise (*Star Wars*).

Doctor Who: The Tom Baker Years

1. Q. What role, in which movie, convinced producer Barry Letts that Tom Baker was the right man to succeed Jon Pertwee?

A. After considering the likes of Jim Dale, Michael Bentine, Fulton Mackay and Bernard Cribbins, Letts was so impressed by Baker's villainous turn as the evil wizard Koura in *The Golden Voyage of Sinbad* (1973) that he offered Tom the role.

2. Q. To supplement his meagre earnings as an actor, what was Tom Baker doing for work when he was cast as the Doctor?

A. He was a labourer on a building site. "I had no skills there," said Baker, "except to make the tea and use a drill." Hauling bricks and mixing cement were likewise specialities.

3. Q. Which of his companions did Baker's Doctor call "a clumsy, ham-fisted idiot"?

A. Harry Sullivan (Ian Marter) in "The Ark in Space" (Season 12, Serial 2, 1975).

4. Q. In which story did John Cleese and Eleanor Bron guest star as art critics who mistake the TARDIS for modern art?

A. "City of Death" (Season 17, Serial 2, 1979).

JC: For me, one of the most curious things about this piece is its wonderful afunctionalism.

EB: Yes, I see what you mean. Divorced from its function and seen purely as a piece of art, its structure of line and colour is curiously counterpointed by the redundant vestiges of its function.

JC: And since it has no call to be here, the art lies in the fact that it is here.

(TARDIS dematerialises)

EB: Exquisite. Absolutely exquisite.

5. Q. What episode of which serial saw the very first appearance of Baker's fourth Doctor?

A. "Planet of the Spiders, Part Six" (Season 11, Serial 5, 1974). There's a brief, uncredited glimpse of Baker as Pertwee's third Doctor regenerates in the dramatic closing seconds of the show.

6. Q. What is the name of the Experimental Prototype Robot built by Professor J.P. Kettlewell (Edward Burnham) in "Robot" (Season 12, Serial 1, 1974–1975)?

A. K1 (Michael Kilgarriff).

7. Q. What was Tom Baker's only two-part *Doctor Who* serial?

A. "The Sontaran Experiment" (Season 12, Serial 3, 1975).

8. Q. What was the real-life reason for the Doctor banging his face on the TARDIS's console in "The Pirate Planet" (Season 16, Serial 2, 1978)?

A. To explain Tom Baker's real-life cut lip from a dog bite! While filming preceding serial "The Ribos Operation" (Season 16, Serial 1, 1978), Baker attempted a trick with a Jack Russell terrier owned by co-star Paul Seed, who played Graff Vynda-K. It did not go well! Consequently, Baker had a scar on his lip for most of the rest of Season 16.

9. Q. When the script for "The Face of Evil" (Season 14, Serial 4) called for the Doctor to threaten one of the tribesmen with a weapon, Tom Baker objected. What did he use instead?

A. A deadly jelly baby!

10. Q. Which serial saw the first appearance of K9 and how many actors have voiced the character?

A. "The Invisible Enemy" (Season 15, Serial 2, 1977). Three actors have voiced K9 – though John Leeson is the character's primary voice artist, when K9 contracts robot laryngitis in "Destiny of the Daleks" (Season 17, Serial 1), Roy Skelton supplied the croaks, while David Brierley voiced the character for the remainder of Season 17.

11. Q. What was the name of the unproduced film Baker wrote with co-star Ian Marter during breaks in filming *Doctor Who*?

A. "Doctor Who Meets Scratchman" (a.k.a. "Doctor Who and the Big Game"), in which the Doctor squares off against Satan, various robots, scarecrows made from bones and the Greek god Pan. More than four decades later, in January 2019, BBC Books published Baker's novelisation of the screenplay, simply called *Scratchman*.

12. Q. What's the final line spoken in "Genesis of the Daleks" (Season 12, Serial 4, 1975)?

A. The Doctor says, "You see, I know that although the Daleks will create havoc and destruction for millions of years, I know also that out of their evil must come something good."

13. Q. In which serial did Tom Baker don an Inverness cape and deerstalker hat, foreshadowing his later role as Sherlock Holmes in a BBC TV adaptation of *The Hound of the Baskervilles* (1982)?

A. "The Talons of Weng-Chiang" (Season 14, Serial 6, 1977).

14. Q. "The Ark in Space" (Season 12, Serial 2, 1975), "The Sontaran Experiment" (Season 12, Serial 3, 1975) and "The Ribos Operation" (Season 16, Serial 1, 1978): Which is the odd one out?

A. "The Ribos Operation": though all three were novelised by Ian Marter, his character, Harry Sullivan, didn't appear in "The Ribos Operation".

15. GUEST STAR Louise Jameson

Q. In which story did Leela's eyes transform from brown to blue? Also, what was the real-life reason behind the change?

A. The story was "Horror of Fang Rock" (Season 15, Serial 1, 1977). When I started playing Leela, I wore red contact lenses that changed my blue eyes to brown. They made everything appear red and were very uncomfortable. Though producer Philip Hinchcliffe wanted Leela to have brown eyes, when producer Graham Williams came on board he was happy for my character to switch to blue. I still had to wear contacts as I'm very short-sighted, but clear ones I could easily cope with.

16. Q. The fourth and final part of which Tom Baker serial had the largest viewing figures for any episode of *Doctor Who* in the history of the series?

A. "City of Death" (Season 17, Serial 2, 1979), which earned a whopping 16.1 million viewers. As ITV was on strike at the time, there was really nothing else to watch though!

17. Q. "We were deliriously happy for weeks," said Tom Baker of his short-lived marriage to which of his *Doctor Who* co-stars?

A. Lalla Ward, who played Romana II from "Destiny of the Daleks" (Season 17, Serial 1, 1979) to "Warriors' Gate" (Season 18, Serial 5, 1981). She and Baker tied the knot in December 1980, but the marriage lasted just 16 months. Recalls Baker, "Somebody at a convention asked her, 'What was your favourite monster?' Quick as a flash, Lalla went, 'Tom Baker!' I remember thinking, 'Ahh, good old Lalla'."

18. Q. It's revealed, in "The Deadly Assassin" (Season 14, Serial 3, 1976), that the Doctor belongs to which Gallifreyan Chapter?

A. The Prydonians: A "notoriously devious" sect.

19. Q. What six serials comprised Season 16's "Key to Time" arc?

A. "The Ribos Operation" (Season 16, Serial 1, 1978), "The Pirate Planet" (Season 16, Serial 2, 1978), "The Stones of Blood" (Season 16, Serial 3, 1978), "The Androids of Tara" (Season 16, Serial 4, 1978), "The Power of Kroll" (Season 16, Serial 5, 1978–1979) and "The Armageddon Factor" (Season 16, Serial 6, 1979).

20. Q. Who does the Doctor say made his signature scarf? Also, how does he describe her?

A. "Madame Nostradamus made it for me. A witty little knitter." ("The Ark in Space", Season 12, Serial 2, 1975.)

21. Q. Sometimes when the Doctor was required to rattle off TARDIS coordinates, Tom Baker would recite what real-life number?

A. The *Doctor Who* production office's telephone number! But no one ever cottoned on.

22. Q. In "The Stones of Blood" (Season 16, Serial 3, 1978), after Romana (Mary Tamm) casually tells K9 to "forget it" in response to a question, what does K9 remove all knowledge of from his memory banks?

A. Tennis.

23. Q. Tom Baker's final serial as the Doctor, "Logopolis" (Season 18, Serial 7, 1981), was the first serial for which companion?

A. Tegan Jovanka (Janet Fielding).

24. Q. Actor Michael Spice menaced Baker's fourth Doctor as the eponymous villains of which two serials?

A. Spice voiced the glowing remains of evil Time Lord Morbius in "The Brain of Morbius" (Season 13, Serial 5, 1976) and later played Weng-Chiang, alias Magnus Greel, The Butcher of Brisbane, in "The Talons of Weng-Chiang" (Season 14, Serial 6, 1977).

25. Q. What was Begonia Pope's wonderful mistake?

A. The knitting professional hired to create a scarf for Baker's Doctor, Pope was given "a wagonload" of wool by costume designer James Acheson. Rather than use a small selection to knit a sensible scarf, which is surely what Acheson intended, Pope mistakenly thought she was supposed to use it all, and an iconic accessory was born! She "was so excited at being asked to work for *Doctor Who*," says Baker, "that she started knitting it and just didn't stop. When we went to her room, it was so full of scarf, we couldn't get in! She offered to cut it up, but Jim wanted to keep it."

26. Q. "The Deadly Assassin" (Season 14, Serial 3, 1976) was the first and only televised series in the show's original run to ditch which key *Doctor Who* element?

A. The companions: Tom Baker felt he could carry the show alone on occasion, and so, after dropping Sarah Jane (Elisabeth Sladen) back home, The Doctor shoots off to Gallifrey unaccompanied. A bold experiment, but ultimately the companions were deemed too integral to the series to leave out again.

27. Q. What is Romana I's (Mary Tamm) full name, and how does the Doctor respond, in "The Ribos Operation" (Season 16, Serial 1, 1978), when she uses it to introduce herself?

A. Romana: My name is Romanadvoratrelundar.
The Doctor: I'm so sorry about that. Is there anything we can do?

28. Q. What is the final piece of the Key to Time disguised as?

A. Princess Astra of Atrios (Lalla Ward in "The Armageddon Factor", Season 16, Serial 6, 1979).

29. Q. What was the name of the French cabaret singer, comedian and nightclub owner who inspired the fourth Doctor's bohemian look? Also, who painted his famous portraits?

A. Aristide Bruant (1851–1925), known to most as the man in the red scarf and black cape in various posters painted by Henri de Toulouse-Lautrec.

30. GUEST STAR Dave Johns

Q. Which three actors played the Master during Tom Baker's era?

A. Peter Pratt, Geoffrey Beevers and Anthony Ainley.

31. Q. What's the only *Doctor Who* television serial to feature a Rutan? Also, who are their mortal enemies?

A. "Horror of Fang Rock" (Season 15, Serial 1, 1977), and they're not terribly fond of Sontarans.

32. Q. Which writer penned three *Doctor Who* serials, all for Tom Baker's Doctor, and all broadcast in 1977?

A. Chris Boucher: "The Face of Evil" (Season 14, Serial 4), "The Robots of Death" (Season 14, Serial 5) and "Image of the Fendahl" (Season 15, Serial 3).

33. Q. According to the 1980 Prime Computer commercial featuring Tom Baker and Lalla Ward, how long is the Doctor's scarf?

A. It is 7.013 metres exclusive of the loose threads!

34. Q. What pocket universe is the Doctor trapped in after the TARDIS accidentally passes through a Charged Vacuum Emboitement?

A. E-Space ("Full Circle", Season 18, Serial 3, 1980).

35. Q. "[He] found it physically impossible to buy a drink. He liked the idea of big sums of money for voiceovers, so I would say in [his] earshot that someone had offered me £15,000 for a voiceover, but I turned it down because it was going to take a whole hour. This wasn't true, but I could hear [his] heart pounding. In fact, he died of a heart attack shortly after that. I think that's why." Who is Tom Baker talking about?

A. The Third Doctor, Jon Pertwee.

36. Q. What English synth-pop band released the instrumental tribute track "Tom Baker" in 1981?

A. The Human League: It was the B-side to their single "Boys and Girls", which reached number 48 in the UK Singles Charts.

37. Q. What unflattering string of adjectives does Romana I (Mary Tamm) hurl at the Doctor in "The Armageddon Factor" (Season 16, Serial 6, 1979)?

A. "Capricious, arrogant, self-opinionated [and] irrational."

38. Q. What's the last thing Sarah Jane (Elisabeth Sladen) says to the Doctor when they finally part company at the end of "The Hand of Fear" (Season 14, Serial 2, 1976)?

A. "You know, travel does broaden the mind." The characters' fond farewells were scripted by Baker and Sladen themselves.

39. Q. What is the Doctor's term for robophobia, mentioned in "The Robots of Death" (Season 14, Serial 5, 1977)?

A. Grimwade's Syndrome, ad-libbed by Baker as an in-joke reference to production assistant Peter Grimwade, who'd been grumbling about always being assigned to work on robot stories.

40. Q. Season 16 of *Doctor Who* saw the series celebrate which trio of major milestones?

A. The 15th anniversary of the first broadcast (November 23, 1978), the 100th serial ("The Stones of Blood", Season 16, Serial 3, 1978) and the 500th episode (part 1 of "The Armageddon Factor", Season 16, Serial 6, 1979).

41. Q. In which *Doctor Who* serial is Davros (Michael Wisher) introduced?

A. "Genesis of the Daleks" (Season 12, Serial 4, 1975).

42. Q. Which author wrote "The Pirate Planet" (Season 16, Serial 2, 1978) while simultaneously pitching what additional project about characters who, like the Doctor, tool through time and space?

A. While writing *The Pirate Planet*, Douglas Adams sold the radio pilot for his most famous creation, *The Hitchhiker's Guide to the Galaxy* (1978–2018), to the BBC. The phrase "Don't Panic" features in both shows.

43. Q. Who is the last of the Osirans? Also, what gift does he have for humanity, in "Pyramids of Mars" (Season 13, Serial 3, 1975)?

A. Sutekh the Destroyer (Gabriel Woolf); "Death to all humans."

44. Q. Which part of the Doctor does mad scientist Mehendri Solon (Philip Madoc) want to complete his Frankensteinian creation with in "The Brain of Morbius" (Season 13, Serial 5, 1976)?

A. His "magnificent head". "I'm glad you like it," says The Doctor. "I have had several. I used to have an old grey model before this. Some people liked it, but I prefer this model."

45. Q. What colour jelly baby is the Doctor's favourite?

A. Orange ("The Invasion of Time", Season 15, Serial 6, 1978).

46. Q. What sad, real-life event occurred between the original UK broadcast of episodes one and two of "Revenge of the Cybermen" (Season 12, Serial 5, 1975)?

A. The First Doctor, William Hartnell, passed away, at the age of 67, on April 23, 1975.

47. Q. "Some of the stories of my era were latched onto as being more frightening, but I don't think we ever overstepped the mark. The ratings were very high, [so] people seemed to like it." Which real-life *Doctor Who* hero is speaking here?

A. The great Philip Hinchcliffe, the show's producer from 1974 to 1977.

48. Q. How many series, serials and episodes comprise Tom Baker's record-setting run as the Doctor?

A. Seven series, 41 serials and 173 episodes – 179, if you count Baker's unaired serial "Shada", which would have rounded off Season 17 (1979–1980) had strike action at the BBC not left it woefully incomplete. "Shada" was finally finished in 2017, with freshly recorded audio and animation filling in the gaps.

49. Q. Which companions were with Tom Baker's Doctor when he regenerated?

A. Adric (Matthew Waterhouse), Nyssa (Sarah Sutton) and Tegan (Janet Fielding) ("Logopolis", Season 18, Serial 7, 1981).

50. Q. Two years after quitting the show, Tom Baker agreed to appear in its 20th-anniversary special, "The Five Doctors" (1983). When he later changed his mind, how did producer John Nathan-Turner compensate for his absence, both in the special itself, and the accompanying publicity photocall?

A. As "The Five Doctors" wouldn't work with just four Doctors, the special included unaired footage of Baker from the unfinished 1980 serial "Shada". When the time arrived for "The Five Doctors" photocall, Peter Davison, Patrick Troughton, Jon Pertwee and Richard Hurndall posed with a waxwork model of Baker that had been created for a 1980 *Doctor Who* exhibition in Madame Tussauds. When asked, years later, why he refused to be a part of the special, Baker explained, "I didn't want to play 20% of the part. I didn't fancy being a feed for other Doctors – in fact, it filled me with horror."

John Carpenter's Apocalypse Trilogy

1. Q. According to *The Thing*'s MacReady (Kurt Russell), what's a hard thing to come by these days?

A. Trust.

2. Q. According to Brian (Jameson Parker) in *Prince of Darkness*, what's a hard thing to come by these days?

A. Faith.

3. Q. According to *In the Mouth of Madness*'s Simon (Wilhelm von Homburg), what's not what it used to be?

A. Reality.

4. Q. *The Thing* was the first of John Carpenter's feature films not to be at least co-scored by the director. Who composed the soundtrack instead?

A. Ennio Morricone.

5. Q. What's the first shot in *Prince of Darkness*?

A. A full moon.

6. Q. Immediately after being thrown into his asylum cell in *In the Mouth of Madness*, Trent (Sam Neill) issues what desperate apology to the limping orderly?

A. "I'm sorry about the balls! It was a lucky shot, that's all."

7. Q. Who shoots the trigger-happy Norwegian who storms into camp chasing the dog, in *The Thing*?

A. Garry (Donald Moffat).

8. Q. On the subatomic level, what does Professor Birack (Victor Wong) say classical reality collapses into, in *Prince of Darkness*?

A. "Ghosts and shadows."

9. Q. What single item does Trent (Sam Neill) ask for in the asylum? Also, what does he use it for, in *In the Mouth of Madness*?

A. A black crayon that he uses to draw crosses on his face, clothes and the padded walls of his cell.

10. GUEST STAR John Carpenter

Q. *The Thing* was shot on the Juneau icefields adjacent to what glacier?

A. The Mendenhall Glacier.

11. Q. What cartoon does Walter (Dennis Dun) watch in the kitchen in *Prince of Darkness*?

A. It's a Tom and Jerry short from 1949 called *Heavenly Puss*.

12. Q. What's the name of Sutter Cane's (Jürgen Prochnow) publisher in *In the Mouth of Madness*?

A. Arcane.

13. Q. Who delivers the first line of dialogue in *The Thing*?

A. Actress Adrienne Barbeau, who was married to John Carpenter from 1979 to 1984, performed uncredited as the voice of MacReady's (Kurt Russell) Chess Wizard computer game. The line is, "Your move: Bishop to Knight four."

14. Q. What does Etchinson (Thom Bray) see at the foot of the alley stairs, shortly before being impaled by the Street Schizo (Alice Cooper), in *Prince of Darkness*?

A. A crucified pigeon. Incidentally, the song Etchinson's listening to on his Walkman in that scene is Alice Cooper's *Prince of Darkness* title song. And the whole impaling gag was taken from Cooper's own stage show – including the prop bike.

15. Q. According to Sutter Cane's (Jürgen Prochnow) editor Linda (Julie Carmen), what effect has his writing been known to have on his less stable readers?

A. Disorientation, memory loss and severe paranoia.

16. Q. According to Dr Blair's (Wilford Brimley) computer projection, how long would it take for the entire world to be infected after *The Thing*'s intruder organism reaches civilised areas?

A. 27,000 hours, which is 3.02 years.

17. Q. What year is the dream broadcast from in *Prince of Darkness*?

A. The future – 1999!

18. Q. Where does Trent (Sam Neill) believe the map he made from Sutter Cane (Jürgen Prochnow) book covers will lead, in *In the Mouth of Madness*?

A. Hobb's End, New Hampshire.

19. Q. What two characters, from which two movies in John Carpenter's Apocalypse Trilogy, wake from a dream, though really they're still dreaming, and it takes another scare to actually wake them from their dream?

A. Brian (Jameson Parker) at the very end of *Prince of Darkness* and then Trent (Sam Neill), after he dozes off while reading, in *In the Mouth of Madness*.

20. Q. What was *The Thing*'s primary source material?

A. John Carpenter's *The Thing* was not a remake of 1951's *The Thing from Another World*, but rather a more faithful adaptation of John W. Campbell, Jr's celebrated sci-fi novella *Who Goes There?*, first published in 1938.

21. Q. Why did John Carpenter write the screenplay for *Prince of Darkness* under the pseudonym Martin Quatermass?

A. As a tribute to British writer Nigel Kneale, specifically his Quatermass shows from the 1950s that, like *Prince of Darkness*, blended science with the supernatural to startling effect. Beside the screen credit, the production notes for *Prince of Darkness* included the following biography of the film's fictitious scribe: "Martin Quatermass, born in London, England, is a former physicist and brother of Bernard Quatermass, the rocket scientist who headed the British Rocket Group during the 1950s. Quatermass graduated from Kneale University with a degree in theoretical physics. *Prince of Darkness* is his first screenplay, and he assures that all the physical principles used in the story, including the ability of subatomic particles to travel backward in time, are true. Author of two novels, *Schrödinger's Revenge* and

Schwarzschild Radius, he currently lives in Frazier Park, California, with his wife, Janet."

22. Q. *The Thing*'s ruined Norwegian camp set cost more to build than the film's main American camp: True or false?

A. False! It actually cost next-to-nothing as the Norwegian camp was simply the scorched remains of the American camp after it was blown up for the movie's climax.

23. Q. Where would *The Thing*'s Garry (Donald Moffat) rather not spend the rest of the winter?

A. "Tied to this fucking chair!"

24. Q. According to Trent (Sam Neill) in *In the Mouth of Madness*, what should one never, never, never do?

A. "Throw chips at a driver."

25. GUEST STAR Sandy King

Q. What actor first worked with John Carpenter on *Prince of Darkness* before appearing in six more of his films?

A. Peter Jason (the other six John Carpenter movies being *They Live* (1988), *Body Bags* (1993), *In the Mouth of Madness* (1994), *Village of the Damned* (1995), *Escape From L.A.* (1996) and *Ghosts of Mars* (2001).

26. Q. What attacks the villagers outside the Black Church after Simon (Wilhelm von Homburg) angrily demands the return of his son?

A. A pack of Doberman Pinschers. If you'd like to visit the exterior location of the Black Church, search online for Canada's Cathedral of the Transfiguration.

27. Q. What's MacReady's (Kurt Russell) job at U.S. Outpost 31 in *The Thing*?

A. Helicopter pilot.

28. Q. What's the name of the secret sect who for centuries kept the lid on Satan, the Anti-God and Alien Jesus in *Prince of Darkness*?

A. The Brotherhood of Sleep.

29. Q. What's under the counter at reception in the Pickman Hotel, in *In the Mouth of Madness*?

A. A whimpering, naked old man, handcuffed to Mrs Pickman's (Frances Bay) ankle.

30. Q. *The Thing* was released on the same day as which other sci-fi favourite, a film that was likewise poorly reviewed but is regarded by many as a classic?

A. Ridley Scott's *Blade Runner* (1982).

31. Q. What's on the crazy Bag Lady's (Joanna Merlin) face when Professor Birack (Victor Wong) first notices her? Also, what's in her cup when she hassles the Priest (Donald Pleasence), in *Prince of Darkness*?

A. Two large ants, then a collection of maggots.

32. Q. What film's playing on the TV in Trent's (Sam Neill) motel room after he flees Hobb's End in *In the Mouth of Madness*?

A. *Robot Monster* (1953).

33. Q. Who's the only U.S. Outpost 31 crew member killed by a human in *The Thing*?

A. Clark (Richard Masur) is shot in the head by MacReady (Kurt Russell).

34. Q. How is Susan (Anne Howard) repeatedly described in *Prince of Darkness*?

A. "Radiologist. Glasses."

35. Q. Name any three of the seven Sutter Cane (Jürgen Prochnow) books featured in *In the Mouth of Madness*.

A. *The Hobb's End Horror*, *The Feeding*, *The Whisperer of the Dark*, *The Breathing Tunnel*, *The Thing in the Basement*, *Haunter Out of Time* and, of course, *In the Mouth of Madness*. Many of these titles pay undisguised homage to the stories of H.P. Lovecraft, most explicitly *The Dunwich Horror*, *The Whisperer in Darkness*, *The Haunter of the Dark*, *The Shadow Out of Time* and, of course, *At the Mountains of Madness*.

36. Q. What song is Nauls (T.K. Carter) listening to when George (Peter Maloney) grumpily complains about the noise, in *The Thing*?

A. "Superstition" by Stevie Wonder.

37. Q. What phrase does Calder (Jessie Lawrence Ferguson) watch Lisa (Ann Yen) type repeatedly in *Prince of Darkness*?

A. I Live!

38. Q. Though the lion's share of *The Thing*'s iconic make-up effects were created by Rob Bottin, who stepped in to make the nightmarish "Kennel-Thing" when Bottin was briefly hospitalised with exhaustion?

A. Stan Winston, who classily chose to work uncredited rather than risk diminishing Bottin's well-deserved limelight. Instead of a credit, Winston received special thanks at the end of the movie.

39. Q. "I've got a message for you and you're not going to like it..." What's the message? Also, do they like it, in *Prince of Darkness*?

A. "Pray for death." As Frank (Robert Grasmere) predicts, they do not like it, especially after his head falls off and he's revealed to be mostly made of beetles.

40. GUEST STAR Sam Neill

Q. While making *In the Mouth of Madness*, who thought that playing The Carpenters' music all day and night would be a good maddening idea in the madhouse?

A. Sam Neill! Originally the script for *In the Mouth of Madness* suggested music by The Rolling Stones.

41. Q. How many spider-like legs burst from the head-thing in *The Thing*?

A. Six.

42. Q. What's the name of the abandoned LA church where the horror happens in *Prince of Darkness*?

A. Saint Goddard's Church. If you'd like to visit the exterior location, search online for Los Angeles Artcore Union Center for the Arts.

43. Q. Which member of the crew is revealed as The Thing during the tense blood test sequence?

A. Palmer (David Clennon).

44. Q. What's written on the cinema marquee in Linda's (Julie Carmen) vision, and again later, when Trent goes to the movies, in *In the Mouth of Madness*?

A. *In the Mouth of Madness* with John Trent.

45. Q. Though long regarded as a classic, and of all his films, John Carpenter's personal favourite, *The Thing*'s original critical reception was frosty at best. Who cruelly dismissed the movie out of hand, saying, "If you want blood, go to the slaughterhouse. All in all, it's a terrific commercial for J&B Scotch."

A. Christian Nyby, director of 1951's *The Thing from Another World*, the first adaptation of John W. Campbell, Jr's *Who Goes There?*

46. Q. Which parts of Satan's body does the Priest (Donald Pleasence) hack off in *Prince of Darkness*?

A. Left arm for starters, then the head, but the arm grows back and the head fits easily back into place.

47. Q. What's the inscription on the doors of the Black Church in *In the Mouth of Madness*?

A. Let these doors be sealed by our Lord God and let any who dare enter this unholy site be damned forever.

48. Q. How long does Vance (Charles Hallahan) estimate the crashed alien spaceship has been in the ice, in *The Thing*?

A. At least 100,000 years.

49. Q. How many people make it out of the church alive at the end of *Prince of Darkness*?

A. Four: The Priest (Donald Pleasence), Professor Birack (Victor Wong), Brian (Jameson Parker) and Walter (Dennis Dun). Arguably five, if you count Catherine (Lisa Blount) making it out of the church in 1999, though she's likely possessed, so not really alive. Also, that might just have been an actual dream, rather than a transmission, so let's say four and leave it at that.

50. Q. What is Sutter Cane's (Jürgen Prochnow) favourite colour, in *In the Mouth of Madness*?

A. Blue.

The 2600: Atari's Electric Dream

1. Q. Which VCS launch game was an unofficial port of 1976 arcade hit *Blockade*, the grandfather of all Snake games?

A. *Surround* (1977).

2. Q. What flag flies in the centre of John Enright's cover art for 1978 strategy game *Flag Capture*?

A. The Union Jack (a.k.a. The King's Colours and Great Union Flag), which was originally only used at sea aboard English and Scottish ships from 1606 to 1707.

3. Q. Name any five of the nine Atari VCS launch games.

A. *Air-Sea Battle*, *Basic Math*, *Blackjack*, *Combat*, *Indy 500*, *Star Ship*, *Street Racer*, *Surround* and *Video Olympics*.

4. Q. What are the names of the four ghosts in *Ms. Pac-Man* (1982)?

A. Blinky (red), Pinky (pink), Inky (cyan) and Sue (orange).

5. Q. What classic 1982 game was recognised by *Softline* magazine as having "earned the ominous distinction of being the game with the most ways to die"? Ways you could croak included being run over on a busy motorway, drowning in a river, being eaten by alligators or riding a log off the side of the screen.

A. Frogger.

6. Q. How many option switches were at the front of the first manufactured version of the Atari VCS? Also, what were they for?

A. Six:

Power: on/off
TV Type: colour/b&w
Left Difficulty: A/B (normal/hard)
Right Difficulty: A/B (normal/hard)
Game Select
Game Reset.

7. Q. *Video Olympics* (1977) offered 50 variants of which classic game, first produced by Atari in 1972?

A. Pong: games included *Super Pong*, *Pong Doubles*, *Quadrapong* and *Robot Pong*.

8. Q. How much did you have to win to break the bank in *Blackjack* (1977)?

A. 1,000 chips.

9. Q. The Atari VCS originally shipped with which game and accessories?

A. Originally priced at $199, which adjusted for inflation is north of $800, the Atari VCS originally came packaged with two joysticks, a conjoined pair of paddle controllers, an RF TV adapter and the *Combat* (1977) game cartridge.

10. Q. "The controls of this game may be a little more complicated than the actual problems," wrote *Video Magazine* of which VCS launch game?

A. *Basic Math* (1977).

11. Q. What are the three main vehicles featured in *Combat* (1977)?

A. Biplanes, jet fighters and tanks.

12. Q. What was the North American launch date of the Atari VCS?

A. September 11, 1977.

13. Q. How many balls could you end up playing with at once in the cavity game mode of *Super Breakout* (1978)?

A. Three: though you only start with one ball, two others are trapped in pockets within the wall and can be freed.

14. Q. What colour dragon is featured in Susan Jaekel's iconic box art for *Adventure* (1979)? Also, what is it holding?

A. Rhindle the red dragon is holding the black key.

15. Q. Which three of the Man of Steel's powers are used in 1979 adventure *Superman*?

A. Flight, X-ray vision and super strength.

16. Q. What's the famous Easter egg hidden in *Adventure* (1979)?

A. A secret room containing the vertical text, "Created by Warren Robinett".

17. Q. In wacky 1980 comedy hit *Airplane!* instead of watching their monitors, flight controllers are seen playing which Atari VCS sports game?

A. *Basketball* (1978).

18. Q. Which title for the Atari VCS was the first official license of an arcade game?

A. *Space Invaders* (1980): Selling over two million units in its first year, it was so popular that people bought the system just to play it, quadrupling sales of the then three-year-old console. It is now considered both Atari's, and the entire games industry's, first "killer app".

19. Q. What company was the first third-party software producer for the Atari VCS? Also, name any two of their first four games for the system.

A. Activision – a portmanteau of “active” and “television” – was formed in 1980 by four former Atari employees who weren’t content to labour in obscurity for peanuts. Their first four games were *Boxing* (1980), *Dragster* (1980), *Fishing Derby* (1980) and *Checkers* (1981).

20. Q. How did Atari reward game programmer Rob Furlop for developing the wildly successful VCS port of *Missile Command* (1981)?

A. For producing a game that sold 2.5 million copies, Atari rewarded Furlop with a certificate for a free turkey, prompting the programmer to quit the company and co-found his own, Imagic.

21. Q. What game for the Atari VCS was the first to use bank switching, a technique that increased available ROM space from 4 KB to 8 KB?

A. *Asteroids* (1981).

22. Q. Which two-dimensional, side-scrolling shooter was originally envisioned as a version of *Space Invaders* rotated 90 degrees?

A. *Defender* (1981): “One of the hardest arcade games ever developed,” wrote *Softline* magazine in 1983. “Initial attempts lasting less than ten seconds are not uncommon for novices.”

23. Q. When, and why, did Atari change the name of the Atari VCS to the Atari 2600?

A. Atari launched its second home console in 1982, christening it the Atari 5200. To standardise the naming of its consoles, the Atari VCS became the Atari 2600 Video Computer System, or the Atari 2600 for short.

24. Q. How much RAM did the Atari 2600 have?

A. 128 bytes.

25. GUEST STAR Dominik Diamond

Q. What Atari 2600 game had a T-shaped plunger handle and is so rare a copy sold in 2012 for $33,000?

A. *Air Raid* (1982).

2600. Q. What was the name of *Berzerk*'s (1982) Big Bad, a bouncing smiley face who couldn't be killed?

A. Evil Otto, named after Dave Otto, the obnoxious security chief at Dave Nutting Associates, a former employer of game designer Alan McNeil. Apparently Otto would smile "while he chewed you out".

27. Q. How many hits does it take to completely destroy a mushroom in *Centipede* (1982)?

A. Four.

28. Q. What was the best-selling Atari 2600 game of all time?

A. Shifting an estimated 7.7 million copies, *Pac-Man* (1982) was by far Atari's best-selling title for the 2600. It was also one of the worst reviewed games for the system, with critics deriding its visuals and controls. Also, as Atari produced 12 million copies of the game, having ever so slightly overestimated demand, they were left with more than four million unsold copies, many of which were secretly buried in an Alamogordo, New Mexico, landfill.

29. Q. What would appear when you reached the roof of every skyscraper in *Crazy Climber* (1982)?

A. A helicopter: To advance to the next level you simply had to reach out and grab its landing gear.

30. Q. What was the name of the five-part miniature comicbook, written by Gerry Conway and Roy Thomas, that in 1982 was included in the boxes for Atari 2600 cartridges *Berzerk*, *Defender*, *Galaxian*, *Phoenix* and *Star Raiders*?

A. *Atari Force*.

31. Q. Mutated houseflies defend their world against an alien attacker in which Atari 2600 game named after Atari CEO Ray Kassar?

A. *Yars' Revenge* (1982): Yar spelled backwards is Ray!

32. Q. *Beat 'Em & Eat 'Em*, *Bachelor Party*, *Jawbreaker* and *Custer's Revenge*: Which one of these 1982 third-party releases for the Atari 2600 is the odd one out?

A. *Jawbreaker*, which was a Pac-Man clone produced by Tigervision. The other three were pornographic games packaged as *Swedish Erotica* by short-lived techno smut-merchants Mystique.

33. Q. What is generally considered to be the very worst Atari 2600 game in the console's history, arguably the worst videogame of all time, a cautionary tale about studio interference and the dangers of rushed development?

A. Often cited as a major contributing factor in the Videogame Industry Crash of 1983, *E.T. The Extra-Terrestrial* (1982) was designed by Howard Scott Warshaw in just five-and-a-half weeks, a ludicrous schedule imposed upon him by Atari, who were determined to get the game in stores for Christmas 1982. According to Atari CEO Ray Kassar, of the four million *E.T.* cartridges produced for the 2600, no more than half a million were sold. Along with *Pac-Man* and other unloved Atari materials, many copies of *E.T. The Extra-Terrestrial* were buried under a layer of concrete in an Alamogordo, New Mexico, landfill.

34. Q. When *Pitfall* was first released in 1982, players scoring over 20,000 points could win a prize from Activision by sending the developers a photo of themselves and their score on TV. What were they sent in return?

A. An Activision Explorers' Club badge featuring Pitfall Harry.

35. Q. Released by Activision in 1982, what vertically-scrolling shooter was the first videogame banned for minors in West Germany by the Federal Department for Writings Harmful to Young Persons?

A. *River Raid*.

36. Q. How was the player represented in *Haunted House* (1982), one of the earliest examples of a survival horror videogame?

A. A pair of eyes.

37. Q. What were the names of the three released *Swordquest* games and the unreleased fourth adventure?

A. *Earthworld* (1982), *Fireworld* (1983) and *Waterworld* (1984) made it into stores, but sadly Airworld never saw the light of day.

38. Q. What was the in-house name for the Atari VCS while it was in development?

A. Stella! Named after engineer Joe Decuir's Stella bicycle.

39. Q. What was the first space-related game for the Atari VCS?

A. *Star Ship* (1977), based on Atari's 1976 arcade hit *Starship 1*.

40. Q. What was the first licensed *Star Wars* videogame, a scrolling shooter for the 2600 described by science fiction author Harlan Ellison as a "time-wasting" and "shamelessly exploitative little toy" with "the potential to emerge as the most virulent electronic botulism of all"?

A. *Star Wars: The Empire Strikes Back* (1982), a Hoth-set game that, though impossible to beat, was actually lots of fun as it allowed young *Star Wars* obsessives to finally get in on the action themselves.

41. Q. When was the Atari 2600 finally released in Japan, and what was it called?

A. It was released in Japan in October 1983 under the name Atari 2800.

42. Q. What game saw an eccentric hopping hero menaced by Slick, Sam, Ugg, Wrongway and Coily the snake?

A. *Q*bert* (1983).

43. Q. What controversial horror game saw players chasing and murdering trespassers while avoiding such obstacles as wheelchairs and cow skulls?

A. *The Texas Chainsaw Massacre* (1983), by Wizard Video Games.

44. Q. What was the name of the 1983 game created by Atari exclusively for Coca-Cola to give to their top 125 sales executives?

A. *Pepsi Invaders*! It was a cheeky modification of *Space Invaders*, with each blastable row consisting of the letters P, E, P, S and I followed by an alien.

45. Q. What colours were the knights, and what creatures did they ride, in early co-op classic *Joust* (1983)?

A. Player One controlled a yellow knight on a flying ostrich; Player Two controlled a blue knight on a stork.

46. Q. How was 1983 US release *Taz* retooled and retitled for Europe?

A. Originally a game in which Looney Tunes' beloved Tasmanian Devil, represented by a tornado, has to whirl into hamburgers and avoid dynamite, *Taz* was made more palatable for European audiences by renaming it *Asterix*, in which Goscinny and Uderzo's feisty creation, represented by his head, has to run into Getafix's magic potion cauldrons and avoid Cacofonix's lyres.

47. Q. The last official release for the 2600 in North America, what 1989 sci-fi adventure game was inspired by NES game-changer *The Legend of Zelda* (1987)?

A. *Secret Quest*.

48. Q. What was the last official release for the Atari 2600?

A. *Klax*, a puzzle game released on June 4, 1990, in PAL regions only.

49. Q. When was the Atari 2600 formally discontinued?

A. January 1, 1992.

50. Q. How many Atari 2600 consoles were estimated to have been sold over the system's lifetime?

A. 30 million.

Retrofuturistic: Fifties' Sci-Fi Cinema

1. Q. Where did "It" come from?

A. Then at a deadly pace...*It Came from Outer Space* (1953).

2. Q. What trio of colours radiate from the Martians' electronic eye in *The War of the Worlds* (1953)?

A. Green, blue and red.

3. Q. What's the name of Captain Nemo's (James Mason) mighty vessel in the father of all steampunk sci-fi movies, *20,000 Leagues Under the Sea* (1954)?

A. The *Nautilus*.

4. Q. What are the first signs of Scott Carey's (Grant Williams) dwindling stature in *The Incredible Shrinking Man* (1957)?

A. His trousers are loose and his shirt is baggy.

5. Q. June 1956, in London's *Evening Standard* newspaper: "Shakespeare takes a journey into space" read the headline of Alan Brien's film review for which stellar sci-fi adventure?

A. *Forbidden Planet*: "The most rumbustiously enjoyable of all Hollywood planetary melodramas," wrote Brien, "apparently by dressing *The Tempest* in space suits."

6. Q. "Please doctor, I've got to ask this," says Scotty (Douglas Spencer). "It sounds like, well, just as though you're describing some form of super carrot." What classic film gave birth to this immortal line?

A. *The Thing from Another World* (1951), the tale of an "intellectual carrot" gone mad.

7. Q. To what event in *The Day the Earth Stood Still* (1951) does the title refer?

A. As a non-lethal demonstration of his power, Klaatu (Michael Rennie) neutralises all electricity around the world for 30 minutes, with essential exceptions like planes in flight and hospitals.

8. Q. What's wrong with the title of George Pal's *When Worlds Collide* (1951)?

A. Although in the novel the movie's based on – *When Worlds Collide* by Philip Wylie and Edwin Balmer (1933) – the Earth is destroyed by a rogue planet called Bronsol Alpha, in the 1951 movie adaptation, the world's end comes courtesy of a rogue star called Bellus. So really the film should have been called *When Astronomical Bodies Collide*, but obviously, that's not nearly as catchy.

9. Q. "Keep your eyes a little wide and blank. Show no interest or excitement..." When Miles (Kevin McCarthy) and Becky (Dana Wynter) hit the street, posing as Pod People, how does Becky immediately blow their cover, in *Invasion of the Body Snatchers* (1956)?

A. When a dog's almost flattened by a truck, Becky squeals and cries, "Watch out!"

10. GUEST STAR Neil Brand

Q. Bernard Herrmann famously used two theremins for *The Day the Earth Stood Still* (1951), but what was the concert instrument he also amplified electronically for the score?

A. He used an electronically amplified violin.

11. Q. What nourishes the rampaging extra-terrestrial vegetable man (James Arness) in *The Thing from Another World* (1951)?

A. Human blood!

12. Q. Which visionary artist, dubbed the "Father of Modern Space Art", created special-effects art for George Pal's

Destination Moon (1950), *When Worlds Collide* (1951), *The War of the Worlds* (1953) and *Conquest of Space* (1955)?

A. Chesley Bonestell, whose "remarkable technique", said Arthur C. Clarke in 1969, "produces an effect of realism so striking that his paintings have sometimes been mistaken for actual colour photographs by those slightly unacquainted with the present status of interplanetary flight. In the years to come it is probably destined to fire many imaginations, and thereby to change many lives."

13. **Q.** According to actor Ross Martin, why did the funeral sequence in *The Colossus of New York* (1958) have to be reshot?

A. Martin, who played a scientist whose premature death leads to his brain being transplanted into a terrifying cyborg, couldn't help but fall asleep while playing dead during the funeral shoot. When it turned out his snoring could be heard over the dialogue, the scene was reshot, presumably with Martin amply caffeinated beforehand.

14. **Q.** Incorporating greater advances than hitherto known in the field of electronics, what's the name of the communication device that Cal (Rex Reason) and Joe (Robert Nichols) build in *This Island Earth* (1955)? Also, what's the secret purpose of the challenge?

A. Comprised of 2,486 parts, the device is called an interocitor. Building it is a secret aptitude test to see if Cal's qualified to join Exeter's (Jeff Morrow) squad of scientists of exceptional ability. He is!

15. **Q.** What was designer Paul Blaisdell's nickname for the bizarre Venusian monster he fashioned for Roger Corman's *It Conquered the World* (1956)?

A. While the crew's more impertinent nicknames for the creature ranged from The Carrot Monster, The Tee-Pee Terror and The Cucumber Critter, Blaisdell favoured the name Beulah.

16. **Q.** How were the effects guys able to simulate giant drops of water in *The Incredible Shrinking Man* (1957)?

A. With hundreds of water-filled condoms.

17. Q. In *Forbidden Planet* (1956), in the underground Krell laboratory, what is Morbius (Walter Pidgeon) able to conjure with the plastic educator?

A. A hologram of his daughter, Altaira (Anne Francis).

18. Q. What's the jaunty sea shanty sung by Ned Land (Kirk Douglas) in Disney's *20,000 Leagues Under the Sea* (1954)?

A. *A Whale of a Tale*, written by Al Hoffman and Norman Gimbel. Apparently Douglas was taught to play the guitar by the film's uncredited production designer, Harper Goff. Though Disney originally intended for the movie to be animated, it was Goff who convinced Uncle Walt to take the live-action route. But that's a whale of a tale for another time.

19. Q. "When an armed and threatening power lands uninvited in our capitol," reasons General Edmunds (Grandon Rhodes) in *Earth vs. the Flying Saucers* (1956), "we don't meet him with…" What?

A. "Tea and cookies!"

20. Q. Years before making his name as a legendary filmmaker, who had a small role in *Invasion of the Body Snatchers* (1956) as Charlie the meter reader, also working on the movie as a dialogue coach?

A. Sam Peckinpah.

21. Q. Emblazoned across the movie poster for *It! The Terror from Beyond Space* (1958) was the eye-catching phrase, "$50,000 Guaranteed!" On closer inspection, how was one to earn this generous bounty?

A. "$50,000 Guaranteed! By a World-renowned insurance company," read the poster, "to the first person who can prove 'IT' is not on Mars now!" Though today, we're within spitting distance of finally exploring the Red Planet, sadly the small print specified that the offer closed on 1/1/60.

22. Q. According to Mac (Robert Nichols) in *The Thing from Another World* (1951), "The Air Force has discontinued investigating and evaluating reported flying saucers on the basis that there is no evidence", and that "reports of unidentified flying objects are the result of..." What three things?

A. One: Misinterpretation of various conventional objects; Two: A mild form of mass hysteria; Three: Jokes.

23. Q. Regarding the Martians, "Their senses could be quite different from ours," speculates Dr Forrester in *The War of the Worlds* (1953). "They may, for instance, be able to smell..." What?

A. Colours!

24. Q. What's unusual about the single-passenger Douglas DC3 plane that collects Cal (Rex Reason), to fly him to Exeter (Jeff Morrow), in *This Island Earth* (1955)?

A. There's no pilot! And no seatbelts, either.

25. GUEST STAR Don Coscarelli

Q. Which low-budget British creature invasion film was released in the States as *Enemy From Space* (1957)?

A. *Quatermass II*: This Hammer Films' production absolutely terrified me when I watched it on television as a child. Starring the terrific Brian Donlevy as Professor Bernard Quatermass, the story begins with a freak meteorite swarm landing in a seemingly targeted area of the countryside. Shot in beautiful black and white, the film's mood is stark and strange as Quatermass investigates a remote industrial facility where he ultimately finds an interstellar invader intent on world domination. It's one of the best of the 1950's sci-fi horror films and was directed by Val Guest, the filmmaker behind such other classics as *The Day the Earth Caught Fire* (1961) and *When Dinosaurs Ruled the Earth* (1970). It's a personal favourite of mine so seek it out. You won't be disappointed!

26. Q. In *The Incredible Shrinking Man* (1957), what causes poor Scott Carey (Grant Williams) to shrink incredibly?

A. He's engulfed in a glittery, radioactive mist that combines with traces of insecticide in his system to trigger a "deadly chemical reversal of the growth process".

27. Q. Why does Robby the Robot rarely partake of Altair IV's high oxygen content?

A. It promotes rust (*Forbidden Planet*, 1956).

28. Q. Long before the release of George Pal's *Destination Moon* (1950), a massive publicity campaign ensured the public were mad keen to see it. Taking advantage of the sudden national interest in space travel, indy producer Robert L. Lippert shot a low-budget sci-fi adventure in just 18 days and sneaked it into cinemas more than three weeks before the release of *Destination Moon*. What was the name of his cheeky film?

A. Co-written by Dalton Trumbo, *Rocketship X-M* (1950) starred Lloyd Bridges as a scientist who shoots for the moon but ends up travelling to Mars by mistake. The posters crowed, "The screen's FIRST story of man's conquest of space!" Legal action forced Lippert to distance his knock-off from Pal's impending release by including the clarifying phrase "This is not *Destination Moon*" on materials sent to exhibitors.

29. Q. In *The Day the Earth Stood Still* (1951), what alien command does Klaatu (Michael Rennie) teach Helen (Patricia Neal), and why?

A. "Klaatu barada nikto" – an order for Gort (Lock Martin) to cease his world-wrecking rampage. If the phrase sounds particularly familiar, that's because it's been sneaked into everything from *The Rockford Files* (1974—1980) to *Army of Darkness: The Medieval Dead* (1992). George Lucas even got in on the act, naming three of Jabba the Hutt's guards Klaatu (John Simpkin), Barada (Dickey Beer) and Nikto (Peter Ross-Murray) in *Return of the Jedi* (1983). Though uncredited in the movie, there are official action figures bearing those names. Hailed by The Robot Hall of Fame (est. 2003) as "one of the most famous commands in science fiction", the phrase was originally coined by *The Day the Earth Stood Still*'s co-writer

Edmund H. North, who revealed, "it's just something I kind of cooked up. I thought it sounded good." As for what the phrase means, opinion is wildly divergent, with North suggesting "There's hope for Earth, if the scientists can be reached", and Tauna Le Marbe, "Alien Linguistics Editor" of the magazine *Fantastic Films* (1978–1985), offering "I die, repair me, do not retaliate". Meanwhile, Robert Wise, the film's revered director, offered his own take on the phrase in 1998, while accepting his AFI Life Achievement Award. "I'd like to say 'Klaatu barada nikto'," he said, "which, roughly translated tonight, means 'Thank you very much from the bottom of my heart'."

30. Q. When Ned (Kirk Douglas) and Conseil (Peter Lorre) are pursued to the submarine by cannibals in *20,000 Leagues Under the Sea* (1954), how does Nemo (James Mason) repel them?

A. By electrifying the hull.

31. Q. In *Invasion of the Body Snatchers* (1956), what does the pod person who replaces Dan Kauffman (Larry Gates) insist that life is so much simpler without?

A. "Love, desire, ambition, faith."

32. Q. The first score for a mainstream film performed entirely by electronic instruments, Louis and Bebe Barron's soundtrack for *Forbidden Planet* (1956) confused and upset the Musician's Union. As the Barrons didn't belong to the union, they were blocked from being credited as composers on the movie. How were they credited instead?

A. *Electronic Tonalities* by Louis and Bebe Barron.

33. Q. It creeps...It crawls...It strikes without warning! What is it?

A. *The Thing from Another World* (1951).

34. Q. Shot in four days on a shoestring budget, *Robot Monster* (1953) told the angry tale of Ro-Man Extension XJ-2 (George Barrows), an evil robot from the Moon with a dream of killing all humans. Although notable for its Elmer Bernstein score, and unexpectedly decent 3-D photography, it is perhaps best known for its thrown-together robot costume consisting of what two elements?

A. It's a guy in a gorilla costume wearing a space helmet.

35. Q. What does the last wire photo out of Paris depict in *The War of the Worlds* (1953)?

A. The city in ruins with the Eiffel Tower shattering in the centre.

36. Q. In *The Incredible Shrinking Man* (1957), what happens the moment after Louise (Randy Stuart) tells her insecure husband Scott (Grant Williams), "As long as you've got this wedding ring on, you've got me"?

A. It falls off.

37. Q. Originally published in the October 1940 issue of *Astounding Science Fiction*, what was the name of the short story, written by Harry Bates, that *The Day the Earth Stood Still* (1951) was based on? Also, what was the original name of Klaatu's robot, named Gort in the movie?

A. "Farewell to the Master" was the title of Bates' short story. 20th Century Fox paid the author just $500 for the rights. The robot's name was originally Gnut.

38. Q. Who is the only member of Nemo's (James Mason) original crew to survive till the end of *20,000 Leagues Under the Sea* (1954)?

A. His pet sea lion Esmerelda, who didn't exist in Jules Verne's original novel, originally published in 1870.

39. Q. The tunnel where Miles (Kevin McCarthy) and Becky (Dana Wynter) hide from the Pod People in *Invasion of the Body Snatchers* (1956) was shot in Griffith Park's Bronson Cave, a popular filmmaking location in Los Angeles due to its remote look but easy access. What do locals call the cave, and why?

A. Everyone calls it the Batcave, as the West Portal was used as the entrance to Bruce Wayne's secret hideout in *Batman* (1966–1968).

40. GUEST STAR Jeremy Dyson

Q. There is a strong link between *Forbidden Planet* (1956) and absurd comedy in the form of Leslie Nielsen who plays Commander Adams in the former and would go on to essay numerous roles for the Zucker/Abrahams/Zucker partnership later in his career. But what is the connection between *Forbidden Planet* and absurd British TV comedy show *The League of Gentlemen* (1999–2017)?

A. There is a recurring character in *The League of Gentlemen*, a dissolute cleaning lady named Iris Krell (played by Mark Gatiss), in honour of the unfortunate self-destroying former citizens of Altair IV.

41. Q. What is Plan 9 in Ed Wood's hilariously loony *Plan 9 from Outer Space* (1959)?

A. "Plan 9 deals with the resurrection of the dead," reveals The Ruler (John Breckinridge). "Long distance electrodes shot into the pineal and pituitary gland of the recently dead."

42. Q. Why do the Metaluna Mutants in *This Island Earth* (1955) wear trousers?

A. Because the special effects department couldn't figure out how to build matching, working legs. Pressed by the studio to finish the job, they grudgingly completed their iconic creature with space slacks.

43. Q. The sound effects accompanying the Martians' heat and death rays in *The War of the Worlds* (1953) were heard again, years later, in what classic sci-fi series?

A. Red Alert: Trivia to Maximum! It was *Star Trek* (1966): The heat ray sound effect, which was a blend of three electric guitars played backwards with a little harp, became the sound of phaser fire. The death ray sound effect, which was created by hitting a high-tension wire with a hammer, became the sound of photon torpedoes.

44. Q. What are the aliens' intentions in *It Came from Outer Space* (1953)?

A. They just want to repair their ship and leave Earth. All they need is a little time. "Time, or terrible things will happen. Things so terrible, you have yet to dream of them." Really though, they're OK. They don't even kill a single person during their stopover.

45. Q. In *The Day the Earth Stood Still* (1951), when Klaatu (Michael Rennie) requires cash to take Bobby (Billy Gray) to the movies, what does he offer to give the lad in exchange for his $2?

A. Two space diamonds!

Klaatu: In some places, these are what people use for money. They're easier to carry and they don't wear out.

Bobby: Let's not say anything to mom about this, huh?

Klaatu: Why not Bobby?

Bobby: She doesn't like me to steal from people.

46. Q. *They Come from Another World*, *Better Off Dead*, *Sleep No More*, *Evil in the Night* and *World in Danger* were rejected title suggestions for which 1956 sci-fi thriller?

A. *Invasion of the Body Snatchers*: Also rejected was the name of the novel the film was based on, *The Body Snatchers* (1954), by Jack Finney. Apparently the producers wanted to avoid confusion with *The Body Snatcher*, a Robert Wise chiller from 1945.

47. Q. While zooming to Metaluna in *This Island Earth* (1955), how does Cal (Rex Reason) describe the feeling of being squeezed into the snug conversion tube?

A. He says, "I feel like a new toothbrush."

48. Q. Following a close encounter with an enormous alien, an alcoholic heiress (Allison Hayes) grows incredibly in *Attack of the 50 Foot Woman* (1958). What motivates her wild rampage?

A. An overwhelming desire to kill her philandering husband (William Hudson).

49. **Q.** Who was the American realist artist responsible for creating the iconic movie posters for *This Island Earth* (1955), *The Incredible Shrinking Man* (1957), *Attack of the 50 Foot Woman* (1958) and scores more besides?

A. Reynold Brown.

50. **Q.** How is the murderous Martian stowaway (Ray "Crash" Corrigan) finally defeated in *It! The Terror from Beyond Space* (1958)?

A. Fleeing to the control deck of their spaceship, the crew throw on their spacesuits and open the airlock into space. Without oxygen, "IT" quickly bites the dust.

Crossing Over Into *The Twilight Zone*

1. **Q.** Rod Serling uttered his signature phrase "Submitted for your approval" an epic 94 times over *The Twilight Zone*'s 156-episode run. True or false?

A. False: He actually only said it three times, in "Cavender is Coming" (S03E36), "In Praise of Pip" (S05E01) and "A Kind of Stopwatch" (S05E04).

2. **Q.** What was the title of *The Twilight Zone*'s pilot episode, and who was the star?

A. "Where is Everybody?" (S01E01) starred Earl Holliman, who was apparently terribly unwell during production, running a temperature in excess of a hundred degrees. What a pro!

3. **Q.** Who is the Howling Man?

A. The Devil! As played by Robin Hughes in "The Howling Man" (S02E05).

4. **Q.** Who played Mr Death in "Nothing in the Dark" (S03E16)?

A. Robert Redford.

5. Q. What's the first book we see Mr Bemis (Burgess Meredith) reading in all-time classic episode "Time Enough at Last" (S01E08)?

A. *David Copperfield* (1850), by Charles Dickens.

6. Q. What's the name of the mysterious travelling salesman who gives drunken former gunslinger Al Denton (Dan Duryea) a second chance in "Mr. Denton on Doomsday" (S01E03)?

A. Henry J. Fate (Malcolm Atterbury).

7. Q. Rod Serling's initial deal with CBS stipulated that he write 80% of *The Twilight Zone*'s first season scripts himself. To make up the difference, Serling invited the show's viewers to send in manuscripts for consideration. Within five days of his request, Serling's staff received approximately 14,000 submissions. Of the 500 they read, how many did they end up using?

A. None. Serling felt every one of them fell short of the show's high standards and so did what he probably should have done from the start: he brought established writers Richard Matheson and Charles Beaumont on board, and between the three of them, with one additional script by Robert Presnall, Jr ("The Chaser", S01E31), *The Twilight Zone*'s sterling first season was completed.

8. Q. With nuclear war imminent, scientists Will Sturka (Fritz Weaver) and Jerry Riden (Joe Maross) plan to steal a spaceship and blast off with their families to which relatively safe planet?

A. Earth! ("Third from the Sun", S01E14).

9. Q. What is Lt William "Fitz" Fitzgerald's (William Reynolds) regrettable ability in WWII tale "The Purple Testament" (S01E19)?

A. Whenever he sees a strange light shining on someone's face, he knows they're about to die.

10. GUEST STAR Mark Scott Zicree

Q. How many lead actors from the original *Star Trek* (1966–1969) are in *The Twilight Zone*?

A. Four: William Shatner ("Nick of Time", S02E07; "Nightmare at 20,000 Feet", S05E03), Leonard Nimoy ("A Quality of Mercy", S03E15), James Doohan ("Valley of the Shadow", S04E03) and George Takei ("The Encounter", S05E31).

11. Q. "The tools of conquest do not necessarily come with bombs and explosions and fallout. There are weapons that are simply thoughts, attitudes, prejudices – to be found only in the minds of men." Which first season episode includes this line in Rod Serling's closing narration?

A. "The Monsters Are Due on Maple Street" (S01E22).

12. Q. Why doesn't Professor Sam Kittridge (Edgar Stehli) want his daughter to marry Walter Jameson (Kevin McCarthy)?

A. Because Walter Jameson is more than 2,000 years old and would abandon her when she grows old ("Long Live Walter Jameson", S01E24).

13. Q. What does the sign say in the room prepared for astronaut Sam Conrad (Roddy McDowall) by his Martian captors?

A. "Earth Creature in his native habitat" ("People Are Alike All Over", S01E25).

14. Q. A familiar face to *Twilight Zone* fans, Jack Klugman starred in which four classic episodes of the show?

A. Best known outside of *The Twilight Zone* for hit spin-off sitcom *The Odd Couple* (1970–1975) and lively crime drama *Quincy M.E.* (1976–1983), Jack Klugman's four trips into *The Twilight Zone* were "A Passage for Trumpet" (S01E32), "A Game of Pool" (S03E05), "Death Ship" (S04E06) and "In Praise of Pip" (S05E01).

15. Q. What is Henry Temple's (Steven Perry) big, tall wish?

A. For the washed-up boxer he idolises (Ivan Dixon) to magically win the match he was about to lose ("The Big Tall Wish" S01E27).

16. Q. Where and when does harassed, exhausted New York executive Gart Williams (James Daly) decide he'd rather live?

A. In Willoughby, July 1888, a sleepy town "where a man can slow down to a walk and live his life full measure" ("A Stop at Willoughby", S01E30).

17. Q. What disconcerting fact eludes fretful, forgetful Marsha White (Anne Francis) until the bitter end of "The After Hours" (S01E34)?

A. She's a department store mannequin!

18. Q. Which season one episode of *The Twilight Zone* marked Rod Serling's first on-screen appearance? Also, how does the show's main character react after Serling describes the story as "ridiculous nonsense"?

A. The episode was "A World of His Own" (S01E36), in which playwright Gregory West (Keenan Wynn) reveals he has the godlike power to not only create life, by describing someone into his dictation machine, but also take it away, by destroying the relevant section of tape. Displeased by Rod's comments, he produces an envelope with the author's name on it, pulls out some tape, throws it on the fire and Serling promptly disappears! It was a perfectly hilarious way to end the final episode of the show's Emmy Award-winning first season.

19. Q. What did *The Twilight Zone* win an Emmy for in 1960?

A. Rod Serling won the Emmy for Outstanding Writing Achievement in Drama for the show's first season, describing the honour as "probably the happiest moment of my professional career". He won again for *The Twilight Zone* the following year.

20. Q. What's the first reply that Don Carter (William Shatner) gets from the Mystic Seer fortune teller machine in "Nick of Time" (S02E07)?

A. "It is quite possible."

21. Q. What is Arthur Castle (Luther Adler) left with, by the end of "The Man in the Bottle" (S02E02), as a result of the genie's (Joseph Ruskin) intervention?

A. Besides a more positive perspective on life...Just five bucks.

22. Q. How does Lew Bookman (Ed Wynn) initially cheat Death (Murray Hamilton) in "One for the Angels" (S01E02)?

A. A small-time salesman, he convinces Death to allow him to live until he's had a chance to do a truly big pitch. "A pitch big enough for the skies to open up. A pitch for the angels."

23. Q. Which episode of *The Twilight Zone* cast different actresses to play masked and unmasked versions of the same character?

A. Mellifluous Maxine Stuart played the bandaged Janet Tyler while beautiful Donna Douglas played Janet for the big reveal in "The Eye of the Beholder" (S02E06).

24. Q. Who wrote *The Twilight Zone*'s familiar guitar-and-bongo theme that ran from the second season onwards? Also, whose eerie season one theme did it replace?

A. Marius Constant's famous theme replaced Bernard Herrmann's initial offering.

25. GUEST STAR Ron Fogelman

Q. What's the connection between *The Twilight Zone* and the black triangle stickers found above certain airplane windows?

A. The triangles mark the windows with the best view of the wings, used by the crew to check potential issues with the engines, slats or flaps. The seats below the triangles are nicknamed "The Shatner Seat" after the classic episode "Nightmare at 20,000 Feet" (S05E03), written by Richard Matheson.

26. Q. What is the final line delivered by actress Agnes Moorhead in "The Invaders" (S02E15)?

A. Trick question! She doesn't say a single word in the episode.

27. Q. "A vacuum-cleaner salesman whose volume of business is roughly that of a valet at a hobo convention", Mr Dingle (Burgess Meredith) first catches the eye of a two-headed Martian (Douglas Spencer and Michael Fox), then a pair of Venusians (Donald Losby and Greg Irvin), who each give him what special powers?

A. The Martian briefly gives him the strength of 300 men. The Venusians boost his intelligence three hundred-fold ("Mr. Dingle, The Strong", S02E19).

28. Q. In "Long Distance Call" (S02E22), who does five-year-old Billy Bayles (Billy Mumy) chat with on his toy telephone?

A. His recently deceased grandmother (Lili Darvas).

29. Q. How do the two aliens differ physically from humans in S02E28's "Will the Real Martian Please Stand Up"?

A. The Martian (John Hoyt) has three arms and the Venusian (Barney Phillips) has three eyes.

30. Q. Why does Dr Stockton (Larry Gates) suddenly find himself at odds with his friends and neighbours?

A. Because everyone thinks the bomb's about to drop and only Stockton has a shelter ("The Shelter", S03E03).

31. Q. How should one respond if Anthony (Billy Mumy) wishes a loved one into the cornfield?

A. "It's a good thing you did, Anthony. A real good thing!" ("It's a Good Life", S03E08).

32. Q. Who were the "Five Characters in Search of an Exit" (S03E14)?

A. They were a Major (William Windom), a Clown (Murray Matheson), a Ballerina (Susan Harrison), a Tramp (Kelton Garwood) and a Bagpipe Player (Clark Allen).

33. Q. Who was Rod Serling's original choice of narrator?

A. Fifties' film star Richard Egan, an athletic leading man with deep, honeyed tones, was Serling's only choice for narrator. "It's Richard Egan or no one," insisted Serling. "It's Richard Egan, or I'll do the thing myself." When contractual issues arose that made it impossible for Egan to join the show, Serling stuck to his guns and cast himself as narrator.

34. Q. "I'd never known a critic, but it was my idea of what a critic was like." Which character, from what episode, is writer Earl Hamner describing?

A. Mr Fitzgerald Fortune (Barry Morse), an acid-penned theatre critic and all-round terrible human being, in "A Piano in the House" (S03E22).

35. Q. What is "To Serve Man"?

A. "It's a cookbook!" ("To Serve Man", S03E24).

36. Q. Which Serling-penned episode of *The Twilight Zone* was inspired by a sequence in British chiller *Dead of Night* (1945) and by a 1957 episode of *Alfred Hitchcock Presents*, "The Glass Eye" (S03E01)?

A. "The Dummy" (S03E33) – The tale of a troubled ventriloquist (Cliff Robertson) who ultimately trades places with his dummy. The show was inspired by the final tale in portmanteau classic *Dead of Night* in which a ventriloquist (Michael Redgrave) believes his dummy is alive, and Hitch TV classic "The Glass Eye", in which a handsome ventriloquist (Tom Conway) turns out to be the dummy, and vice versa.

37. Q. *Twilight Zone* writers Charles Beaumont and Richard Matheson both considered fantasy author Ray Bradbury a mentor. Rod Serling himself was a fan, often dropping Bradbury references into the show. How fortunate, then, that Bradbury was eager to contribute. How many of his scripts were ultimately produced, and what were the show titles?

A. Ultimately the series only shot one of Bradbury's scripts, adapted from his own short story "I Sing the Body Electric" (S03E35). Reasons cited for not using more of his teleplays include Bradbury's penchant for poetic language that reads beautifully but maybe doesn't translate so well into authentic dialogue, and the unbound scope of his imagination that conjured visuals so dizzying, they were either impossible to realistically render at the time or just much too expensive to produce.

38. **Q. Which** significant change to *The Twilight Zone*'s format was forced upon the show by CBS for its relatively short fourth season?

A. The episodes were expanded from tight half-hours to bloated hour-long slogs. In his wonderful episode guide, *The Twilight Zone Companion*, Marc Scott Zicree recounts the thoughts of series scribe Richard Matheson: "The ideal Twilight Zone started with a really smashing idea that hit you right in the first few seconds, then you played that out, and you had a little flip at the end; that was the structure." Stretching the shows to an hour was a doomed concept, noted Serling. "We'd have to fleshen our stories, soap-opera style. Viewers could watch 15 minutes without knowing whether they were in a Twilight Zone or Desilu Playhouse." Though the series managed to produce a few fine episodes during its fourth season, by its fifth and final season, it wisely returned to its original half-hour format.

39. **Q.** "What you have just witnessed could be the end of a particularly terrifying nightmare. It isn't – it's the beginning. Although Alan Talbot doesn't know it, he's about to enter a strange new world, too incredible to be real, too real to be a dream. It's called The Twilight Zone." Which episode of *The Twilight Zone*'s fourth season opens with this narration?

A. "In His Image" (S04E01).

40. **GUEST STAR Phil Nobile Jr**

Q. One episode of *The Twilight Zone* is an Oscar-winner. How is that possible?

A. Robert Enrico's short 1962 film adaptation of Ambrose Bierce's *An Occurrence at Owl Creek Bridge*, in which a Civil War soldier attempts to escape his own execution, won the 1963 Oscar for Live-Action Short film. In 1964, Twilight Zone producer William Froug bought the rights to the short and aired it – with explanatory narration from Rod Serling – as a season 5 episode of the series (S05E22). It only aired twice and was not included in syndication packages, though today it's included on home video and streaming releases.

41. Q. What do the three astronauts (Jack Klugman, Ross Martin and Fredrick Beir) aboard Spaceship E-89 discover when they land on the 13th Planet of Star System 51 in the year 1997?

A. A wrecked duplicate of their own ship, and inside it, their own dead bodies! ("Death Ship", S04E06).

42. Q. Which episode of *The Twilight Zone* sees Satan (Burgess Meredith) publishing a local newspaper with such outrageous but true headlines as "MAYOR'S WIFE GIVES BIRTH TO BABY HIPPOPOTAMUS" and "BANK PRESIDENT'S WIFE CLAIMS DIVORCE – EXPLAINS CAUGHT HUSBAND TRIFLING WITH THREE MERMAIDS IN A BATHTUB"?

A. "Printer's Devil" (S04E09).

43. Q. Described by Serling in his introduction as "a would-be writer who, if talent came 25 cents a pound, would be worth less than car fare", Julius Moomer (Jack Weston) inadvertently conjures up which legendary writer, in what amusing episode of *The Twilight Zone*?

A. William Shakespeare (John Williams), in "The Bard" (S04E18).

44. Q. During the opening narration for seasons four and five of the show, what visuals accompany Serling's phrases "A dimension of sound" and "A dimension of mind"?

A. A shattering window frame and Albert Einstein's Theory of Relativity, $E = mc^2$.

45. Q. Which three episodes of *The Twilight Zone* starred sci-fi icon Robby the Robot?

A. "The Little People" (S03E28), "The Brain Center at Whipple's" (S03E33) and "Uncle Simon" (S05E08). Mainly shot by Rod Serling's Cayuga Productions at the MGM studio in Culver City, *The Twilight Zone* made frequent use of props, costumes, sets and even effects shots from sci-fi classic *Forbidden Planet* (1956).

46. Q. Who directed the classic *Twilight Zone* episode "Nightmare at 20,000 Feet" (S05E03)?

A. Richard Donner, who later directed *The Omen* (1976), *Superman: The Movie* (1978), *Ladyhawke* (1985), *The Goonies* (1985) and all four *Lethal Weapons* (1987–1998).

47. Q. Voiced by June Foray, what does Tina say to Annabelle (Mary LaRoche) at the end of "Living Doll" (S05E06)?

A. "My name is Talky Tina... and you'd better be nice to me!"

48. Q. Pioneering filmmaker and actress Ida Lupino was the only person during *The Twilight Zone*'s five-season run to star in one episode and direct another. What were those two episodes?

A. Lupino starred in "The Sixteen-Millimeter Shrine" (S01E04) and directed "The Masks" (S05E25). Lupino was the only woman to direct an episode of the show.

49. Q. How many of *The Twilight Zone*'s 156 episodes were written by Rod Serling over the show's five-year run?

A. 56
B. 77
C. 92
D. 113

A. C. 92.

50. Q. After CBS cancelled *The Twilight Zone* in 1964, ABC President Tom Moore seemed keen to pick it up. As CBS owned the rights to the title *Twilight Zone*, what did Moore suggest as an alternative?

A. As Serling had edited a paperback anthology in 1963 called *Rod Serling's Triple W: Witches, Warlocks, and Werewolves*, Moore suggested *Witches, Warlocks, and Werewolves*. Not wanting to "be hooked into a graveyard every week", Serling suggested an alternative title to Moore's alternative title: *Rod Serling's Wax Museum*. Ultimately neither idea came to pass.

Walt's Wonderful World of Disney

1. Q. Where do the seven dwarfs keep the key to their jewel vault?

A. On a peg beside the door! (*Snow White and the Seven Dwarfs*, 1937).

2. Q. What three nationalities of marionettes does Pinocchio (Dickie Jones) sing and dance with during Stromboli's puppet show?

A. Dutch, French and Russian (*Pinocchio*, 1940).

3. Q. Featured in *Fantasia*'s (1940) "Night on Bald Mountain" sequence, the demon Chernabog was based upon which iconic horror movie star's facial expressions, mannerisms and dramatic poses?

A. Bela Lugosi.

4. Q. What do the warning signs say on the front of Mrs Jumbo's makeshift cage in *Dumbo* (1940)?

A. "DANGER" and "MAD ELEPHANT".

5. Q. During which season is Bambi's mother brutally gunned down?

A. Winter (*Bambi*, 1942).

6. Q. Now, Sala-gadoola means menchicka-boolaroo, but the thing-a-ma-bob that does the job is?

A. "Bibbidi-bobbidi-boo!" A novelty song written by Al Hoffman, Mack David and Jerry Livingston in 1948, "Bibbidi-bobbidi-boo" is, of course, sung by Fairy Godmother (Verna Felton) in *Cinderella* (1950).

7. Q. What can one celebrate 364 days a year?

A. A very merry unbirthday! (*Alice in Wonderland*, 1951).

8. Q. According to Peter Pan's (Bobby Driscoll) instructions, how would one fly to Never Land from London's Big Ben?

A. "Second star to the right and straight on till morning" (*Peter Pan*, 1953).

9. **Q.** What breed of dog is Lady (Barbara Luddy)?

A. She's an American Cocker Spaniel (*Lady and the Tramp*, 1955).

10. **Q.** Princess Aurora (Mary Costa) hides out in the forest under which assumed name?

A. Briar Rose (*Sleeping Beauty*, 1959).

11. **Q.** America's first animated feature, *Snow White and the Seven Dwarfs* (1937) was the greatest gamble of Walt Disney's career. Had it failed at the box office, there'd be no Walt Disney Productions, and the general consensus around Hollywood was that it was a fool's errand. Prior to its release, then, what did industry sceptics call the movie?

A. "Disney's folly". Three years in the making, ultimately it proved the naysayers wrong by succeeding spectacularly at the box office, the highest-grossing film of all time until *Gone with the Wind* (1939) knocked it off the top spot.

12. **Q.** According to *Pinocchio*'s (1940) Jiminy Cricket (Cliff Edwards), how does one make their dreams come true?

A. Wishing upon a star.

13. **Q.** Which Disney classic was described by olden-days film critic Otis Ferguson as "one of the strange and beautiful things that have happened in the world"?

A. *Fantasia* (1940).

14. **Q.** What do *Dumbo*'s (1941) Mr Stork, *Bambi*'s (1942) Adult Flower and *Alice in Wonderland*'s (1951) Cheshire Cat all have in common?

A. They were all voiced by Disney Legend Sterling Holloway, who later also voiced Kaa the Snake in *The Jungle Book* (1967), Roquefort in *The Aristocats* (1970) and, most famously, Winnie the Pooh in multiple Disney productions.

15. GUEST STAR Carrie Henn

Q. In the 1950 classic *Cinderella*, how many times does Cinderella (Ilene Woods) lose her shoe: once, twice or three times?

A. Cinderella loses her shoe three different times throughout the film. First, when she is delivering breakfast to her stepsisters and stepmother. Second, when she is fleeing the prince's (William Phipps) castle at midnight, and third, when she runs down the stairs after her wedding.

16. Q. Walt Disney holds the record for winning the most Academy Awards. Including his honorary Oscars, what's the magic number?

A. 26! That includes 22 wins in competitive categories (from a staggering 59 nominations), three honorary Oscars and an Irving Thalberg Memorial Award.

17. Q. What does Peter Pan (Bobby Driscoll) break into the Darling household to recover?

A. His shadow (*Peter Pan*, 1953).

18. Q. What does Tramp (Larry Roberts) call Lady's (Barbara Luddy) part of town?

A. "Snob Hill": a lid on every trash can and a fence around every tree (*Lady and the Tramp*, 1955).

19. Q. What precious resource was shared by 1959 releases *Plan 9 from Outer Space* and *Sleeping Beauty*?

A. Maila Nurmi, a.k.a. iconic horror hostess Vampira, played the Vampire Girl in Ed Wood's *Plan 9 from Outer Space* and was the secret real-life model for *Sleeping Beauty*'s evil fairy Maleficent.

20. Q. What does Adult Flower (Sterling Holloway) name his pungent offspring?

A. Bambi (*Bambi*, 1942).

21. Q. What evidence does the Queen (Lucille La Verne) demand the Huntsman return to her as proof of his dark deed?

A. Snow White's (Adriana Caselotti) heart (*Snow White and the Seven Dwarfs*, 1937).

22. Q. By what name is *Pinocchio*'s (1940) Jiminy Cricket (Cliff Edwards) known in Carlo Collodi's original 1883 novel, and how does he die in the book?

A. In Collodi's novel he was simply known as Talking Cricket. After criticising Pinocchio for not wanting to go to school, the puppet cruelly squishes him with a mallet. Later in the story though, Talking Cricket returns as a ghost, and then, inexplicably, to life.

23. Q. Though unnamed in *The Sorcerer's Apprentice*, what did Disney's animators dub Mickey's magical master?

A. Yen Sid, which is Disney spelled backwards! The sorcerer's eyebrow, when raised in disapproval, was considered a dead giveaway that the famous *Fantasia* (1940) character was partly based upon Walt Disney, a man of famously exacting standards who wasn't afraid to read his employees the riot act.

24. Q. According to the scornful crows in *Dumbo* (1940), though they've not yet seen an elephant fly, what sort of flies have they previously observed?

A. Horse-flies, dragonflies and houseflies.

25. Q. What is Bambi's first word?

A. Bird (*Bambi*, 1942).

26. Q. By what name were legendary animators Les Clark, Marc Davis, Ollie Johnson, Milt Kahl, Ward Kimball, Eric Larson, John Lounsbery, Wolfgang Reitherman and Frank Thomas collectively known? Also, what was the first feature they all collaborated on?

A. The first film that Disney's "Nine Old Men" all collaborated on was *Cinderella* (1950).

27. Q. What could a rabbit possibly be late for?

A. A very important date: No time to say hello, goodbye, he's late, he's late, he's late! (*Alice in Wonderland*, 1951).

28. Q. According to the Josh Billings quote that opens *Lady and the Tramp* (1955), what's the one thing that money can't buy?

A. The wag of a dog's tail.

29. Q. Which Disney villain is dispatched by the Mighty Sword of Truth?

A. The Mistress of all Evil, Maleficent (Eleanor Audley), during her battle with Prince Phillip (Bill Shirley) in *Sleeping Beauty* (1959).

30. GUEST STAR Dave Bossert

Q. *Cinderella* (1950) represents a stylistic transition from the more European-influenced book illustration look of *Snow White and the Seven Dwarfs* (1937) and *Pinocchio* (1940) to the more graphic design look of animation in the 1950s. What artist's style was most influential on *Cinderella*?

A. Mary Blair was responsible for the more graphic stylistic look of *Cinderella*.

31. Q. What wood is Pinocchio (Dickie Jones) made of?

A. Pine (*Pinocchio*, 1940).

32. Q. For introducing him to Felix Salten's 1923 novel, *Bambi: A Life in the Woods*, Walt Disney planned to thank animator Maurice Day by holding *Bambi*'s (1942) world premiere in his home town of Damariscotta, Maine, USA. That plan had to be scrapped, however, after Maine officials officially objected to Disney's plan for what reason?

A. They were afraid the movie might offend sports hunters. A popular destination for moose, bear and, yes, deer hunting, Maine was perhaps not the best place to unveil a major motion picture that painted hunters as bloodthirsty, environmentally ruinous monsters.

33. Q. What does Alice (Kathryn Beaumont) think Wonderland's flowers could learn a few things about?

A. Manners (*Alice in Wonderland*, 1951).

34. Q. Marilyn Monroe was the real-life model for Tinker Bell: True or false?

A. False! Despite rumours to the contrary, it was actress Margaret Kerry, who also voiced the red-haired mermaid in *Peter Pan* (1953).

35. Q. What was Disney's first widescreen animated feature?

A. *Lady and the Tramp* (1955): As the decision to switch to the CinemaScope widescreen film process was made after production had begun, many of the backgrounds had to be extended to accommodate the new format. Disney animators also had to adjust their thinking and find new ways of filling the screen as single characters no longer dominated the wider image as they once had. When the film was finally ready for release, Disney was hardly thrilled to discover that many cinemas weren't even equipped yet to screen films in CinemaScope, forcing the studio to create an alternate version of the film in the original boxy aspect ratio.

36. Q. Which one of the seven dwarfs wears glasses?

A. Doc (Roy Atwell) (*Snow White and the Seven Dwarfs*, 1937).

37. Q. During *Fantasia*'s (1940) *Rite of Spring* sequence, which two dinosaurs fight to the death? Also, which of them emerges victorious?

A. The Tyrannosaurus rex kills then eats the Stegosaurus.

38. Q. Dopey, Gideon, Mrs Dumbo, Lucifer and Tinker Bell: Who's the odd one out?

A. Mrs Jumbo, because while Dopey in *Snow White and the Seven Dwarfs* (1937), Gideon in *Pinocchio* (1940), Lucifer in *Cinderella* (1950) and Tinker Bell in *Peter Pan* (1953) are all mute, Mrs Jumbo, voiced by Verna Felton in *Dumbo*

(1940), manages to utter two whole words when naming her son: "Jumbo Jr". Instantly nicknamed Dumbo by the chattier pachyderms, Dumbo is also mute.

39. Q. According to Cinderella (Ilene Woods), what is a dream?

A. A dream is a wish your heart makes when you're fast asleep (*Cinderella,* 1950).

40. Q. Which character in *Alice in Wonderland* (1951) recites lines from Lewis Carroll's epic nonsense poem "Jabberwocky"?

A. The Cheshire Cat (Sterling Holloway): Although the full Jabberwocky poem appears in Carroll's *Alice's Adventures in Wonderland* (1865) sequel, *Through the Looking-Glass, and What Alice Found There* (1871), the first stanza was printed in an 1855 issue of *Mischmasch*, a periodical produced by Carroll and his siblings to amuse their family. It's this lone verse, originally entitled *A Stanza of Anglo-Saxon Poetry*, that the Cheshire Cat sings and repeats throughout Disney's adaptation:

> *Twas bryllyg, and the slythy toves*
> *Did gyre and gymble in the wabe:*
> *All mimsy were the borogoves;*
> *And the mome raths outgrabe.*

41. Q. Where would two dogs in love best go for the best-a spaghetti in-a town?

A. Tony's Restaurant (*Lady and the Tramp*, 1955).

42. Q. Who are the three good fairies and what colour outfits do they wear?

A. Mistress Flora (Verna Felton) wears pink, Mistress Fauna (Barbara Jo Allen) wears green and Mistress Merryweather (Barbara Luddy) wears blue (*Sleeping Beauty*, 1959).

43. Q. What was the first Disney feature – actually the first film in cinema history – to release a soundtrack album

A. *Snow White and the Seven Dwarfs* (1937).

44. Q. Who teaches grown-up Bambi (John Sutherland), Thumper (Sam Edwards) and Flower (Sterling Holloway) about the birds and the bees? Also, who's the first of the trio to get "twitterpated"?

A. Friend Owl (Will Wright) teaches the boys about love, and Flower's the first to succumb (*Bambi*, 1942).

45. Q. In the *Star Trek* (1966–1969) episode "Shore Leave" (S01E12), Dr McCoy (DeForest Kelley) stumbles across live action versions of which two characters from Disney's *Alice in Wonderland* (1951)?

A. Alice and the White Rabbit.

46. Q. As a lad, Walt Disney played which character – later immortalised in one of his movies – in a school play?

A. Peter Pan! "No actor ever identified himself with the part he was playing more than I," said Disney, whose older brother Roy hoisted him up on a rope for the flying scenes.

47. Q. What does the word maleficent mean?

A. The Oxford English Dictionary defines maleficent as an adjective meaning "Causing harm or destruction, especially by supernatural means", and that's certainly appropriate (*Sleeping Beauty*, 1959).

48. Q. Give a bad boy enough rope and what will he make of himself?

A. A jackass (*Pinocchio*, 1940).

49. Q. What's the first mythological species that appears in *Fantasia*'s (1940) *Pastoral Symphony* sequence?

A. A herd of unicorns.

50. Q. While playing croquet in *Alice in Wonderland* (1951), what do Alice (Kathryn Beaumont) and the Queen of Hearts (Verna Felton) use instead of traditional mallets and balls?

A. Flamingos and hedgehogs.

Stephen King: *Carrie* to *Christine*

1. Q. What was Stephen King's first published novel?

A. Though it was the fourth novel King wrote, *Carrie* was the first of his to be published, in 1974. It was also the first story of his to be adapted into a movie, courtesy of Brian De Palma, in 1976.

2. Q. "Almost everyone thought the man and the boy were father and son." Which Stephen King novel opens with this line?

A. "Salem's Lot" (1975): "An opening line should invite the reader to begin the story," says King. "It should say: 'Listen. Come in here. You want to know about this.'"

3. Q. A stickler for authenticity, Sissy Spacek insisted that it be her hand, rather than a stunt double's, shooting out the grave in the shocking final moments of Brian De Palma's *Carrie* (1976): True or false?

A. True!

"Sissy, come on, I'll get a stunt person," reasoned De Palma. "What do you want? To be buried in the ground?!"

"Brian, I have to do this," she insisted. So they buried her!

"We had to put her in a box and stick her underneath the ground," remembers De Palma.

Spacek was likewise committed to maintaining the continuity of her bloodstains during the climactic prom sequence, refusing to wash off the fake blood, and actually sleeping in her bloody clothes, for three days while shooting the scene.

4. Q. What does all work and no play make Jack?

A. A dull boy (*The Shining*, 1980): According to Stanley Kubrick's daughter Vivian, her dad insisted his secretary spend weeks – if not months, typing the phrase "All work and no play makes Jack a dull boy" on dozens of pages for the scene in which Wendy takes an alarmed peek at her husband's mental manuscript.

5. Q. Convicted in 1948 for the double murder of his wife and her lover, where in Maine is banker Andy Dufresne sent to serve a double life sentence?

A. Shawshank State Penitentiary: As featured in the novella "Rita Hayworth and Shawshank Redemption", which was published in 1982's *Different Seasons*, a book collecting four previously unpublished novellas with a more serious dramatic vibe than King was generally known for. The other three novellas in the book were "Apt Pupil", "The Body" – filmed in 1986 as *Stand By Me* – and "The Breathing Method".

6. Q. What's the first Stephen King novel set in his signature fictional town of Castle Rock, Maine?

A. *The Dead Zone* (1979).

7. Q. What was the first novel credited to Stephen King's nom de plume, Richard Bachman?

A. *Rage* (1977). A psychological thriller about a high school shooting and hostage situation that's now out of print, withdrawn by the author, due to its unsettling resemblance to several subsequent real-life school shootings.

8. Q. What breed of dog is Cujo?

A. He's a St Bernard (*Cujo*, 1981).

9. Q. What's the name of the weaponised strain of influenza that kills 99.4% of the world's population in *The Stand* (pub. 1978)?

A. Project Blue, a.k.a. "Captain Trips" and the superflu.

10. Q. Written by King in the grand, ghastly tradition of EC horror comics of the 1950s, what are the titles of the five terrifying tales told in *Creepshow* (1982)?

A. "Father's Day", "The Lonesome Death of Jordy Verill", "Something to Tide You Over", "The Crate" and "They're Creeping Up On You".

11. **Q.** The posters for which Stephen King feature adaptation included the tagline "How do you kill something that can't possibly be alive?"?

A. *Christine* (1983).

12. **Q.** How did Carrie kill her crackpot mother in King's 1974 novel of the same name?

A. She used telekinesis to stop her heart. In the film, of course, she (Sissy Spacek) used the same power, though rather more visually, hurling knives and other pointy utensils at her mum (Piper Laurie), crucifying her in the kitchen.

14. **Q.** "There were fourteen steps exactly fourteen. But the top one was smaller, out of proportion, as if it had been added to avoid the evil number." To what phobia, suffered by King, does this line from *Salem's Lot* (pub. 1975) allude?

A. Triskaidekaphobia, which is an irrational fear of the number 13. "The number 13 never fails to trace that old icy finger up and down my spine," says King. "When I'm writing, I'll never stop work if the page number is 13 or a multiple of 13; I'll just keep on typing till I get to a safe number. I always take the last two steps on my back stairs as one, making 13 into 12. There were after all 13 steps on the English gallows up until 1900 or so. When I'm reading, I won't stop on page 94, 193, or 382, since the sums of these numbers add up to 13."

15. **GUEST STAR Dan Lloyd**

Q. For Stanley Kubrick's *The Shining*, in any snowy exterior scene with actors present, the snow was not, in fact, snow. There was so much of this anti-snow around that it ended up in all our coat pockets by the end of the day. Which of these four options served as our snow?

A. Sodium bicarbonate
B. Salt
C. Styrofoam
D. Rice

A. B. Salt.

16. Q. How does Cujo contract rabies?

A. He's bitten on the nose by a rabid bat after poking his head into a small cave in search of a rabbit he'd been chasing (*Cujo*, 1981).

17. Q. What was the title of Stephen King's 1981 non-fiction exploration of horror fiction, a book in which he states that radio is a superior medium for horror than film and TV, as it requires more active use of the imagination?

A. *Danse Macabre*: "I recognize terror as the finest emotion and so I will try to terrorize the reader," wrote King of his own literary goals. "But if I find that I cannot terrify, I will try to horrify, and if I find that I cannot horrify, I'll go for the gross-out. I'm not proud."

18. Q. Stephen King's performance in *Creepshow* (1982) was informed by which choice bit of acting advice from director George Romero?

A. "To play the role as broadly as Wile E. Coyote might have played it," remembered Romero, "for which Steve has never forgiven me!"

19. Q. How is Marty able to identify the werewolf terrorising the residents of Tarker's Mills, Maine, in Stephen King's novella *Cycle of the Werewolf* (1983)?

A. After blasting out the creature's left eye with a package of Black Cat firecrackers on July 4, come Halloween, he sees Reverend Lowe wearing an eyepatch and makes the connection, later shooting and killing him with two silver bullets on New Year's Eve.

20. Q. What poem does Johnny (Christopher Walken) read his class at the beginning of David Cronenberg's *The Dead Zone* (1983)?

A. *The Raven* (1845), by Edgar Allan Poe.

21. Q. What song plays during *Christine*'s (1983) opening scene, as the cars roll down the production line and the star of the show claims her first victim?

A. "Bad to the Bone", released in September, 1982, by George Thorogood and the Destroyers (*Christine*, 1983).

22. Q. Having already scored two of Brian De Palma's movies – 1972's *Sisters* and 1976's *Obsession* – it's likely Bernard Herrmann would have scored 1976's *Carrie* too. Sadly, though, he passed away in 1975, before that was possible. Ultimately, the film was scored by Pino Donaggio, who, let's say, "paid homage" to Herrmann in what distinctive way?

A. By using his piercing four-note violin theme from Alfred Hitchcock's *Psycho* (1960), over and over again. As De Palma was, in the parlance of Annie Wilkes, Hitchcock's "number one fan", it was two tributes for the price of one.

23. Q. Which film adaptation of one of his novels did Stephen King famously dislike, dismissing it as "cold" and "misogynistic"?

A. *The Shining* (1980): "I'm not a cold guy," explained the author. "One of the things that people relate to in my books is there's a warmth. There's a reaching out that says to the reader, 'I want you to be a part of this.' But with Kubrick's *The Shining*, I felt it was very cold." It was a film, felt King, that held you at arm's length. Like "a Cadillac with no engine in it. You can't do anything with it except admire it as sculpture." Also, "Shelley Duvall, as Wendy, is really one of the most misogynistic characters ever put on film. She's basically just there to scream and be stupid, and that's not the woman I wrote about." Regarding Jack, King says the character "has no arc in that movie. Absolutely no arc at all. When we first see Jack Nicholson, he's in the office of Mr. Ullman, the manager of the hotel, and you know [immediately] he's crazy as a shit house rat. All he does is get crazier. In the book, he's a guy who's struggling with his sanity and finally loses it. To me, that's a tragedy. In the movie, there's no tragedy because there's no real change."

24. Q. Which character died in King's novel *Cujo* (1983), but survived in the 1983 film adaptation?

A. Little Tad, played by Danny Pintauro. King apparently regretted allowing the lad to die of dehydration and heat stroke in the book, so made sure the kid at least survived the movie version.

25. Q. What kind of car is Christine?

A. Officially, she's a red and white 1958 Plymouth Fury, though a combination of 1957 and 1958 models were used in the film, along with a number of Belvederes and Savoys. Approximately 28 cars were purchased, several just for parts, with roughly 17 Christines created for the 1983 movie – no more than a couple of which survived the shoot. King said he decided to make Christine a 1958 Plymouth Fury as it was a forgotten car. "I didn't want a car that already had a legend attached to it," he said, "like the '50s Thunderbird."

26. Q. Who's that scratching at Mark Petrie's (Lance Kerwin) bedroom window?

A. It's Danny Glick (Brad Savage), decked out in his funeral best, in Tobe Hooper's *Salem's Lot* (1979).

27. Q. "For a long time," said King, "ten years at least, I had wanted to write a fantasy epic like *The Lord of the Rings*, only with an American setting." Set in a plague-decimated USA, what's the name of that oft-revised novel? Also, what location served as the book's Mordor, and which characters did King consider his Frodo and Sauron?

A. *The Stand* (1978), wrote King, was "my American fantasy epic. The land of Mordor was played by Las Vegas. Instead of a hobbit, my hero was a Texan named Stu Redman, and instead of a Dark Lord, my villain was a ruthless drifter and supernatural madman named Randall Flagg."

28. Q. "By the time he graduated from college, John Smith had forgotten all about the bad fall he took on the ice that January day in 1953." Which Stephen King novel begins with this line?

A. *The Dead Zone* (1979): "When I'm starting a book, I compose in bed before I go to sleep," King told *The Atlantic*'s Joe Fassler in 2013. "I will lie there in the dark and think. I'll try to write a paragraph. An opening paragraph. And over a period of weeks and months and even years, I'll word and reword it until I'm happy with what I've got. If I can get that first paragraph right, I'll know I can do the book. Because of this, I think, my first sentences stick with me. They were a doorway I went through."

29. Q. Besides King's crazy performance as doomed, dumb Jordy Verrill in *Creepshow* (1982), which other member of the King household played a role in the film?

A. King's son Joe, better known to most as Joe Hill, author of *Heart-Shaped Box* (2007), *Horns* (2010), *NOS4A2* (2013) and *The Fireman* (2016). It was Joe, age nine, who played vengeful little Billy in *Creepshow*'s bookend sequences. "I'll teach you to throw away my comicbooks!"

30. GUEST STAR Steve Casino

Q. What are Tad's (Danny Pintauro) two nicknames in *Cujo* (1983)?

A. He's called "Tadder" by his parents and "Tadpole" by his mother's lover Steve (Christopher Stone).

31. Q. In Kubrick's *The Shining* (1980), what does Ullman (Barry Nelson) tell Wendy (Shelley Duvall) the Overlook Hotel was built over?

A. An old Indian burial ground. It's always an old Indian burial ground.

32. Q. As *Christine* (1983) wasn't violent enough to earn an "R" rating, and the last thing the producers wanted to release was a PG horror movie, what was their solution?

A. They added lots of swearing, mainly F-bombs.

33. Q. Which early film adaptation of one of his books does King prefer to his own original novel?

A. Brian De Palma's *Carrie* (1976), adapted from King's 1974 novel. "De Palma's approach to the material was lighter and more deft than my own," said King, "and a good deal more artistic. The book seems clear enough and truthful enough in terms of the characters and their actions, but it lacks the style of De Palma's film. The book attempts to look at the ant farm of high school society dead on; De Palma's examination of this 'High School Confidential' world is more oblique and more cutting...Carrie is a good movie. It hasn't aged as well as some of the other ones, but it's still pretty good."

34. Q. According to Stephen King's 1977 novel *The Shining*, which Overlook Hotel room is best avoided?

A. Room 217: The Overlook Hotel was inspired by Colorado's Stanley Hotel, where Stephen King and his wife Tabitha spent a spooky night in the hotel's supposedly haunted room 217. Stanley Kubrick is said to have changed the room number in his 1980 adaptation to 237 as a favour to the management of Oregon's Timberline Lodge, which served as the Outlook's exterior in the movie. Apparently they were afraid that no one would ever want to sleep in room 217 again, so Kubrick changed it to the non-existent 237.

35. Q. Though it wasn't the first of his novels to be published, what was the first novel ever written by Stephen King?

A. *The Long Walk*, a dystopian teen tale written during King's freshman year (1966–1967) at the University of Maine. Finally published in 1979, it was the second King novel credited to Richard Bachman.

36. Q. Which of King's early novels did the author reveal he "barely remembers writing at all"?

A. *Cujo* (pub. 1981): In his 2000 biography, *On Writing: A Memoir of the Craft*, King revealed that he wrote the book during a cocaine binge, and that while he likes it, he wishes he could remember enjoying the good parts as he put them down on the page.

37. Q. For whom does The Gunslinger gun?

A. The Man in Black (*The Dark Tower: The Gunslinger*, 1982).

38. Q. Plume's comicbook adaptation of *Creepshow* (1982) marked Stephen King's first collaboration with which master monster illustrator?

A. Bernie "Berni" Wrightson.

39. Q. In Kubrick's *The Shining* (1980), what does Jack (Jack Nicholson) say he'd give his goddamned soul for?

A. Just a glass of beer.

40. Q. While shooting *Cujo* (1983), actress Dee Wallace was bitten by one of the canines in the cast: True or false?

A. False! Though she was bitten by Danny Pintauro, the kid playing her son Tad, after she put her fingers in his mouth during a scene in which he's having a seizure.

41. Q. Carrie is responsible for all of the deaths in King's 1974 novel, with which exception?

A. Tommy, who dies after being knocked unconscious by a bucket of blood dropped by Chris.

42. Q. "Children of the Corn", "Graveyard Shift", "The Mangler" and "The Lawnmower Man" lurk among the twenty tales gathered in Stephen King's first collection of short stories. What was its title?

A. *Night Shift* (1978).

43. Q. What is Danny Torrance's (Danny Lloyd) nickname in Stanley Kubrick's *The Shining* (1980)? Also, what's the name of the little boy who lives in his mouth?

A. Danny's parents call him Doc , "...like in the Bugs Bunny cartoons". The little boy with the croaky voice is called Tony.

44. Q. In *Creepshow* (1982), what was effects wiz Tom Savini's nickname for the ferocious, bitey creature in the crate?

A. Fluffy: Apparently all the creatures in the movie had nicknames. The skeleton at the window, for example, was called Raoul.

45. Q. Which Stephen King feature adaptation was described in its print ads as a terrifying blend of *American Graffiti* (1973) and *Psycho* (1960)?

A. *Carrie* (1976).

46. Q. Introduced in the novel *Firestarter* (pub. 1980), and featured in several Stephen King projects since, what's the name of the fictional, top-secret US government agency specialising in largely evil scientific research?

A. The Shop: A reference to Canadian sci-fi author A. E. van Vogt's *The Weapon Shops of Isher* (1951).

47. Q. In Cronenberg's *The Dead Zone* (1983), what vision terrifies Johnny (Christopher Walken) when he shakes hands with vile senatorial candidate Greg Stillson (Martin Sheen)?

A. He sees Stillson as President, mad as a bag of badgers, launching a pre-emptive nuclear strike against Russia, triggering the end of the world.

48. Q. What's the name of Ellie Creed's cat, back from the grave but still "a little dead" in *Pet Sematary* (pub. 1983)?

A. Winston Churchill, or Church for short.

49. Q. King had originally planned for his pseudonym to be Guy Pillsbury – his maternal grandfather's name. When this secret was accidentally spilled, and King had to come up with a last-minute replacement, Richard Bachman was born. How did the author arrive at this name?

A. "I was reading a paperback novel by Richard Stark [itself a pen name of Donald E. Westlake's] and Bachman-Turner Overdrive was on the stereo," remembers King, "so I said, 'Call me Richard Bachman,' and that's what happened."

50. Q. In *Creepshow* (1982), what does grating Nathan Grantham (Jon Lormer) demand?

A. It's Father's Day – he wants his cake!

51. Q. "His single-minded purpose. His unending fury." Which Stephen King novel ends with these lines?

A. *Christine* (1983).

Ray Harryhausen's Creature Features

1. Q. What film inspired Ray Harryhausen to become a stop-motion animator?

A. *King Kong* (1933): "I wandered innocently into Grauman's Chinese Theatre one afternoon with my mother," Ray told me, "and I haven't been the same since." He was 13 years old. "I fell in love with the movie, with the fantasy, with the fact that someone dared put a 50-foot gorilla with a girl in his hand on the screen. Nobody had ever done that sort of thing before. It was so outrageous, and so convincing, that it titillated my imagination.

"Kong haunted me. I kept going back to see it again and again. I desperately wanted to know how they'd brought the creatures to life, but unlike today there were no books on the subject, no DVD extras or magazines full of movie secrets. And that's the way it should be. If you know too much about a film it destroys the fantasy. Today's audiences are jaded by inside information. Back in 1933, I had no idea how Kong was made and I had no way to find out, so I had to be imaginative and devise my own methods. I started experimenting with a camera and animation models, then I started making my own dinosaurs, and gradually it turned from a hobby into a profession."

2. Q. What is Mr Joseph Young's favourite tune?

A. "Beautiful Dreamer", a parlour song by Stephen Foster, first published in 1864, and featured throughout *Mighty Joe Young* (1949).

3. Q. *The Beast from 20,000 Fathoms* (1953) inspired which Japanese monster movie? Also, what was Ray's opinion of the film?

A. *Gojira* (aka *Godzilla*; 1954), and he hated it! "I gave a lecture at the National Film Theatre a few years ago," said Ray, "and someone in the audience asked, 'Why do you go to all the trouble of stop motion? Why don't you just put a man in a suit?' I didn't know what to say. What do you say to a person like that? I felt like wringing his neck. People who can't see the difference between *Godzilla* and what I do shouldn't be allowed to see my films. They should only be allowed to watch *Attack of the Killer Tomatoes* (1978) and rubbish like that."

4. Q. How did Ray Harryhausen famously cut costs on *It Came from Beneath the Sea* (1955)?

A. By adapting his octopus model into a "sixtopus" and only animating six tentacles, shooting it so that the missing limbs appeared to be underwater or were in other ways out of view.

5. Q. In *Jason and the Argonauts* (1963), who are the Children of the Hydra's Teeth?

A. Seven skeleton warriors conjured by King Aeetes (Jack Gwillim) to keep Jason (Todd Armstrong) from robbing the legendary Golden Fleece from Colchis.

6. Q. What incantation does Sokurah the Magician (Torin Thatcher) recite to summon the Genie (Richard Eyer) from his lamp in *The 7th Voyage of Sinbad* (1958)?

A. "From the land beyond beyond... From the world past hope and fear... I bid you, Genie, now appear."

7. Q. After the castaways overpower the giant crab in *Mysterious Island* (1961), what do they do with it?

A. Tip it into a bubbling hot spring and eat it for lunch!

8. Q. In *20 Million Miles to Earth* (1957), when the army attempts to lure the Ymir into an electric net, what do they use for bait?

A. Sulphur – its favourite food.

9. Q. What does Professor Cavor (Lionel Jeffries) name his gravity-defying metallic paste in *First Men in the Moon* (1964)?

A. Cavorite.

10. Q. "Travel back through time and space to the edge of man's beginnings...Discover a savage world whose only law was lust!" This juicy tagline adorned the posters for which movie?

A. *One Million Years B.C.* (1966).

11. Q. "I had to do everything because I couldn't find another kindred soul," said Ray of his arduous and time-consuming creative process. "Now you see 80 people listed doing the same things I was doing by myself." Though Harryhausen famously animated the majority of his projects solo, everyone needs help sometimes. George Lofgren, a taxidermist, co-created many of Ray's furry critters. Willis Cook, an occasional assistant, built some of his miniature sets. But what vital roles did Ray's parents play in the making of his movies?

A. Based on his son's designs, Ray's father machined the metal armatures – the poseable skeletons – for his models, while Ray's mother helped create many of his creatures' miniature costumes.

12. Q. What's in the sack brought back from The Forbidden Valley at the beginning of *The Valley of Gwangi* (1969)? Also, what does T.J. (Gila Golan) name it?

A. A tiny horse, identified by Professor Bromley (Laurence Naismith) as a prehistoric Eohippus. T.J. calls it El Diablo!

13. Q. In *The Golden Voyage of Sinbad* (1973), what does Margiana (Caroline Munro) have tattooed on the palm of her right hand?

A. An eye.

14. Q. In *Sinbad and the Eye of the Tiger* (1977), the bronze colossus Minaton was both a stop-motion creation and a man in a suit. Which 7'3"-tall performer made his uncredited movie debut in the role?

A. Peter Mayhew, whose second screen job was playing Chewie in *Star Wars* (1977), a movie ultimately released three months before *Sinbad and the Eye of the Tiger*.

15. Q. In *Clash of the Titans* (1981), what's the only safe way to view Medusa?

A. In a reflective surface like a shiny shield.

16. Q. Ray's movie-making idol since *King Kong* (1933), who worked with Harryhausen on his first feature, *Mighty Joe Young* (1949)?

A. Willis O'Brien, the grandfather of stop-motion animation, who designed Joe and storyboarded the action, though it was Ray and second technician Peter Peterson who did most of the actual animating. Their efforts earned O'Brien an Oscar for Best Special Effects at the 1950 Academy Awards.

17. Q. What's the name of the generic-sounding secret base, far north of the Arctic Circle, that's featured at the very beginning of *The Beast from 20,000 Fathoms* (1953)?

A. Operation Experiment.

18. Q. What was Ray Harryhausen's first colour feature?

A. *The 7th Voyage of Sinbad* (1958).

19. Q. Who was the one-sandalled man?

A. Jason (Todd Armstrong), lawful King of Thessaly, in *Jason and the Argonauts* (1963).

20. Q. In whose name does Professor Cavor (Lionel Jeffries) claim the Moon, in *First Men in the Moon* (1964)?

A. "In the name of our Sovereign Lady, Queen Victoria."

21. Q. Where does Sinbad (John Phillip Law) find the third golden tablet in *The Golden Voyage of Sinbad* (1973)?

A. Inside the shattered Kali statue.

22. Q. Malcolm McDowell, Michael York, Richard Chamberlain and Arnold Schwarzenegger were all considered for which role in what movie?

A. Perseus in *Clash of the Titans* (1981), a role that eventually went to Harry Hamlin.

23. Q. What triggers Joe's nightclub rampage in *Mighty Joe Young* (1949)?

A. A trio of boozehounds mess with Joe while he's caged in the basement, giving him their liquor, and when he drinks it all, one of them angrily burns his hand with a cigarette lighter.

24. Q. "If you can load it, I can fire it..." Which up-and-coming actor played military sharpshooter Corp. Stone in *The Beast from 20,000 Fathoms* (1953)?

A. Lee Van Cleef, best known for Sergio Leone's *The Good, the Bad and the Ugly* (1966) and John Carpenter's *Escape from New York* (1981).

25. GUEST STAR Joel Hodgson

Q. Was Ray Harryhausen British? Because he sure sounded like it.

A. No! Actually he was born in Los Angeles, California, but moved at age 40, in 1960, to work and live in London, where he became a dual US–UK citizen and lived there till his death, in 2013, age 92.

26. Q. What was the promotional term coined by producer Charles H. Schneer to distinguish Harryhausen's model animation technique from mere cartoon animation?

A. Dynamation. Heralded as "The New Miracle of the Screen" during the opening titles for *The 7th Voyage of Sinbad* (1958), it was a portmanteau of "dynamic animation" that was later renamed SuperDynaMation and finally Dynarama.

27. Q. When the castaways discover a chest washed ashore in *Mysterious Island* (1961), what suitable novel do they discover inside?

A. Daniel Defoe's *Robinson Crusoe* (1719).

28. Q. How does Jason (Todd Armstrong) defeat Talos in *Jason and the Argonauts* (1963)?

A. As advised by Hera (Honor Blackman), Jason unscrews a large plug on Talos' left heel, releasing a torrent of bronze, smoking liquid known as ichor, the ethereal fluid that, according to Greek mythology (and Wikipedia), is the blood of gods and immortals. Clutching his throat, Talos topples to the ground and breaks into pieces.

29. Q. What are the names of the two tribes featured in *One Million Years B.C.* (1966)?

A. The savage Rock tribe and the, relatively chilled, Shell tribe.

30. Q. What actor, best known for playing Doctor Who, appeared in which two Ray Harryhausen movies?

A. Second Doctor Patrick Troughton played the blind prophet Phineas in *Jason and the Argonauts* (1963) and the alchemist Melanthius in *Sinbad and the Eye of the Tiger* (1977).

31. Q. What breaks the steaming surface of the cauldron when the Stygian Witches (Flora Robson, Anna Manahan and Freda Jackson) meet Perseus (Harry Hamlin) in *Clash of the Titans* (1981)?

A. A human hand.

32. Q. "Nobody paid any attention to us. Nobody said, 'Why did you do this?' and 'Why did you do that?' We just did it, and when the picture was finished, they saw it. We had full control, artistic control without any interference. That was worth the price of making a 'B' picture, as opposed to an 'A' picture." Which close collaborator of Ray Harryhausen's said this, and how many films did they make together?

A. Charles H. Schneer, who produced all but four of Ray Harryhausen's features, the exceptions being *Mighty Joe Young* (1949), *The Beast from 20,000 Fathoms* (1953), Irwin Allen documentary *The Animal World* (1956) and Hammer production *One Million Years B.C.* (1966). Schneer and Harryhausen first worked together on 1955's *It Came from Beneath the Sea*. In all, they made 12 movies together over 26 years.

33. **Q.** After the producers of *Monster from the Sea* bought the rights to Ray Bradbury's short story "The Beast from 20,000 Fathoms" (pub. 1951) – principally so they could use his superior title for their creature feature – Bradbury later renamed the story when including it in his 1953 anthology, *The Golden Apples of the Sun*. What was his new name for it?

A. "The Fog Horn".

34. **Q.** Which actor, who played Capt. Patrick Hendry in *The Thing from Another World* (1951) and was often cast as stoic military types, later played Col. Jack Evans in *The Beast from 20,000 Fathoms* (1953) and Cmdr. Pete Mathews in *It Came from Beneath the Sea* (1955)?

A. The inimitable Kenneth Tobey, who, in later life, played cameo roles in a string of Joe Dante films: *The Howling* (1981), *Gremlins* (1984), *Innerspace* (1987) and *Gremlins 2: The New Batch* (1990).

35. **Q.** What guards the entrance to Sokurah's fortress in *The 7th Voyage of Sinbad* (1958)?

A. A dragon named Taro. The model of the dragon was more than three feet long and difficult to animate, but Ray, of course, worked wonders with it.

36. **Q.** Which three Harryhausen films were directed by Nathan Juran?

A. *20 Million Miles to Earth* (1957), *The 7th Voyage of Sinbad* (1958) and *First Men in the Moon* (1964). "I wasn't a born director," said Juran. "I never became caught up in the romance of the movies. I was just a technician who could transfer the script from the page to the stage, and get it shot on schedule and on budget."

37. Q. What's Loana (Raquel Welch) teaching Tumak's (John Richardson) tribe when she's attacked and carried off by a Pteranodon?

A. How to swim, or at least, have fun splashing about.

38. Q. In which two movies, and with which two creatures, do battles with elephants occur?

A. The Venusian Ymir battles an elephant on the streets of Rome in *20 Million Miles to Earth* (1957), while in Mexico, the Allosaurus named Gwangi the Great kills an elephant in *The Valley of Gwangi* (1969).

39. Q. What's the final line, spoken in unison by Sinbad (John Phillip Law) and the Grand Vizier of Marabia (Douglas Wilmer), in *The Golden Voyage of Sinbad* (1973)?

A. "But tie up your camel!" A recurring line in the movie, said in response to the phrase, "Trust in Allah."

40. Q. Which of Ray Harryhausen's movies features Petra's iconic Treasury (Al-Khazneh), a striking 1st-century temple carved from a sandstone rock face that also appeared in Hergé's *The Adventures of Tintin: The Red Sea Sharks* (1958) and Steven Spielberg's *Indiana Jones and the Last Crusade* (1989)?

A. In *Sinbad and the Eye of the Tiger* (1977), The Treasury doubles as the Castle of Melanthius (Patrick Troughton) on the Isle of Casgar.

41. Q. What do Calibos (Neil McCarthy) in *Clash of the Titans* (1981) and the Id Monster from *Forbidden Planet* (1956) have in common?

A. They're both based on the human/monster hybrid Caliban from William Shakespeare's play *The Tempest* (~1611).

42. Q. Where is Ray's star situated on Hollywood Boulevard's Walk of Fame?

A. "Appropriately enough," remarked Ray, "I'm outside Grauman's [Now TCL] Chinese Theatre, sandwiched between Harold Lloyd and Jane Russell, who's something of a special effect herself." Ray was honoured with a star on June 10, 2003.

43. Q. Besides the usual fatalities associated with sea creature invasion – being eaten, squished or drowned, crushed by toppling masonry or trapped in exploding vehicles – what additional aspect of the Rhedosaurus' assault on New York proves deadly in *The Beast from 20,000 Fathoms* (1953)?

A. The monster's blood hosts a horrible, virulent disease.

44. Q. In *20 Million Miles to Earth* (1957), when McIntosh (Thomas Browne Henry) tells Signore Contino (Jan Arvan) that Calder's (William Hopper) just returned from an expedition to Venus, Contino laughs and corrects him how?

A. "To Venice," he says with a condescending smirk. "Perhaps you mean Venezia?"

45. Q. Although initially Ray Harryhausen was eager for either Miklós Rózsa or Max Steiner to score *The 7th Voyage of Sinbad* (1958), producer Charles H. Schneer persuaded him to go another way. Who did they ultimately hire, and since it went so very well, which additional Harryhausen films did he end up scoring?

A. The incomparable Bernard Herrmann, who, besides delivering a thrilling score for *The 7th Voyage of Sinbad* (1958), also composed the music for *The 3 Worlds of Gulliver* (1960), *Mysterious Island* (1961) and *Jason and the Argonauts* (1963). Incidentally, Harryhausen did get to work with Miklós Rózsa eventually, on *The Golden Voyage of Sinbad* (1973).

46. Q. How long did it take Ray to animate the legendary skeleton scene from *Jason and the Argonauts* (1963)?

A. "Trying to time three men swinging their swords with seven skeletons swinging theirs, was a big challenge. That one scene took four months to film as I couldn't shoot more than 13 frames a day. That's only half a second of film!"

47. Q. What are Professor Cavor's (Lionel Jeffries) thoughts regarding the Selenites' practice of putting their chemical workers to sleep until they're needed again?

A. "Well it's a unique way of dealing with unemployment," he says. "Entirely reasonable, I suppose."

48. Q. When Zenobia (Margaret Whiting) turns from a seagull back to a full-sized human being in *Sinbad and the Eye of the Tiger* (1977), as there wasn't enough magic potion left to effect a full transformation, what souvenir of her shape-shifting adventure remains?

A. Her right foot is a massive gull's foot.

49. Q. What was Ray's final feature?

A. *Clash of the Titans* (1981): "When you're working on a film, you have to think about it 24 hours a day," said Ray. "It's not just an eight-hour job. You have to live and breathe the film, at least that's the way I always approached it. I found it takes an enormous chunk of your life. I worked for three years on *Clash of the Titans* and hardly ever saw my family. Our daughter had to grow up without daddy being around very much. Finally, I felt I'd had enough of it."

50. Q. When Ray Harryhausen received his honorary Oscar – The Gordon E. Sawyer Award – at the Academy's Science and Technical Ceremony in 1992, host Tom Hanks remarked, "Some people say *Citizen Kane* (1941) or *Casablanca* (1942) is the greatest movie ever made. I say..." What film did he name?

A. *Jason and the Argonauts* (1963).

Star Trek: The Original Series

1. Q. What is the registry number of the USS *Enterprise*?
A. NCC-1701.

2. Q. Including the original, how many episodes of *Star Trek* were produced?
A. 79.

3. Q. What does the "T" in James T. Kirk (William Shatner) stand for?
A. Tiberius.

4. Q. What colour is Spock's (Leonard Nimoy) blood?
A. Green.

5. Q. Who convinced Nichelle Nichols not to quit playing Uhura, insisting she was an essential role model for black women in America?

A. Martin Luther King Jr. Remembers Nichols, "He said something along the lines of 'Nichelle, whether you like it or not, you've become a symbol. If you leave, they can replace you with a blonde-haired white girl, and it will be like you were never there. What you've accomplished, for all of us, will only be real if you stay.' That got me thinking about how it would look for fans of colour around the country if they saw me leave. I saw that this was bigger than just me."

6. Q. How do you stop Tribbles from reproducing?

A. Starve them.

7. Q. What is the show's legendary opening monologue?

A. "Space, the final frontier. These are the voyages of the starship *Enterprise*. Its 5-year mission: to explore strange new worlds, to seek out new life and new civilizations, to boldly go where no man has gone before."

8. Q. What three colours of uniform are worn by Command, Sciences and Operations?

A. Gold, Blue and Red.

9. Q. What was the message burnt into the ground by the Horta in "The Devil in the Dark" (S01E25)?

A. "No Kill I."

10. GUEST STAR George Takei

Q. In "The Naked Time" (S01E04), Sulu stalks the corridors of the *Enterprise* with a fencing foil. What weapon was proposed for Sulu in the initial script written by John D.F. Black?

A. A samurai sword was proposed in the original script but as I was a fan of Errol Flynn's 1938 film *The Adventures of Robin Hood*, I proposed that Sulu do some fencing, and the producers approved, so a shirtless Sulu did some fencing!

11. Q. What was the first episode of the show to feature all seven main cast members?

A. "Who Mourns for Adonais" (S02E02).

12. Q. Which one of these three eccentric mutterings was never uttered by cantankerous Dr McCoy (DeForest Kelley)?

A – "I'm a doctor, not a bricklayer!"
B – "I'm a doctor, not a proctor!"
C – "I'm a doctor, not an escalator!"

A. B.

13. Q. What was the name of the book that caused widespread cultural contamination in "A Piece of the Action" (S02E17)?

A. *Chicago Mobs of the Twenties.*

14. Q. What was Gene Roddenberry's nickname?

A. The Great Bird of the Galaxy.

15. Q. What rare crystals power the *Enterprise*'s warp core?

A. Dilithium.

16. Q. In which episode did Kirk (William Shatner) romance a doomed, Great Depression-era missionary (Joan Collins)?

A. "The City on the Edge of Forever" (S01E28).

17. Q. Joining the cast in its second year to increase youth appeal, Chekov's (Walter Koenig) look and attitude were inspired by which singer/actor?

A. Lead singer of The Monkees, Davy Jones.

18. Q. Which alien race invented cloaking technology?

A. Romulans ("Balance of Terror", S01E08).

19. Q. Who wrote *Star Trek*'s theme tune?

A. Alexander Courage.

20. Q. Gene Roddenberry originally wrote lyrics for *Star Trek*'s theme tune: True or false?

A. True! Apparently Roddenberry wrote them, not so they'd ever be used, but so he could take a co-writer credit and receive residual payments for the theme's use alongside composer Alexander Courage, who often complained that Roddenberry had "swindled" him out of 50% of the popular theme's royalties. If you're curious to read and perhaps attempt to sing those ill-fitting lyrics, they're just a Google search away.

21. Q. Many tubes in the hallways of the Enterprise are marked "GNDN". What does this stand for?

A. Goes Nowhere Does Nothing!

22. Q. Why were Spock's (Leonard Nimoy) pointed ears and eyebrows airbrushed out of early publicity pictures for the series?

A. NBC advertising executives feared folks would shun the show because of Spock's resemblance to Satan.

23. Q. Which species of aliens force Kirk (William Shatner) and Uhura (Nichelle Nichols) to kiss?

A. The Platonians ("Plato's Stepchildren", S03E10).

24. Q. Who founded Desilu Productions, the company that produced the first season-and-a-half of *Star Trek*?

A. *I Love Lucy* stars Desi Arnaz and Lucille Ball co-founded the company, though by the time it produced *Star Trek*, Ball was the sole owner, having divorced Arnaz in 1962 and bought his share.

25. GUEST STAR Julie Nimoy

Q. Which instrument did Mr Spock (Leonard Nimoy) play in "Charlie X" (S01E02)?

A. A Vulcan lyrette.

26. **Q.** "Beam me up, Scotty." During the run of the show, how many times did Kirk (William Shatner) utter this immortal catchphrase: never, 12 times, or 62 times?

A. Never! Not even once. Though he often came close with, "Beam me up", "Scotty, beam me up" and "Scotty, beam us up".

27. **Q.** Every seven years, Vulcans experience ponn farr, where they're stricken with a blood fever, become violent and finally die unless they do either one of which two things?

A. Either they mate with a partner they've empathically bonded with or engage in a ritual battle known as kal-if-fee ("Amok Time", S02E05).

28. **Q.** Which two main cast characters didn't have first names in the series?

A. Sulu (George Takei) and Uhura (Nichelle Nichols): Sulu's first name, Hikaru, wasn't spoken on screen until *Star Trek VI: The Undiscovered Country* (1991), and Uhura's first name, Nyota, which is a Swahili word meaning star, wasn't spoken on screen until 2009's *Star Trek*.

29. **Q.** How was writer and script editor Dorothy Fontana credited on the show, and why?

A. Gene Roddenberry told her to go by D.C. Fontana as networks back then didn't generally hire female writers. The "C" stands for Catherine.

30. Q. According to Chekov (Walter Koenig) in "The Trouble with Tribbles" (S02E15), who invented Scotch?

A. "A little old lady from Leningrad."

31. Q. What are the slanting crawlways that lead up to the warp-drive nacelles called? Also, who were they named after?

A. Jefferies tubes were named after *Star Trek* art director and production designer Walter Matthew "Matt" Jefferies, Jr.

32. Q. Which member of *Star Trek*'s main cast also voiced Providers 2 and 3 in "The Gamesters of Triskelion" (S02E16), a radio announcer in "A Piece of the Action" (S02E17), Sargon in "Return to Tomorrow" (S02E20), Commodore Enwright in "The Ultimate Computer" (S02E24) and a NASA technician in "Assignment: Earth" (S02E26)?

A. James Doohan.

33. Q. Rather than knock out evil Kirk (William Shatner) with the butt of Spock's phaser in "The Enemy Within" (S02E05), Leonard Nimoy devised which fascinating alternative?

A. The famous Vulcan neck pinch.

34. Q. Created by writer Gene L. Coon, the Klingons first appeared in which episode of the show? Also, who played the Klingon Kor?

A. The episode was "Errand of Mercy" (S01E26). The actor was John Colicos, best known otherwise for playing treacherous Count Baltar in *Battlestar Galactica* (1978). Incidentally, the Klingons were apparently named after Lieutenant Wilbur Clingan, who served with Roddenberry in the LAPD.

35. Q. Which actors' names appeared in the opening credits of *Star Trek*'s first season?

A. Just William Shatner and Leonard Nimoy. DeForest Kelley was added from season two.

36. Q. Why wouldn't you ever want to see a Medusan?

A. Because their appearance would drive you insane ("Is There in Truth No Beauty?" S03E05).

37. Q. With what message does Trelane, the all-powerful and eccentric Squire of Gothos played by William Campbell, first greet the Enterprise?

A. "Greetings and Felicitations!" Followed by "Hip hip hoorah. Tallyho!" ("The Squire of Gothos", S01E18).

38. Q. Which member of *Star Trek*'s cast claims never to have seen a single episode of the show?

A. William Shatner: "I don't watch myself," he said. Nor did he keep any mementos from the series, or even a single scrap of *Star Trek* memorabilia.

39. Q. Who is the only non-crew character in *Star Trek* to be featured in more than one episode? Also, who played him, and what were the names of the episodes he appeared in?

A. Harry Mudd, played by Roger C. Carmel, appeared in the episodes "Mudd's Women" (S01E06) and "I, Mudd" (S02E08).

40. GUEST STAR James Callis

Q. What did Leonard Nimoy originally want to change about his character?

A. Spock's pointy Vulcan ears! Nimoy hated them so much that Gene Roddenberry promised his character could have an operation to make them appear more human if he still hated them after the first 13 weeks of filming.

41. Q. What is the name of the ancient sleeper ship containing 72 genetically engineered passengers in suspended animation? Also, who was their leader?

A. The SS *Botany Bay*; Eugenics War criminal Khan Noonien Singh (Ricardo Montalbán) ("Space Seed", S01E22).

42. Q. Which intimate Vulcan technique was first featured in the episode "Dagger of the Mind" (S01E09)?

A. A mind meld.

43. Q. Which notorious season three episode was described by William Shatner as one of the show's worst, calling the episode's plot a "tribute" to NBC executives who slashed the show's budget and placed it in a bad time slot?

A. "Spock's Brain" (S03E01).

44. Q. Which member of the cast was nominated for an acting Emmy for each of the show's three seasons? Also, how many Emmys did the series eventually win?

A. Leonard Nimoy received a Best Supporting Actor nomination three years in a row, but in all those years, neither he, nor the show, won a single Emmy.

45. Q. Which two-part episode of the show used footage originally shot for the series' unscreened pilot, "The Cage"?

A. "The Menagerie" (S01E11/12).

46. Q. Why is Kirk (William Shatner) offended when Commodore Wesley (Barry Russo) calls him Captain Dunsel in "The Ultimate Computer" (S02E24)?

A. Because Dunsel is Starfleet Academy slang for a part that serves no useful purpose. Burn!

47. Q. Where would you find the ISS *Enterprise*?

A. In the Mirror Universe ("Mirror, Mirror", S02E04).

48. Q. An RCA advert in 1967 cited *Star Trek* as the best reason to buy which luxury item?

A. A colour television.

49. Q. How do the Melkotians sentence Kirk (William Shatner) and his landing crew to die in "Spectre of the Gun" (S03E06)?

A. In a re-enactment of Tombstone, Arizona's Gunfight at the O.K. Corral. Coincidentally, DeForest Kelley played Morgan Earp in John Sturges' 1957 western, *Gunfight at the O.K. Corral*.

50. Q. What saves Spock (Leonard Nimoy) from being permanently blinded by an intense beam of light in "Operation: Annihilate!" (S01E29)?

A. His Vulcan inner eyelids.

If It Bleeds, We Can Kill It: Eighties' Action Classics

1. Q. According to the hero of *Rambo: First Blood Part II* (1985), what does one have to do in order to survive war?

A. "To survive war," slurs Sly, "you gotta become war."

2. Q. What is best in life?

A. According to Conan the Barbarian (played by Arnold Schwarzenegger in the 1982 sword and sorcery classic), it's "To crush your enemies, see them driven before you, and to hear the lamentation of the women."

3. Q. What might Arjen Rudd (Joss Ackland), South African Minister for Diplomatic Affairs, say if you pointed a gun at him?

A. "Diplomatic immunity!" (*Lethal Weapon 2*, 1989).

4. Q. Which action classic features the characters The Toadie (Max Phipps), The Humungus (Kjell Nilsson), The Gyro Captain (Bruce Spence) and The Feral Kid (Emil Minty)?

A. *Max Max 2: The Road Warrior* (1981).

5. Q. Who's all out of bubblegum? What's the only thing he wants to do besides chew?

A. Rowdy Roddy Piper's John Nada, in John Carpenter's *They Live* (1988), wants to kick alien ass.

6. Q. A daydreaming romantic novelist lives out her fantasies when a treasure map arrives in the post, leading her to Colombia on the trail of a priceless emerald, in which lively 1984 adventure?

A. *Romancing the Stone* (1984).

7. Q. Jon Voight and Eric Roberts earned Oscar nominations for playing fugitive stowaways on what sort of vehicle?

A. A runaway train, in *Runaway Train* (1985).

8. Q. According to the 1987 movie of the same name, what's the highest-rated show in 2019?

A. *The Running Man*: Based on the 1982 novel by Richard Bachman, otherwise known as Stephen King, who wrote it in a week.

9. Q. Crime is a Disease. Meet the Cure." Who's the cure? What's the movie?

A. Sylvester Stallone's Marion Cobretti in 1986's *Cobra*.

10. GUEST STAR Sam J. Jones

Q. During production on *Flash Gordon*, Brian Blessed's Hawkman wings were so large that he couldn't sit on a chair. Instead, a special perch was constructed for him, and whenever he leaned on it, the cast and crew would whistle bird sounds to tease him. True or false?

A. True!

11. Q. Which classic western was remade as sci-fi adventure *Battle Beyond the Stars* (1980)? Also, which actor starred in both?

A. 1960's *The Magnificent Seven* starring Robert Vaughn.

12. Q. Who played The Beastmaster? Who were his closest animal friends?

A. Marc Singer mainly hangs around in the 1982 movie with an eagle, a black panther and comedy ferrets Codo and Podo.

13. Q. According to 1985's *Code of Silence*, what will Eddie Cusack (Chuck Norris) do if he wants your opinion?

A. He'll beat it out of you.

14. Q. What does the acronym JAFO stand for in 'copter classic *Blue Thunder* (1983)? How was it sanitised for the short-lived TV spin-off the following year?

A. "Just Another Fucking Observer" became "Just Another Frustrated Observer".

15. **Q.** What did henchman Jimmy (Marshall Teague) used to do to guys like Dalton (Patrick Swayze) in prison? How does Dalton respond to this information?

A. Jimmy used to fuck guys like Dalton in prison. Unimpressed, Dalton tears Jimmy's throat out (*Road House*, 1989).

16. **Q.** Who are "They"? Where are they? When do they mostly come out?

A. They're Aliens (a.k.a. Xenomorphs), on Planet LV-426, and they mostly come out at night.

17. **Q.** According to his *Commando* (1985) back-story, why was Bennett (Vernon Wells) booted out of Matrix's (Arnold Schwarzenegger) army unit?

A. Because he liked killing too much.

18. **Q.** When a representative of the Teamsters Union contacted director Michael Winner to swearily enquire how he'd had the gall to shoot *Death Wish III* (1985) in New York without hiring a single Teamster, how did the exploitation filmmaker calm them down?

A. By explaining that even though the movie was set in New York, it was actually shot in the heart of London's East End.

19. **Q.** What's better than a shower and a hot cup of coffee after a tiring flight?

A. According to the chatty businessman played by Robert Lesser in *Die Hard* (1988), after you get where you're going, take off your shoes and your socks, then walk around on the rug barefoot and make fists with your toes.

20. **Q.** Who served for one term as mayor of Carmel-by-the-Sea, California? What was his first official act?

A. Clint Eastwood served from 1986 to 1988 and his first official act was to legalise ice-cream stands and parlours.

21. Q. How many people does Rambo (Sylvester Stallone) kill in *First Blood* (1982)?

A. Just the one, actually: Deputy Sergeant Art Galt (Jack Starrett), who falls out of a helicopter after Rambo throws a rock at it in self-defence. And really it was his own stupid fault for not wearing a seat belt (and being a massive jerk).

22. Q. How long do cranky homicide detective Jack Cates and fast-talking convict Reggie Hammond have to catch cop killers on the loose in San Francisco?

A. 48HRS! With Nick Nolte and Eddie Murphy on the case, that's all they need in the 1982 action comedy.

23. Q. When quizzed on the matter by Princess Jehnna (Olivia d'Abo), what is the one thing that drunk Conan (Arnold Schwarzenegger) admits can hurt him, in *Conan the Destroyer* (1984)?

A. "Only pain."

24. Q. In which movie do Kurt Sloane (Jean-Claude Van Damme) and "Tiger" Tong Po (Michel Qissi) "fight the old way, hands wrapped in hemp and resin, dipped in broken glass"?

A. 1989's *Kickboxer*.

25. **GUEST STAR Lea Thompson**

Q. Which two *Red Dawn* stars were former professional ballet dancers?

A. Patrick Swayze and Lea Thompson.

26. Q. Which Aikido master broke Sean Connery's wrist while teaching him martial arts during the production of 1983's *Never Say Never Again*?

A. Steven Seagal.

27. Q. John Woo dedicated *The Killer* (1989) to which one of his filmmaking heroes?

A. Martin Scorsese.

28. Q. Who's too old for this shit? How old is he when we first meet him?

A. Roger Murtaugh turns 50 in *Lethal Weapon*, though actor Danny Glover was actually only 41 when the movie came out in 1987.

29. Q. Which legendary action movie producer parodied his own fast-talking, booming, in-your-face image by playing the aggravated director at the beginning of 1988's *Who Framed Roger Rabbit*?

A. Joel Silver, producer of *48 HRS.* (1982), *Commando* (1985), *Lethal Weapon* (1987), *Die Hard* (1988), *Road House* (1989) and way more besides.

30. Q. Who once remarked of his *Lone Wolf McQuade* (1983) co-star that "David Carradine is about as good a martial artist as I am an actor"?

A. Chuck Norris.

31. Q. What are RoboCop's three Prime Directives and secret Fourth Directive?

A. 1. Serve the public trust; 2. Protect the innocent; 3. Uphold the law; 4. Any attempt to arrest a senior OCP employee results in shutdown.

32. Q. What ability does Remo Williams (Fred Ward) share with Superman? Also what does he have in common with James Bond?

A. They can both dodge bullets; 1985's *Remo: Unarmed and Dangerous* was directed by Guy Hamilton, veteran Bond director of *Goldfinger* (1964), *Diamonds Are Forever* (1971), *Live and Let Die* (1973) and *The Man with the Golden Gun* (1974).

33. Q. Who teaches troubled Seattle youth Jason Stillwell (Kurt McKinney) martial arts in 1986's *No Retreat, No Surrender*?

A. Bruce Lee's ghost (Kim Tai Chong).

34. Q. What does Jesse Ventura not have time for?

A. He ain't got time to bleed, though bleed he does, in 1987's *Predator*.

35. Q. Who flew the Gullfire over Leningrad?

A. Snake Plissken (Kurt Russell), prior to his escapades in *Escape from New York* (1981).

36. Q. What, according to Mark Kaminski (Arnold Schwarzenegger) in *Raw Deal* (1986), should you never do while drinking?

A. You should not drink and bake.

37. Q. Which one of these four frantic sequels has the highest body count: *Mad Max 2: The Road Warrior* (1981), *Rambo: First Blood Part II* (1985), *A Better Tomorrow II* (1987) or *Lethal Weapon 2* (1989)?

A. *Lethal Weapon 2* features 33 killings, *Mad Max 2* has 44, *Rambo 2* delivers 67 deaths, but *A Better Tomorrow II* rules the roost with 199 fatalities, making it the deadliest film of the Eighties.

38. Q. What 1984 sci-fi thriller predicted the Internet, social media, tablet PCs, voice-activated computers, wireless headsets, video mail, camera drones, biometric security and domestic robots? Which visionary filmmaker wrote and directed it?

A. *Runaway*, from *Westworld* writer/director Michael Crichton.

39. Q. Which action superstar originally worked as a gym teacher and dorm bouncer at a Swiss boarding school for girls, and as a lion cage cleaner at the Central Park Zoo?

A. Sylvester Stallone.

40. GUEST STAR Clancy Brown

Q. How many people won Oscars after working on *Highlander*, can you name them, and how many total Oscars did they win?

A. Three people won Oscars: Sean Connery won Best Supporting Actor for *The Untouchables*, Lois Burwell won Best Makeup for *Braveheart* and James Acheson won Best Costume Design for *The Last Emperor*, *Dangerous Liaisons* and *Restoration*. So five Oscars in all!

41. Q. Which legendary action movie star was once described by the Guinness Book of World Records as "the most perfectly developed man in the history of the world"?

A. Four-time Mr. Universe winner and seven-time Mr. Olympia winner Arnold Schwarzenegger, a.k.a. The Austrian Oak.

42. Q. What does a guy have to do to sleep with Red Sonja?

A. "No man may have me unless he has beaten me in a fair fight," says Brigitte Nielsen in the 1985 actioner.

43. Q. Californian character actor Brion James plays Requin, a wild-eyed, pony-tailed henchman with a cockney accent even Dick Van Dyke wouldn't stoop to – favourite phrases include "I'll cut your bloody froat" and "You ain't werf a toss" – in what crazy team-up classic?

A. *Tango & Cash* (1989).

44. Q. What is Tso (Conan Lee) and Fai's (Gordon Liu) weapon of choice for their climactic battle in 1988's *Tiger on the Beat*?

A. Chainsaws!

45. Q. Which martial arts master cites Charlie Chaplin, Buster Keaton and Harold Lloyd as his greatest influences?

A. Jackie Chan.

46. Q. Which 1989 blockbuster did Sylvester Stallone claim led to the decline of muscle-bound action entertainment, stating, "It was the beginning of a new era. The visuals took over. The special effects became more important than the single person. I wish I had thought of Velcro muscles myself. I didn't have to go to the gym all those years, all those hours wedded to the iron game, as we call it."

A. Tim Burton's *Batman* (1989).

47. Q. The Chinese characters in the main title screen for which lively 1986 actioner literally translate to "Evil Spirits Make a Big Scene in Little Spiritual State"?

A. John Carpenter's *Big Trouble in Little China* (1986).

48. Q. Who ran the often notorious Cannon Group production company throughout the Eighties? What was their nickname?

A. Israeli cousins Menahem Golan and Yoram Globus were known as the Go-Go Boys.

49. Q. "The Dancing's Over. Now it gets dirty." Which film's UK quad poster bore this shameless tagline?

A. *Road House* (1989) starring *Dirty Dancing*'s (1987) Patrick Swayze.

50. GUEST STAR Gale Anne Hurd

Q. What was the name of the nightclub in *The Terminator* where The Terminator first targets Sarah Connor?

A. Tech Noir: Jim and I thought it was a good name for a sub-genre of science fiction films dealing with the darker side of technological advances.

2000 AD: The First 500 Thrill-Powered Progs

1. Q. "It sums up the facelessness of justice – justice has no soul. So it isn't necessary for readers to see his face, and I don't want you to." Who is John Wagner describing here?

A. Judge Dredd.

2. Q. Bastich, Drokk, Grud, Sneck, Stomm: which is the odd one out?

A. Sneck, a universal swear word from John Wagner and Carlos Ezquerra's Strontium Dog (#86, 1978). The other four are all expletives from Judge Dredd (#2, 1977).

3. Q. What does the acronym M.A.C.H. stand for?

A. Man Activated by Compu-puncture Hyperpower: M.A.C.H. 1 (#1, 1977) creator Pat Mills was inspired by the phenomenal success of *The Six Million Dollar Man* (1974–1978) to create a like-minded series.

4. **Q.** What's the term for Mega-City One citizens who attempt to cross the Cursed Earth for a fresh start in the New Territories?

A. Helltrekkers: "Better to die in Hell than live in Mega-City One." The Helltrekkers (#387, 1984) was created by John Wagner, Alan Grant, Horacio Lalia and Jose Ortiz.

5. **Q.** What free gifts came with the first and third Progs in 1977?

A. Prog 1 came with the Space Spinner and Prog 3 came with the Red Alert Survival Wallet.

6. **Q.** What trio of Harry Harrison novels were adapted for *2000 AD* by Kelvin Gosnell and Carlos Ezquerra?

A. "The Stainless Steel Rat" (#140, 1979), "The Stainless Steel Rat Saves the World" (#166, 1980) and "The Stainless Steel Rat for President" (#393, 1984).

7. **Q.** What comedy sci-fi series created by John Wagner, Alan Grant and Massimo Belardinelli included the 1982 adventures "Lugjack" (#244, 1982), "The Great Mush Rush" (#251, 1982) and "Stoop Coop Soup" (#288, 1982)?

A. Ace Trucking Co. (#232, 1981).

8. **Q.** Who are the four Dark Judges, and in which story do they first appear together?

A. Judges Fire, Fear and Mortis first joined Judge Death in John Wagner, Alan Grant and Brian Bolland's "Judge Death Lives" (#224, 1981).

9. **Q.** Who is *2000 AD*'s fictional editor and from where does he hail?

A. Tharg the Mighty (a.k.a. The Mighty One) comes from Quaxxann, a fictional planet orbiting the star Betelgeuse.

10. Q. Which treasured 1950s comicbook character was resurrected for the launch of *2000 AD* in 1977?

A. Dan Dare: Originally featured in *Eagle*, Dan was created in 1950 by Frank Hampson and then returned to life, after 200 years in suspended animation, by Ken Armstrong, Pat Mills and Massimo Bellardinelli.

11. Q. The ABC Warriors are a squad of war 'bots designed to withstand which three varieties of warfare?

A. Atomic, Bacterial and Chemical: Created by Pat Mills, Kevin O'Neill, Mike McMahon and Brendan McCarthy, The ABC Warriors first appeared in *2000 AD*'s Prog 119 (1979).

12. Q. Where does Kano keep a secret he refuses to share?

A. In a little box, as detailed in Peter Milligan, Brett Ewins and Jim McCarthy's "Bad Company" (#500, 1986).

13. Q. What's the sport – described as "Football, Boxing, Kung Fu and Basketball rolled into one!" – featured in "Harlem Heroes" (#1, 1977)?

A. Aeroball.

14. Q. What stories did *2000 AD* inherit from struggling sister comics *Starlord* and *Tornado*?

A. When *2000 AD* merged with *Starlord* in Prog 86 (1978), it brought John Wagner and Carlos Ezquerra's Strontium Dog and Pat Mills and Kevin O'Neill's Ro-Busters aboard. When it merged with Tornado in Prog 127 (1979), it added Gerry Finley-Day and Alfonso Azpiri's Blackhawk (though helmed by a new creative team), Tom Tully and Vanyo's The Mind of Wolfie Smith and Dave Angus and Kevin O'Neill's Captain Klep to the line-up.

15. GUEST STAR Pat Mills

Q. What was the name of the art editor who laid out most of the early Progs and was thus responsible for its unique look?

A. Doug Church.

16. Q. January 1, 1999: Bombed in the morning and defeated by teatime, Britain is defeated by what force, during which conflict, in what series?

A. Britain is defeated by the Volgan Republic of Asia during the blink-and-you'd-miss-it Eight-Hour War detailed in Pat Mills and Jesús Blasco's "Invasion!" (#1, 1977).

17. Q. "It's only three pages long, written and drawn by Kevin O'Neill showing some really unsettling artwork. I read this when I was very young and couldn't help feeling concern for the kid that Tharg psychologically damages. If he's alive today I hope he's okay," wrote artist Henry Flint of which short tale from Prog 24 (1977)?

A. "Tharg and the Intruder": "Readers who go space-happy looking at this will have their minds refunded."

18. Q. Where did she go? What did she do?

A. Out. Everything. From Alan Moore and Ian Gibson's "The Ballad of Halo Jones" (#376, 1984).

19. Q. What was the first Judge Dredd story to exceed twenty episodes?

A. Pat Mills, Mike McMahon and Brian Bolland's "The Cursed Earth" (#61, 1978). It was also the first Dredd story featured in *2000 AD*'s colour centre pages.

20. Q. Who were the four original members of the Angel Gang, introduced and promptly killed off in "The Judge Child" (#156, 1980)?

A. Link Angel, Elmer "Pa" Angel, Mean "Mean Machine" Angel and Junior Angel. Created by John Wagner, Alan Grant and Mike McMahon.

21. Q. During the Scrawl War documented in John Wagner, Alan Grant and Ron Smith's "Unamerican Graffiti" (#206, 1981), Chopper is provoked into defacing which enormous relocated landmark?

A. The White Cliffs of Dover.

22. Q. What is Waldo Dobbs' alias, and what do those initials stand for?

A. D.R. stands for Diminished Responsibility. As featured in Alan Moore and Alan Davis's "D.R. & Quinch" (#317, 1983).

23. Q. Who was named "Character Most Worthy of Own Title" in the British Section of the 1984 Eagle Awards?

A. Judge Anderson: By popular demand, the character earned her own title in 1985. The first story of the newly minted Anderson: Psi-Division was "Four Dark Judges" (#416, 1985), by Alan Grant, John Wagner and Brett Ewins.

24. Q. What range of Mega-City One confectionery was known as the sweet that was too good to eat?

A. "Uncle Ump's Umpty Candy" (#145, 1979): Too delicious for its own good, and quickly banned for enslaving anyone with a sweet tooth, varieties of the irresistible confectionery included Bat Ump, Dairy Ump, Five Umps, Mivvump, Opal Umps, Sherbet Umpty, Suck Ump, Ump Dust, Ump Magic, Umpties, Umpty Bar, Umpty Chews, Umpty Street, Ump Gums and Ump Lump.

25. Q. How much did Prog 1 (1977) cost in UK Earth Money, and also, on Mercury?

A. Here on Earth, in the UK, it was 8p. On Mercury it was 17g.

26. Q. A short-lived series by Alan Hebden and César López Vera, "Death Planet" (#62, 1978) featured what important first for *2000 AD*?

A. Captain of the Starship *Eternity*, Commander Lorna Varn was *2000 AD*'s first female lead, fighting to survive a hostile alien world in the face of shameless chauvinism.

27. Q. To illustrate his line of thinking, and inspire artist Carlos Ezquerra, John Wagner handed him an advert featuring what character, from which movie, suggesting he use it as a guideline when designing the look of Judge Dredd?

A. The homicidal anti-hero Frankenstein, played by a black-leather-clad David Carradine, in Paul Bartel's violent post-apocalyptic parody *Death Race 2000* (1975). When he first saw Ezquerra's over-the-top take on the character, Wagner reportedly blurted, "He looks like a Spanish pirate!"

28. Q. "NO! Please let me drown before the GIANT SCORPIONS get to me!" Accompanied by similarly sensational art, this legendary cover line from Prog 93 (1978) promoted what gory tale in the pages within?

A. "Flesh" (#1, 1977): A cowboys vs. dinosaurs classic created by Pat Mills and Ramon Sola.

29. Q. How is The Jam's Paul Weller connected with Nemesis the Warlock, a fire-breathing demonic alien sworn to defeat the fanatical Torquemada, Grand Master of the Terran Empire?

A. The Comic Rock tale "Terror Tube" (#167, 1980), by Pat Mills and Kevin O'Neill. "Terror Tube" was the first of a planned series of one-off stories inspired by pop hits, with The Jam's "Going Underground" apparently inspiring this six-page chase tale between Torquemada's hordes and the mysterious Nemesis. Though the Comic Rock idea was quickly ditched, Nemesis proved popular enough to inspire a two-part follow up, "Killer Watt" (#178, 1980), and then a full, ongoing Nemesis the Warlock series.

30. GUEST STAR Matt Smith

Q. What frozen – and canned – vegetable figurehead made an appearance in Judge Dredd to much controversy?

A. The Jolly Green Giant: Four episodes of the Judge Dredd story "The Cursed Earth" (#61, 1978) weren't reprinted until 2016, as they featured villainous parodies of copyrighted corporate mascots like Ronald McDonald, the Burger King, the Michelin Man, KFC's Colonel Sanders, and more. A half-page retraction strip was published in Prog 84, in which Dredd is seen enjoying some of Green Giant Foods' produce.

31. Q. What's the name of the extra-dimensional agency dedicated to the maintenance and repair of breaks and distortions across the multiverse? Also, what is most unusual about its agents?

A. Indigo Prime, whose agents are all dead. Created by John Smith and Chris Weston, the agency first appeared in the Future Shock "A Change of Scenery" (#490, 1986). In that first story, though, it was named Void Indiga, but that changed after Smith learned of Steve Gerber's almost identically titled graphic novel *Void Indigo* (1983).

32. Q. 5 Men plus 1 Droid plus 1 Alien plus 1 Panther equals what?

A. "The Mean Team" (#437, 1985): In the annals of the sport of Death-Bowl, no names stand higher than the all-galaxy champions of 2882–2886. Written by "The Beast" (a.k.a. John Wagner and Alan Grant), with art by Massimo Belardinelli.

33. Q. What was the first Judge Dredd story ever created? Also, what was the first Judge Dredd story ever published?

A. The first Judge Dredd story ever created was "Bank Raid". Written by John Wagner and Pat Mills, with art by Carlos Ezquerra, it was likely withheld for being too violent, and finally published in 1981's *2000 AD Annual*. Published in its place, in Prog 2 (1977), "Judge Whitey" became the first published Judge Dredd story. Written by Peter Harris and Pat Mills, with art by Mike McMahon and cut-and-pasted panels of Ezquerra's original "Bank Raid" art.

34. Q. A former S.A.S. officer who's blasted into the future by a mighty nuclear boom, the adventures of Nick Stone and his Yujee chums – cat girl Liana, wolf man Gruff, bull man T-Bone and dog man Billy the Pup – are detailed in which eye-popping series?

A. "Meltdown Man" (#178, 1980).

35. Q. Who are Sam Slade's two robotic sidekicks?

A. Joining Slade on his 'bot-busting adventures is his idiot kit-built robot assistant Hoagy, and a Cuban robot cigar named Stogie ("Robo-Hunter", #76, 1978).

36. Q. Prior to "The Apocalypse War" (#245, 1982), by John Wagner, Alan Grant and Carlos Ezquerra, approximately how many people were unemployed in Mega-City One?

A. As the population of Mega-City One is 800,000,000 and the unemployment rate is 98%, the answer is 784,000,000.

37. Q. The last of Nu Earth's Genetic Infantrymen, Rogue Trooper pursues the despicable Traitor General with help from three fallen comrades whose consciousnesses are stored on biochips implanted in his equipment. What are their names and which items do they inhabit?

A. Helm is in his helmet, Gunnar works his rifle and Bagman runs his backpack. Created by Gerry Finley-Day and Dave Gibbons, "Rogue Trooper" first appeared in Prog 228 (1981).

38. Q. Who is the only bear on the CIA Death List?

A. Created by Pat Mills and Juan Arancio, it could only be "Shako!" (#20, 1977).

39. Q. What does Birmingham schoolgirl Roxie prefer to call Interpreter Zhcchz, of the Tau Ceti Imperium, after he crash lands on Earth and she takes him in?

A. "Skizz": Created by Alan Moore and Jim Baikie, the series often described as "*E.T.* meets *Boys from the Blackstuff*" debuted in Prog 308 (1983). The second and third parts of the series were written and drawn by Baikie alone: "Alien Cultures" (#767, 1992) and "Skizz Book 3" (#912, 1994).

40. Q. What was Judge Dredd's first extended storyline, and which long-running character did it introduce?

A. "Robot Wars" (#10, 1977) introduced Dredd's loyal, lisping, comic relief-delivering servant, Walter the Wobot.

41. Q. Based on the body-distorting battle frenzy of the Irish hero Cú Chulainn, what is the power that transforms Sláine into a terrifying and prodigiously powerful warrior?

A. The mighty Warp Spasm, as featured in Pat Mills and Angela Kincaid's equally powerful "Sláine" (#330, 1983).

42. Q. Johnny Alpha's mutated eyes give him which two key abilities?

A. He can see through walls and read minds. As featured in John Wagner and Carlos Ezquerra's "Strontium Dog" (#86, 1978).

43. Q. Who killed Halo Jones' flatmate Brinna, and why?

A. Brinna's robot dog Toby killed her as he'd fallen in love with Halo and learned that in the event of Brinna's death, Halo would inherit him. Sadly for Toby, his love remained unrequited. From Alan Moore and Ian Gibson's "The Ballad of Halo Jones" (#376, 1984).

44. Q. What do "Borag Thungg" and "Splundig vur thrigg" mean?

A. They're Betelgeusian for "Galactic Greetings" and "Farewell".

45. Q. Who is the only member of the ABC Warriors to lead the team besides Hammerstein? Also, what is the name of his signature weapon, and what does it enable him to do?

A. Khaos magician Deadlock wields the fearsome X-Caliber, with which he can drain the souls of the living to use as psychic nourishment. Tasty! ("ABC Warriors", #119, 1979)

46. Q. What are the six basic settings available to wielders of the Lawgiver MK I?

A. Standard Execution, Heat Seeker, Ricochet, Incendiary, Armour-Piercing and High-Explosive.

47. Q. Following his vengeful attack on the Trans Time Base, where does the Nothosaurus known as Big Hungry end up in

Geoffrey Miller and Massimo Belardinelli's "Flesh: Book II" (#86, 1978)?

A. In modern-day Scotland, where he becomes known as the Loch Ness Monster.

48. Q. Your skin and surface muscular tissue have become transparent. You are the first man to see inside his own body. To see his own bones, heart, lungs and liver! You are unique. You are...?

A. The Visible Man! Created by Pat Mills and Carlos Trigo, the first Visible Man story debuted in Prog 47 (1978).

49. Q. Created by John Wagner and Brian Bolland, how does Psi-Judge Anderson save Mega-City One in her debut adventure, "Judge Death" (#149, 1980)?

A. While possessed by Judge Death, she demands Judge Dredd encase her in the miracle plastic Boing, "forever" trapping the superfiend in her own coma.

50. Q. Released on the short-lived Zarjazz record label in February 1985, what was the name of the Judge Dredd tribute single by The Fink Brothers?

A. "Mutants in Mega-City One". The Fink Brothers were actually Suggs and Chas Smash from two-tone ska band Madness. The single reached #50 in the charts.

Universal Monsters Unleashed!

1. Q. What was Lon Chaney's well-earned nickname?

A. The Man of a Thousand Faces: Rarely did audiences get to see his real one. "My whole career has been devoted," said Chaney, "to keeping people from knowing me."

2. Q. When Bela Lugosi died in 1956, aged 73, at his request he was buried in the cape he wore in 1931's *Dracula*: True or false?

A. False! Although that's what Lugosi's fifth wife and widow Hope Lininger told the press, it was actually Bela's fourth wife, Lillian Arch, and their son Bela Lugosi Jr, who decided to bury him in one of his Dracula capes – but not the one he wore in the 1931 movie. That cape Lillian kept for herself, and when she died in 1981, it passed to Bela Jr who tried to sell it at auction in 2011, but frightened bidders away with a steep $1,200,000 starting price.

3. **Q.** Commonly mistaken for bolts, what items actually protrude from The Monster's (Boris Karloff) neck in *Frankenstein* (1931)?

A. Electrodes.

4. **Q.** Who is the only actor to portray all four of Universal's major monsters: Dracula, Frankenstein's Monster, The Mummy and The Wolf Man?

A. Lon Chaney Jr, who followed *The Wolf Man* (1941) by playing Frankenstein's Monster in *The Ghost of Frankenstein* (1942), Dracula in *Son of Dracula* (1943) and Kharis the Mummy in *The Mummy's Tomb* (1942), *The Mummy's Ghost* (1944) and *The Mummy's Curse* (1944). Though several actors played Dracula, The Mummy and The Monster, no one but Chaney ever played The Wolf Man. "He was my baby," said the star, who played The Wolf Man in the 1941 original, then in *Frankenstein Meets the Wolf Man* (1943), *House of Frankenstein* (1944), *House of Dracula* (1945) and *Abbott and Costello Meet Frankenstein* (1948).

5. **Q.** What side effect of the drug monocane is Dr Jack Griffin (Claude Rains) unaware of when he uses it to create his invisibility formula?

A. Madness! "The drugs I took seemed to light up my brain," says Griffin. "Suddenly I realised the power I held, the power to rule, to make the world grovel at my feet!" (*The Invisible Man*, 1933).

6. **Q.** Eager to drink to his new partnership with Henry Frankenstein (Colin Clive), Doctor Pretorius (Ernest Thesiger) pours them each a gin and makes what memorable toast?

A. "To a new world of gods and monsters!" *Gods and Monsters* was, decades later, the title of Bill Condon's 1998 biopic of *Bride of Frankenstein* (1935) director James Whale.

7. **Q.** Described by *New York Times* film critic Frank S. Nugent as a "charming bit of lycanthropy", what was the world's first feature-length werewolf movie?

A. *Werewolf of London* (1935).

8. **Q.** The poster for which Universal creature feature included the suggestive tagline, "She gives you that weird feeling!"?

A. *Dracula's Daughter* (1936).

9. **Q.** In *The Wolf Man* (1941), while flirting with Gwen (Evelyn Ankers) in her antique shop, what curious item does Larry Talbot (Lon Chaney Jr) purchase for the princely sum of £3?

A. A cane with a silver wolf head handle.

10. **Q.** What was the first Universal horror movie featuring more than one of the studio's classic monsters?

A. *Frankenstein Meets the Wolf Man* (1943): Starring Lon Chaney Jr as The Wolf Man, with Bela Lugosi as The Monster, it established the shared universe of the Universal Monsters and led to many additional all-star team-up flicks.

11. **Q.** What's the name of the boat in *Creature from the Black Lagoon* (1954)?

A. *Rita*.

12. **Q.** Which iconic monster make-up involved the application of fish skin to the actor's nose, and egg membrane to his eyeballs?

A. Both were required to complete Lon Chaney Jr's skull-like visage as, and for, *The Phantom of the Opera* (1925). The undisputed master of early movie make-up techniques,

Chaney's painstaking process and his insistence on absolute secrecy were well documented in these excerpts from a story in Ohio's *Dayton Daily News*, dated October 26, 1924: At no time during the production is his picture, in the make-up of the weird creature he is playing, to be made public. In every scene photographed for publicity or lobby display in which Lon Chaney appears, the face will be "blanked out" by a patch... At no time will any screen actor other than one playing in the picture be allowed on the set to see his make-up – and the actors in the production are pledged to secrecy. No one will see him [apply his] make-up – for Chaney applies his make-up at home and comes to the studio wearing a mask – a molded, flesh-colored affair that is within the law on the public streets, but still conceals his strange disguise from the onlookers. Chaney has experimented for months on the make-up, and does not want the public to see it except in the actual production, when completed and released. "It is not fair to have me experiment, work up a make-up that is really something of an achievement, then spoil the public's appreciation of it by broadcasting pictures of it, so that by the time the picture is released there is no surprise to it."

13. Q. What is the life?

A. "The blood is the life" (*Dracula,* 1931).

14. Q. Who was known as "The Uncanny", and what was his real name?

A. Boris Karloff, whose real name was William Henry Pratt.

15. GUEST STAR Xander Berkeley

Q. Who designed the iconic make-up and prosthetics used in Universal's *Frankenstein* (1931), *The Mummy* (1932) and *The Wolf Man* (1941)?

A. Jack Pierce, who was head of Universal's make-up department in the 1930s and early 1940s. He is now cited as an influence to horror make-up artists everywhere, among them Tom Savini and Rick Baker.

16. Q. For what sacrilege was Imhotep (Boris Karloff) condemned to the Nameless Death, in *The Mummy* (1932)?

A. For attempting to resurrect his forbidden lover, Princess Ankh-es-en-amon (Zita Johann).

17. Q. After seeing *The Invisible Man* (1933), who told director James Whale that while he liked the picture, he had one grave fault to find with it: it had taken the novel's brilliant scientist and changed him into a lunatic – a liberty he could not condone?

A. Author H.G. Wells, whose 1897 novel the movie was based on. Whale defended the change by explaining he'd made the film for the "rationally minded motion picture audience", and that "in the minds of rational people, only a lunatic would want to make himself invisible".

18. Q. What inspired Elsa Lanchester's piercing hiss as the Monster's frightened, scornful bride in 1935's *The Bride of Frankenstein*?

A. The swans in London's Regent's Park. "They're really very nasty creatures," she insisted.

19. Q. What's the name of the striking, iconic rock formation, in northern Los Angeles, that doubled for Tibet in *Werewolves of London* (1935) and was most famously featured in the classic *Star Trek* episode "Arena" (S01E18), where Captain Kirk (William Shatner) battles the fearsome Gorn?

A. Vasquez Rocks: Named after the bandit Tiburcio Vásquez who, in 1874, used the rocks to hide out from the law. Vásquez is also thought to have at least partially inspired author Johnston McCulley's creation of Zorro in 1919.

20. Q. Which Universal frightener marked the launch of Lon Chaney Jr's prolific career as a horror movie star?

A. *Man-Made Monster* (1941), a.k.a. *The Atomic Monster*, *The Electric Man* and *The Mysterious Dr. R.*

21. Q. "Even a man who is pure in heart,
And says his prayers by night...

A. "...May become a Wolf when the Wolfbane blooms,
And the autumn Moon is bright."

This fine, fabricated folklore from writer Curt Siodmak was first featured in *The Wolf Man* (1941), then used in all its sequels, though the final stanza was changed in those to "When the moon is full and bright".

22. Q. What is the only Oscar-winning Universal horror film?

A. *Phantom of the Opera* (1943), which actually won two Academy Awards, for Best Cinematography, Colour and Best Art Direction – Interior Decoration, Colour.

23. Q. "The LAUGHS Are MONSTERous", and "It's SCARE-EWY", teased the trailer for which hit horror comedy?

A. *Abbott and Costello Meet Frankenstein* (1948): "With MORE HOWLS Than You Can Shake a SHIVER At!"

24. Q. Which Universal monster movie did acclaimed art-house filmmaker Ingmar Bergman screen for himself every year as a birthday treat?

A. *Creature from the Black Lagoon* (1954).

25. Q. Whose premature demise led to Bela Lugosi winning the title role in *Dracula* (1931)?

A. Silent screen legend Lon Chaney would have been director Tod Browning's original choice, the two being close friends who'd worked together several times before. Sadly Chaney died in 1930, aged just 47. Bela Lugosi was a reasonable substitute, however, as he'd played Dracula on Broadway in 1927, in the play the film was based on.

26. Q. Though it sneaked past the censor during the film's initial run, which line of dialogue from *Frankenstein* (1931) was later deemed blasphemous and replaced with a loud clap of thunder when the film was re-released in the late 1930s?

A. "Now I know what it's like to BE God!"

27. Q. Though no direct sequels to *The Mummy* (1932) were ever produced, Universal released a quartet of chillers in the 1940s that told terrifying tales of a different Mummy, Kharis, first played by Tom Tyler, then three times in a row by Lon Chaney Jr. What were the titles of those four fearsome films?

A. *The Mummy's Hand* (1940), *The Mummy's Tomb* (1942), *The Mummy's Ghost* (1944) and *The Mummy's Curse* (1944).

28. Q. What varieties of homunculi does Doctor Pretorius (Ernest Thesiger) reveal to Henry (Colin Clive) in *Bride of Frankenstein* (1935)?

A. A queen, king, archbishop, devil, ballerina and mermaid. Though it was largely cut from the movie, a wide shot reveals a seventh tiny person in a jar, a baby in a highchair, played by ten-year-old Billy Barty.

29. Q. What phrase does Baron Wolf von Frankenstein (Basil Rathbone) find scrawled in chalk on his father's sarcophagus in *Son of Frankenstein* (1939)?

A. MAKER OF MONSTERS.

30. GUEST STAR Tony Todd

Q. Who played Universal's terrifying Gill-man in *Creature from the Black Lagoon* (1954) and its two sequels, *Revenge of the Creature* (1955) and *The Creature Walks Among Us* (1956)?

A. Ricou Browning: While other actors portrayed the Gill-man on land, Browning performed virtually all of the creature's underwater sequences. He later co-created *Flipper* (1963) and directed the underwater scenes in Sean Connery Bond movies *Thunderball* (1965) and *Never Say Never Again* (1983).

31. Q. Which classic chiller endured multiple reshoots after the test audience at its initial preview judged it too horrific for release, causing up to 60% of the original film to be scrapped?

A. *The Phantom of the Opera* (1925).

32. Q. What film was shot at night, at the same time and on the same sets as *Dracula* (1931)?

A. A Spanish-language version of the movie, *Drácula* (1931), which ran about a half-hour longer than the English-language version and starred Carlos Villarías in the title role.

33. Q. Insisting he'd been a star in his native Hungary, and had not moved to America to be a "scarecrow", Bela Lugosi rejected which iconic role?

A. Lugosi refused to play The Monster, in *Frankenstein* (1931), primarily as it didn't speak. He later played the role in *Frankenstein Meets the Wolf Man* (1943), in part because, in the film's original shooting script, The Monster speaks. However, Lugosi's dialogue scenes were ultimately all cut from the finished picture.

34. Q. Years before co-writing the screenplay for *The Mummy* (1932), John L. Balderston covered which momentous Egyptian event for the *New York World* newspaper?

A. English archaeologist Howard Carter's 1922 discovery, 1923 opening, and the subsequent excavation of the tomb of King Tutankhamen. It was the alleged Curse of the Pharaohs, triggered by those tomb-raiding shenanigans, that inspired Universal to make *The Mummy*.

35. Q. What's the only time in *The Invisible Man* (1933) that Claude Rains is visible?

A. In the final moments of the movie, on his deathbed, as soon as he snuffs it.

36. Q. What three staples of classic werewolf lore were invented for 1935's *Werewolf of London*?

A. First, that someone who's bitten by a werewolf becomes a werewolf. Prior to the movie, according to legend, folks willingly practised witchcraft to transform into werewolves. Second, that victims are compelled by the full moon to transform into howling monsters. Again, folklore suggests that in days gone by, witches and the like transformed any time they pleased. Finally, that werewolves were wolf/man hybrids, though it's likely this third development was born more from necessity than design as real-life werewolves are hard to come by, and, back in the day, could only be conjured by human beings in furry make-ups.

37. Q. Count Alucard, Baron Latos and Dr Lahos are all names assumed in different movies by which fiendish character?

A. Count Dracula: He poses as Count Alucard (Lon Chaney Jr) in *Son of Dracula* (1943), as Baron Latos (John Carradine) in both *House of Frankenstein* (1944) and *House of Dracula* (1945), and finally as Dr Lahos (Bela Lugosi) in *Abbott and Costello Meet Frankenstein* (1948).

38. Q. Clint Eastwood made his first screen appearance, as lab technician Jennings, in which Universal monster movie?

A. *Revenge of the Creature* (1955).

39. Q. "My mind drifted off, and I thought, 'If one vampire is scary, what if the whole world is full of vampires?'" Which author was inspired by *Dracula* (1931) to write what masterpiece of horror fiction?

A. Richard Matheson was inspired by *Dracula* (1931) to write *I Am Legend* (1954).

40. Q. What's the name of Henry's hunchback assistant in *Frankenstein* (1931)?

A. Not Igor, but Fritz: Played by Dwight Frye, he's strangled by The Monster (Boris Karloff) in *Frankenstein* (1931) after antagonising it with a flaming torch. Frye returned in *Bride of Frankenstein* (1935) to play a hobbling assistant who's neither a hunchback nor called Igor, but Karl, and again is murdered by The Monster, tossed screaming from the battlements of Castle Frankenstein. There's an Ygor in sequels *Son of Frankenstein* (1939) and *The Ghost of Frankenstein* (1942), both times played by Bela Lugosi, but while he does a little light assistant work, he's really more an evil blacksmith and besides, has a lumpy, broken neck, not a hunchback. There was another hunchbacked lab assistant in *House of Frankenstein* (1944), but in that one his name was Daniel (J. Carrol Naish), so again, not Igor. Why then do most people believe Frankenstein's hunchback lab assistant was named Igor? Certainly it's not the book's doing, as Mary Shelley's original novel features neither a hunchbacked lab assistant nor any character named Igor. It seems instead, mysteriously, the name, profession and deformity somehow assembled of its own volition in the collective consciousness, and the misconception was cemented by Mel Brooks' classic parody *Young Frankenstein* (1974), in which finally, a hunchbacked lab assistant name Igor (Marty Feldman) finally appears. Only in that film, of course, his name was pronounced "Eye-gor". Honestly it's enough to turn a brain Abby Normal.

41. Q. What was Boris Karloff's tragic final line as The Monster in *The Bride of Frankenstein* (1935)?

A. "We belong dead." Karloff, though, didn't approve of the decision to give the monster dialogue. "Speech! Stupid! My argument was," he explained, "that if the monster had any impact or charm, it was because he was inarticulate."

42. Q. In *Son of Frankenstein* (1939), what crime was Ygor (Bela Lugosi) hung for, only to survive and swear vengeance on the jurors who sent him to the gallows?

A. Grave robbing.

43. Q. What Universal classic was known as *El Hombre Lobo* in Argentina and O *lykanthropos* (*ο λυκανθρωπος*) in Greek?

A. *The Wolf Man* (1941).

44. Q. How many times did Bela Lugosi play Count Dracula?

A. Just twice: Though it's the role he'll forever be remembered for, besides taking the lead in Universal's original *Dracula* (1931), Lugosi only played the Count one more time, in 1948's *Abbott and Costello Meet Frankenstein.*

45. Q. Which Universal monster was known to The Munsters as Uncle Gilbert, appearing in the episode "Love Comes to Mockingbird Heights" (S01E31)?

A. Gill-man, a.k.a. The Creature from the Black Lagoon, played in *The Munsters* by Richard Hale.

46. Q. Eager to avoid even a whiff of homoeroticism, Universal nixed a sequence in *Dracula* (1931) where The Count (Bela Lugosi) has Renfield (Dwight Frye) for dinner. To clarify the studio's position, a memo was sent to director Tod Browning. What did it say?

A. "Dracula is only to attack women."

47. Q. How is the esteemed author of *Frankenstein; or, The Modern Prometheus* (1818) credited at the beginning of Universal's celebrated 1931 adaptation?

A. Mrs. Percy B. Shelley: Researchers have since unearthed, however, that while the author was indeed married to romantic poet and philosopher Percy Bysshe Shelley, she was also an author and actual person with her own identity called Mary Wollstonecraft Shelley (*Frankenstein*, 1931).

48. Q. What did Boris Karloff describe as "the most trying ordeal I ever endured"?

A. His transformation into The Mummy, an eight-hour torment wrought upon him, not by the Ancient Egyptians, but by make-up wiz Jack Pierce. Cotton, collodion and spirit gum were applied to his face, then clay to his hair, and finally he was swathed in linen bandages that had been treated with acid and burnt in an oven. By 7pm, Karloff was ready to shoot the one scene in the movie where he appears in full Mummy regalia. After filming finished at 2am, Karloff suffered a final two hours of torment as the gum was painfully removed from his face. In all, it was a terrible 21-hour day, but all things considered, totally worth the trouble.

49. Q. The great spell by which Isis raised Osiris from the dead is inscribed on which cursed artefact?

A. The Scroll of Thoth: "Oh! Amon-Ra – Oh! God of Gods – Death is but the doorway to new life – We live today – we shall live again – In many forms shall we return – Oh, Mighty One" (*The Mummy*, 1932).

50. Q. "Certainly, I was typed. But what is typing? It is a trademark, a means by which the public recognises you. Actors work all their lives to achieve that. I got mine with just one picture. It was a blessing." Whose wise words were these, and what film was he talking about?

A. Boris Karloff, who played mostly bit parts in minor movies for more than a decade until his role as The Monster in *Frankenstein* (1931) made him a star overnight. Prior to *Frankenstein*'s release, Karloff was considered so anonymous that he wasn't even invited to the film's premiere. Within a year of its release, however, his fame was so far-reaching that he was often billed simply as Karloff. "My dear old monster," he'd often say. "I owe everything to him. He's my best friend."

Hanna-Barbera: The General Motors of Animation

1. Q. They would have gotten away with it too, if it weren't for what?

A. Those meddling kids! (*Scooby-Doo, Where Are You!* 1969–1970).

2. Q. What was Hanna-Barbera's first original animated television series?

A. *The Ruff and Reddy Show* (1957–1960).

3. Q. What's the song that Huckleberry Hound was so fond of singing, badly but with great enthusiasm?

A. "Oh My Darling, Clementine" (*The Huckleberry Hound Show*, 1958–1961).

4. **Q.** When visiting Jellystone Park, what must you keep your eye on at all times?

A. Your pic-a-nic basket! (*The Yogi Bear Show*, 1961–1962).

5. **Q.** What's playing at the Drive-In Movie featured in *The Flintstones* opening titles?

A. *The Monster* (*The Flintstones*, 1960–1966).

6. **Q.** Whose alter ego was El Kabong, a Zorro type who'd bash bad guys with his guitar?

A. Quick Draw McGraw (*The Quick Draw McGraw Show*, 1959–1962).

7. **Q.** At a charity speaking engagement in London, shortly before his death in 1997, voice actor Don Messick performed many of his most popular Hanna-Barbera characters, yet neglected to perform arguably his most famous, claiming that giving up smoking had robbed him of the rasp he needed to do the voice justice. Which character was he talking about?

A. Scooby-Doo (*Scooby-Doo, Where Are You!* 1969–1970).

8. **Q.** What are the names of the cats in T.C.'s gang?

A. Top Cat's (Arnold Stang) crew was Benny the Ball (Maurice Gosfield), Choo-Choo (Marvin Kaplan), Fancy-Fancy (John Stephenson), Brain and Spook (both voiced by Leo De Lyon) (*Top Cat*, 1961–1962).

9. **Q.** What was Touché Turtle's catchphrase?

A. "Touché away!" (*Touché Turtle and Dum Dum*, 1962–1963).

10. GUEST STAR James Arnold Taylor

Q. Besides Yogi, what do Boo-Boo Bear and Mr Ranger have in common?

A. They were both performed by legendary voice actor Don Messick, who provided the voices for hundreds of characters for Hanna-Barbera, from the very beginning of the company in 1957, alongside voice acting great Daws Butler. Don is most famously known for the lovable Scooby-Doo!

Don was a hero of mine whom I got to work with from his home studio when I was 19 years old. After our session I got up the nerve to call him, after finding his phone number in the phone book, and asked him to breakfast. He spent a couple of hours with me telling me stories of his adventures as a voice actor and was extremely kind...He also picked up the cheque for breakfast. He set the tone for me and my career and while Mel Blanc is more recognised, Don is the quintessential voice-actor in my book. Extremely humble and giving and rarely got accolades for his brilliant work and contribution to the world of animation.

11. Q. What was the first Hanna-Barbera show to win an Emmy?

A. *The Huckleberry Hound Show* (1958–1961) won an Emmy in 1960 for Outstanding Achievement in the Field of Children's Programming. It was the first animated series ever honoured with an Emmy.

12. Q. Wally Gator, Yogi Bear, Captain Caveman, Elroy Jetson and Huckleberry Hound: who's the odd one out?

A. Captain Caveman, as he was voiced by Mel Blanc. All of the others were voiced by Daws Butler.

13. Q. What was Hanna-Barbera's first prime-time animated series?

A. *The Flintstones* (1960–1966).

14. Q. What company employs George Jetson to press a button for an hour a day, two days a week?

A. Spacely Space Sprockets (*The Jetsons* 1962–1963).

15. Q. What was Hanna-Barbera's first action show, an adventure serial with the working title *The Saga of Chip Baloo*?

A. *Jonny Quest* (a.k.a. *The Adventures of Jonny Quest*, 1964–1965).

16. Q. How, in 1957, did Bill Hanna and Joe Barbera decide who'd come first in their new company name?

A. A coin toss!

17. Q. Which one of the vintage comedy legends featured in animated spin-offs *Laurel and Hardy* (1966) and *The Abbott and Costello Cartoon Show* (1967–1968) lived long enough to voice his own character?

A. Bud Abbot voiced himself in *The Abbott and Costello Cartoon Show*, with his longtime partner Lou Costello voiced by nightclub manager and friend of the duo Stan Irwin. Larry Harmon, meanwhile, played Stan, and Jim MacGeorge played Ollie, in Laurel and Hardy.

18. Q. Which three heroes formed Beatlesque superteam *The Impossibles*?

A. Multi-Man (Don Messick), Coil-Man (Hal Smith) and Fluid-Man (Paul Frees) (*Frankenstein Jr. and The Impossibles*, 1966–1968).

19. Q. Of the four fleecy, anthropomorphised animal musicians who formed bubblegum rock quartet The Banana Splits, what was unique about Snorky? Also, what species was he, and what instrument did he play?

A. Snorky was the only member of The Banana Splits not to speak English, communicating instead with honking noises. An elephant, he was on keyboards.

20. Q. What are the names of the Flintstones' pets?

A. Dino is a Snorkasaurus and the main Flintstone pet. Sabre-toothed cat Baby Puss rarely appeared in the show outside of its opening and closing titles (*The Flintstones*, 1960–1966).

21. Q. In the Top Cat episode "Top Cat Falls in Love" (S01E07), what does T.C. do to spend time with Miss LaRue (Jean Vander Pyl), a pretty cat nurse he has a crush on?

A. He pretends to have a rare illness (*Top Cat*, 1961–1962).

22. Q. Which Hanna-Barbera production was the first TV show broadcast in colour on ABC-TV?

A. *The Jetsons* (1962–1963), though in 1962 only 3% of the US public owned colour televisions.

23. Q. Which long-running Eighties' 'toon was based on a comic strip by Belgian cartoonist Pierre "Peyo" Culliford?

A. *The Smurfs* (1981–1989). Peyo's original strip debuted in 1958 in the Belgian magazine *Spirou*.

24. Q. Who never won a single Wacky Race and what was their atrocious auto?

A. Dick Dastardly (Paul Winchell) and Muttley (Don Messick), who drove The Mean Machine (*Wacky Races*, 1968–1969).

25. GUEST STAR Brad Meltzer

Q. What were the three team names in the Laff-a-Lympics?

A. The Yogi Yahooeys, The Scooby Doobies and The Really Rottens: Still the best underrated show for giant team-ups all owned by the same company (*Laff-A-Lympics*, 1977–1978).

26. Q. What vintage sitcom inspired Hanna-Barbera's *Top Cat* (1961–1962). Also, which actor appeared in both shows?

A. Key among *Top Cat*'s inspirations was *The Phil Silvers Show* (1955–1959), a hilarious military sitcom starring Silvers as scheming Master Sergeant Ernest G. Bilko. Maurice Gosfield, who played the gloriously dopey Private Duane Doberman opposite Silvers, also voiced, and resembled, *Top Cat*'s Benny the Ball.

27. Q. Who is the adopted son of Dr Benton Quest?

A. Hadji (Danny Bravo), an 11-year-old orphan from the streets of Calcutta with mystical powers and mad Judo skills (*Jonny Quest*, 1964–1965).

28. Q. What were Clyde, Dum Dum, Pockets, Snoozy, Softy, Yak Yak and Zippy collectively known as, and which two shows did they feature in?

A. The Ant Hill Mob starred first in *Wacky Races* (1968–1969) and later in spin-off series *The Perils of Penelope Pitstop* (1969–1970).

29. Q. What inspired CBS's head of daytime programming, Fred Silverman, to christen Hanna-Barbera's Greatest Dane, Scooby-Doo?

A. A scat vocal at the end of Frank Sinatra's 1966 hit, *Strangers in the Night*. Frank sang 'doo-be-doo-be-doo' and Fred, on his way to a development meeting, had a bright idea (*Scooby-Doo, Where Are You!* 1969–1970).

30. Q. In the first episode of which series does Melody Valentine (Jackie Joseph/Cherie Moor) adopt Bleep, a fluffy, pink-limbed alien who makes bleep sounds only she can understand, and generates invisible sound waves from its mouth and eyes?

A. *Josie and the Pussycats in Outer Space* (1972).

31. Q. Who's got style, a groovy style, and a car that just won't stop?

A. *Hong Kong Phooey* (1974).

32. Q. Why did the BBC rename *Top Cat* a month into the show's 1962 UK TV debut, and what did they call it instead?

A. As there was a popular British brand of cat food at the time called Top Cat, rather than run the risk of inadvertently promoting a product on the ad-free channel, the BBC renamed the series *The Boss Cat*, and later, simply, *Boss Cat* (*Top Cat*, 1961–1962).

33. Q. What was unusual about the tandem motorbike ridden by the Hair Bear Bunch?

A. It was invisible (*Help!...It's the Hair Bear Bunch!* 1971–1972).

34. Q. Superman, Wonder Woman, Aquaman, Batman and Robin assembled in 1973 to form which team for Hanna-Barbera?

A. Super Friends.

35. Q. Barney Rubble was voiced by Mel Blanc for all but five episodes of *The Flintstones* (1960–1966). Who covered for him while he was absent, and what was the extraordinary story behind his sooner-than-expected return to work?

A. Daws Butler covered for Blanc while the legendary voice actor was recovering from a near-fatal car accident in 1961. Though he was in a full body cast for much of the series' second season, and obviously couldn't get into the studio to record his lines, Blanc was a trooper, so Joe Barbera set up a temporary recording studio for the entire cast by his bedside, first in the hospital and later at his home. Often as many as 16 people would squeeze into the room for a group recording, with Blanc laid flat on his back.

36. Q. How old is Captain Cavemen?

A. Captain Cavemen (Mel Blanc) is approximately 2 million years old (*Captain Caveman and the Teen Angels*, 1977–1980).

37. Q. Who voiced Frankenstein Jr, Meteor Man and Godzilla for Hanna-Barbera?

A. Ted Cassidy, who also voiced his most famous live-action character, Lurch, in Hanna-Barbera's animated adaptation of *The Addams Family* (1973).

38. Q. "The problem with the show was simply this: When they start telling you in Standards and Practices, 'Don't shoot any flame at anybody, don't step on any buildings or cars,' then pretty soon, they've taken away all the stuff he represents." What show is Joe Barbera describing here?

A. *Godzilla* (1978–1979).

39. Q. What are the full names of those four meddling teens and their cowardly Great Dane?

A. Frederick Herman Jones, Daphne Blake, Velma Dinkley, Norville "Shaggy" Rogers and Scoobert "Scooby" Doo (*Scooby-Doo, Where Are You!* 1969–1970).

40. GUEST STAR Eric Lewald

Q. In the mid-1980s, Hanna-Barbera had their own hit transforming-vehicles action series that was NOT called Transformers. What was its full name and who were its lead hero and villain?

A. *Challenge of the GoBots* (1984–1985), starring good guy and head Guardian LEADER-1 (Lou Richards, Jr) versus leader of the Renegades, CY-KILL (Bernard Erhard).

41. Q. Which classic 'toon antagonist was known as Sharshabeel in Arabic, Drakoumel in Greek and Lão Gà Mên in Vietnamese?

A. The evil wizard Gargamel (Paul Winchell) in *The Smurfs* (1981–1989).

42. Q. The appearance of which recurring character, during the final season of *The Flintstones* (1960–1966), is considered by many fans to be the series' shark-jumping moment?

A. The Great Gazoo, an alien from the future voiced by Harvey Korman.

43. Q. Who did Dastardly and Muttley spend weeks on end fruitlessly trying to nab, jab, tab and/or grab?

A. Yankee Doodle Pigeon (*Dastardly and Muttley in Their Flying Machines*, 1969–1970).

44. Q. Larry, Curly and Moe with bionic powers, fighting crime in superhero show *The Robonic Stooges*. Was that really a thing?

A. Indeed it was, and it lasted two seasons (1977–1978).

45. Q. Which super-powered sidekicks joined DC's finest in *The All-New Super Friends Hour*, and what were their abilities?

A. Shape-shifting extra-terrestrials The Wonder Twins were a brother and sister superhero duo with a Space Monkey pet named Gleek. Jayna (Liberty Williams) could transform into any animal, both real and mythological, while Zan (Michael Bell) could transform into any state of water, from ice to liquid nitrogen. "Wonder Twin powers, activate!" (*The All-New Super Friends Hour*, 1977–1978).

46. Q. Where does mild-mannered janitor Penrod "Penry" Pooch transform into his fan-riffic alter-ego?

A. Penrod jumps into the bottom drawer of the police station's filing cabinet and emerges from the top drawer as Hong Kong Phooey (Scatman Crothers), number one super guy (*Hong Kong Phooey*, 1974).

47. Q. Which troubled superstar gave Joe Barbera an autographed photo of himself with the inscription, "To my hero of yesterday, today, and tomorrow, with many thanks for all the many cartoon friends you gave me as a child. They were all I had."

A. Michael Jackson.

48. Q. Who was born in St Bernard's Memorial Hospital to Scooby's sister, Ruby-Doo?

A. Scrappy-Doo (*Scooby-Doo and Scrappy-Doo*, 1980–1982).

49. Q. Which three *Happy Days* (1974–1984) castmates reunited for time-travelling spin-off 'toon *The Fonz and the Happy Days Gang* (1980–1982)?

A. Though Ron Howard (Richie Cunningham) and Donny Most (Ralph Malph) left the live-action show in 1980, returning only occasionally for special episodes, they starred in Hanna-Barbera's wacky spin-off with Henry Winkler (The Fonz).

50. Q. What phrase would Bez the Beast (Henry Corden) have to incant if he wanted to shapeshift into, say, an elephant, in *Arabian Knights* (1968–1969)?

A. "Size of an elephant!"

Steven Spielberg: *Jaws* to *Jurassic Park*

1. Q. You yell shark and what?

A. "We've got a panic on our hands on the Fourth of July" (*Jaws*, 1975).

2. Q. Shaving cream, mud, sand, clay, mashed potato: what's the odd one out?

A. Sand: Everything else is used by Roy (Richard Dreyfuss) to make Devils Tower sculptures in *Close Encounters of the Third Kind* (1977).

3. Q. *1941* (1979) opens with a parody of which classic monster movie?

A. Spielberg's own *Jaws* (1975): Actress Susan Backlinie, who played poor, doomed Chrissie in *Jaws*, parodied her iconic role by playing the girl whose frosty early morning skinny dip in *1941* (1979) is rudely interrupted by Mitamura's (Toshirô Mifune) surfacing sub.

4. Q. What is packed in Top Secret Army Intelligence crate #9906753?

A. The Ark of the Covenant.

5. Q. In *E.T. The Extra-Terrestrial* (1982), what does Elliott (Henry Thomas) use to lure E.T. back to his house?

A. A breadcrumb-like trail of Reese's Pieces. Spielberg originally wanted to use M&Ms, but Mars turned him down as they felt E.T. was so ugly, he'd frighten children away from their products. Ultimately the opposite proved true, with sales of Reese's Pieces going through the roof.

6. Q. What delicacies are served at the infamous feast of Pankot Palace in *Indiana Jones and the Temple of Doom* (1984)?

A. Snake Surprise, Giant Beetles, Eyeball Soup and, of course, Chilled Monkey Brains.

7. Q. What scares Professor Henry Walton Jones Sr (Sean Connery)?

A. Rats (*Indiana Jones and the Last Crusade*, 1989).

8. Q. What is the first dinosaur that Hammond's (Richard Attenborough) visitors see in *Jurassic Park* (1993)?

A. A towering Brachiosaurus.

9. Q. The first film to make over $100 million at the box office, *Jaws* (1975) was crowned the highest-grossing film of all time, holding the title until which film snatched it away?

A. *Star Wars* (1977).

10. Q. I wanted the aliens to look like aliens," said Steven Spielberg of *Close Encounters of the Third Kind*'s (1977) design process. "I did not want the aliens to look like people in costumes." To that end, what was Spielberg's first, frankly crazy, idea for portraying visitors from outer space?

A. Picture, if you will, an orangutan in an alien costume, wearing roller skates: "My first idea was to get an orangutan," explained Spielberg, "and dress the orangutan up in an E.T. suit, and let the orangutan behave almost simian-like. So we dressed this orangutan up in a spandex body suit, with a head on, and I also thought it would be interesting to put him on roller skates and push him off a Mylar ramp, so he'd come down like he's floating. Well, it all went wrong. We had a couple of cameras set up for the test and the first image was, you saw the handler bringing out the orangutan, then the orangutan running back and jumping into the handler's arms. You'd see the orangutan pushed out by human hands, and the minute the guy would let go, the orangutan would turn and grab hold of his hands, then climb up his body." The one time they managed to get the orangutan down the ramp, it panicked, pulled off its mask and rolled down backwards. "I realised," concluded Spielberg, "that that wasn't going to work."

11. Q. Where are Claude (Murray Hamilton) and Herbie (Eddie Deezen) stationed on watch in *1941* (1979)?

A. At the top of the Ocean Amusement Park's ferris wheel.

12. Q. What does the student in Indy's classroom have written on her eyelids in *Raiders of the Lost Ark* (1981)?

A. LOVE you.

13. Q. When are the first three Indiana Jones movies set?

A. *Raiders of the Lost Ark* (1981) is set in 1936. *Indiana Jones and the Temple of Doom* (1984) is a prequel set in 1935. *Indiana Jones and the Last Crusade* (1989) opens with a flashback set in 1912, before skipping ahead to 1938.

14. Q. How did Henry (Sean Connery) know Ilsa (Alison Doody) was a Nazi in *Indiana Jones and the Last Crusade* (1989)?

A. She talks in her sleep.

15. **GUEST STAR Jerry Ordway**

Q. What's the connection between Nick Fury and Indiana Jones?

A. Artist and writer Jim Steranko, who pushed the boundaries of the Comic Code with his ground-breaking work on Marvel's *Nick Fury, Agent of S.H.I.E.L.D.* (1966–1968), and created pulp-style conceptual art for *Raiders of the Lost Ark* (1981), helping to design and define the character of Indiana Jones.

16. Q. Which John Williams score did Spielberg insist was "clearly responsible for half the success of that movie"?

A. *Jaws* (1975): Williams himself described his score as "grinding away at you, just as a shark would do, instinctual, relentless, unstoppable".

17. Q. What are close encounters of the first, second and third kinds?

A. First is sighting a UFO. Second is physical evidence. Third is contact. J. Allen Hynek, the famous ufologist who coined these terms in his book *The UFO Experience: A Scientific*

Study (1972), appears in *Close Encounters of the Third Kind* (1977) as the grey-haired man with glasses, pipe and a pointy beard who waits to greet the returnees at the end of the movie.

18. Q. "Can't it just beam up?"

A. "This is reality, Greg" (*E.T. The Extra-Terrestrial*, 1982).

19. Q. Before conspiring with the Nazis in *Indiana Jones and the Last Crusade* (1989), actors Julian Glover (who played Walter Donovan) and Michael Sheard (who played Adolf Hitler) served which other evil army?

A. The Empire! Glover played General Veers and Sheard played Admiral Ozzel in *The Empire Strikes Back* (1980).

20. Q. What is Alan Grant's (Sam Neill) first line in *Jurassic Park* (1993)?

A. "I hate computers."

21. Q. Which Spielberg movie holds the record for longest theatrical run?

A. *E.T. The Extra-Terrestrial* (1982), which screened in cinemas for over a year.

22. Q. What, according to Hammond (Richard Attenborough), does Malcolm (Jeff Goldblum) suffer from?

A. "A deplorable excess of personality – especially for a mathematician."

23. Q. What does Hooper (Richard Dreyfuss) pull out of the tiger shark that he cuts open in *Jaws* (1975)?

A. A whole fish, a fish head, a tin can and a number plate.

24. Q. When Roy (Richard Dreyfuss) boards the Mothership at the end of *Close Encounters of the Third Kind* (1977), John Williams' soaring score references what Oscar-winning song from which vintage Disney classic?

A. *When You Wish Upon a Star*, from *Pinocchio* (1940): Music by Leigh Harline and lyrics by Ned Washington.

25. Q. Where do Loomis (Tim Matheson) and Donna (Nancy Allen) crash land in *1941* (1979)?

A. The La Brea Tar Pits, in Los Angeles, California.

26. Q. How does Indy (Harrison Ford) respond to Marion's (Karen Allen) observation that he's not the man she knew ten years ago?

A. "It's not the years, honey. It's the mileage." Apparently the line in *Raiders of the Lost Ark* (1981) was ad-libbed by Harrison Ford.

27. Q. What does E.T. dress as to sneak out of the house during All Hallows' Eve?

A. A ghost (*E.T. The Extra-Terrestrial*, 1982).

28. Q. Which three characters in *Indiana Jones and the Temple of Doom* (1984) were named after the filmmaker's dogs?

A. Indiana was named after George Lucas' dog, Short Round was named after screenwriters' Willard Huyck and Gloria Katz's dog, and Willie was named after Steven Spielberg's dog.

29. Q. What make of gun does Donovan (Julian Glover) shoot Henry (Sean Connery) with in *Indiana Jones and the Last Crusade* (1989)?

A. A Walther PPK: the same gun Connery carried as Bond in the film franchise that inspired the Indiana Jones series.

30. GUEST STAR Ed Solomon

Q. What was the on-set nickname of the shark in *Jaws* (1975)?

A. Bruce: named after Steven Spielberg's lawyer, Bruce Raymer.

31. Q. What's the first toy that activates in Barry's (Cary Guffey) bedroom when the aliens visit his house?

A. A cymbal-playing monkey.

32. Q. According to Jack Nicholson, what did Stanley Kubrick say to Steven Spielberg about *1941* (1979)?

A. That it was "great, but not funny". He also suggested the film should have been marketed as a drama, not a comedy.

33. Q. Who was famously offered the role of Indiana Jones in *Raiders of the Lost Ark* (1981), but forced to turn it down due to a prior commitment?

A. Tom Selleck: That prior commitment being the first season of his smash-hit TV show *Magnum, P.I.* (1980–1988), though as it turned out, season one didn't start shooting until after Raiders wrapped, so Selleck could have done both.

34. Q. What song does famous American female vocalist Willie Scott (Kate Capshaw) sing, mostly in Mandarin, during *Indiana Jones and the Temple of Doom*'s (1984) sparkling opening credits?

A. *Anything Goes*, originally written by Cole Porter for the 1934 musical of the same name.

35. Q. What do Quint (Robert Shaw) and Hooper (Richard Dreyfuss) toast to, in *Jaws* (1975)?

A. Their legs.

36. Q. Following a demonstration in which Dennis Muren proved that full-body dinosaur effects for *Jurassic Park* (1993) could be achieved digitally, what did creature designer and go motion pioneer Phil Tippett whisper to Steven Spielberg?

A. "I think we're extinct." Spielberg liked the line so much, he worked it into the screenplay. "We're out of a job," says Grant (Sam Neill) at the Visitor Centre. Quips Malcolm (Jeff Goldblum), "Don't you mean extinct?"

37. Q. Why did wee Cary Guffey, who played adorable Barry Guiler in *Close Encounters of the Third Kind* (1977), find the scene where he exits the Mothership embarrassing to shoot?

A. Because, to prevent him from slipping on the ramp, he was forced to wear ballet shoes.

38. Q. When it seemed Spielberg's career might be a casualty of the relative failure of *1941* (1979), John Belushi took to wearing a t-shirt bearing what hilariously spiteful message?

A. "Steven Spielberg 1946–1941"

39. Q. Whose signature stunt inspired the memorable moment in *Raiders of the Lost Ark* (1981) where Indy (played by stuntman Terry Leonard, doubling for Harrison Ford) drops from the front of a German transport truck and is dragged underneath, between the wheels?

A. Yakima Canutt: Although his version of the stunt, first performed in *Riders of the Dawn* (1937), then more famously in John Ford's *Stagecoach* (1939), saw him dart between the legs of six charging horses, then the wheels of a stagecoach.

40. Q. In *Jurassic Park* (1993), what is the girl on Nedry's (Wayne Knight) computer wallpaper wearing?

A. A zebra-print bikini.

41. Q. What are E.T.'s final words to Gertie (Drew Barrymore), Michael (Robert MacNaughton) and Elliott (Henry Thomas) in *E.T. The Extra-Terrestrial* (1982)?

A. E.T. says "Be good" to Gertie, "Thank you" to Michael and "I'll be right here" to Elliott.

42. Q. Besides Harrison Ford, who's the only actor to appear in each of the first three Indiana Jones films?

A. Former wrestler and veteran big screen bruiser Pat Roach. In *Raiders of the Lost Ark* (1981) he played the giant sherpa who tackles Indy in Marion's bar, and later, the bald, boxing mechanic who's shredded by the Flying Wing's propeller. In *Indiana Jones and the Temple of Doom* (1984), Roach played the giant, bearded Thuggee who's mashed in the rock crusher, and finally, in *Indiana Jones and the Last Crusade* (1989), he appeared as a Gestapo officer, though his role was reduced to a cameo after his fight scene was cut.

43. Q. What do you call a blind dinosaur's dog?

A. Do-you-think-he-saurus Rex (*Jurassic Park* 1993).

44. Q. What's the name of Quint's (Robert Shaw) boat in *Jaws* (1975)?

A. *Orca*: Killer whales, also known as orcas, are the only known predators of great white sharks.

45. Q. Which celebrated fantasy author declared that *Close Encounters of the Third Kind* (1977) was the greatest science fiction film ever made?

A. Ray Bradbury

46. Q. What film does General Stilwell (Robert Stack) insist on seeing in *1941* (1979)?

A. Walt Disney's *Dumbo* (1941).

47. Q. What happens to Belloq (Paul Freeman), Toht (Ronald Lacey) and Dietrich's (Wolf Kahler) heads during the climactic Ark-opening sequence in *Raiders of the Lost Ark* (1981)?

A. Dietrich's head implodes, Toht's head melts and Belloq's head explodes.

48. Q. "X never, ever…"?

A. "…marks the spot!" Except when it does (*Indiana Jones and the Last Crusade*, 1989).

49. Q. Which of Spielberg's monster movies has a higher human body count: *Jaws* (1975) or *Jurassic Park* (1993)?

A. Trick question – it's a tie! *Jaws* has five kills (Chrissie Watkins, Alex Kintner, Ben Gardner, "Estuary Victim" and, of course, Quint), as does *Jurassic Park* ("Worker in Raptor Pen", Donald Gennaro, Dennis Nedry, Ray Arnold and Robert "Clever Girl" Muldoon).

50. Q. In *Raiders of the Lost Ark* (1981), who does Major Eaton (William Hootkins) insist will be researching the unspeakable power of the new-found Ark?

A. Top. Men.

Batman: The Animated Series

1. Q. Although "On Leather Wings" (S01E02) was the first produced episode of *Batman: The Animated Series*, what was the first episode that actually aired?

   A. "The Cat and the Claw Part I" (S01E01), which premiered on September 5, 1992. For the record, the S0/E0 designations assigned to each episode in this chapter reflect the order in which they originally aired.

2. Q. What does The Joker (Mark Hamill) ask of Charlie (Ed Begley Jr) in "Joker's Favor" (S01E07)?

   A. To open a door.

3. Q. What colour are Pamela Isley's eyes?

   A. What else could Poison Ivy's (Diane Pershing) eyes be but green?

4. Q. What links The Bookworm, from *Batman* (1966–1968), to The Mad Hatter, from *Batman: The Animated Series*?

   A. Roddy McDowall, who played both roles.

5. Q. What has kept Ra's Al Ghul (David Warner) alive for 600 years?

   A. The Lazarus Pit ("The Demon's Quest", S01E57/58).

6. Q. In "Harley and Ivy" (S01E47), after Poison Ivy (Diane Pershing) boasts that "No man can take us prisoner", who, then, does?

   A. Officer Renée Montoya, GCPD (Ingrid Oliu).

7. Q. Eager to understand how he'd earned the role of The Joker, Mark Hamill approached casting director Andrea Romano. "I asked [her], 'How did I get it? How did you know you wanted me?'" What did she tell him?

   A. "The laugh." It was a laugh Hamill refined playing Mozart in *Amadeus*, during its first national tour, and later on Broadway, in 1983. "Mozart had this ghastly laugh that threw everybody. I played with it a lot," says the actor. "I'd do a little Dwight Frye. I'd do a little Sydney Greenstreet. Sometimes I'd get notes like, 'It was a little too Jerry Lewis at the matinée. Reel it back.'"

8. Q. In "The Cat and the Claw Part I" (S01E01), when Catwoman (Adrienne Barbeau) says to Batman, "You can't deny there's something between us," how does he respond?

A. "You're right, and I'm afraid it's the law."

9. Q. Who was Bruce Wayne's boyhood TV hero?

A. The Gray Ghost – and he still is! Voiced, of course, by Adam West, who as Batman in the iconic 1966–1968 show became everyone's childhood TV hero ("Beware the Gray Ghost", S01E32).

10. GUEST STAR Paul Dini

Q. How did sadistic Arkham guard Lyle Bolton (a.k.a. Lock Up, voiced by Bruce Weitz) torture Scarface (George Dzundza)?

A. He held him over a can filled with termites ("Lock-Up", S03E09).

11. Q. Using dark paper instead of white to lay down their moody art deco backgrounds, artists Eric Radomski and Ted Blackman refined a style dubbed what, by storyboard artist Bruce Timm?

A. Dark Deco.

12. Q. *Batman: The Animated Series* features a much older Robin than in the comicbooks. Voiced by Loren Lester, Dick Grayson's about 20 years old in the cartoon. This was partly because the creators of the show didn't want him around all the time, a constant sidekick who'd "diminish Batman's role", says Paul Dini, "as a brooding, solitary hero". However, there was another key reason why Robin couldn't be a kid in the series. Any idea what that was?

A. Strict rules laid down by the censor, zealously enforced by the Fox Kids network, prohibiting the depiction of child endangerment. Blood, open wounds, strangulation, smoking, drugs, nudity and religion were also off the table.

13. Q. Which actress and former classmate of writer Paul Dini inspired the creation of Harley Quinn, originally intended as a one-time character in "Joker's Favor" (S01E07), but now a staple of Batman's comicbook and live-action universe as well?

A. Arleen Sorkin: Apparently Dini was inspired by a dream sequence from the soap opera *Days of Our Lives* in which Sorkin wore a harlequin's costume, later factoring in aspects of the actress's personality when writing the role. All of which made it super-appropriate that Sorkin was eventually cast to voice Harley, the final, perfect puzzle piece in the creation of a fan-favourite character.

14. Q. In "Pretty Poison" (S01E09), District Attorney Harvey Dent (Richard Moll) is sentenced to death by Poison Ivy (Diane Pershing) for committing what terrible crime?

A. For "murdering" a field of beautiful flowers, ploughing the Wild Thorny Rose to near-extinction, to build a "silly penitentiary".

15. Q. During the casting process for *Batman: The Animated Series*, which actor originally set his sights on playing The Joker, Jim Gordon or Harvey Bullock?

A. Kevin Conroy, who "settled" for Batman after casting director Andrea Romano pulled him aside and said, "Don't you get it? It's called Batman. You would be in every episode! This is the role you should want!"

16. Q. How much is the contract that crime boss Rupert Thorne (John Vernon) puts on Two-Face in "Two-Face Part II" (S01E18)?

A. $2 million – "A million dollars a face for the man who brings me Two-Face!"

17. Q. While masquerading as Jekko the Clown, who does The Joker (Mark Hamill) identify as his mentor?

A. The Great Proscuitto: "Now *there* was a ham!" ("Be a Clown", S01E11).

18. Q. "Setting the look and tone for all that was to come," says Paul Dini, the dramatic, two-minute 'toon that sold the studio on *Batman: The Animated Series* saw the Caped Crusader interrupt a daring rooftop heist. How was that specific scene later repurposed for the series?

A. The show's original opening sequence was essentially a remake of that vital, in-house pilot.

19. Q. What is the name of the ancient, forbidden martial art detailed in "Day of the Samurai" (S01E55) that is so efficient and terrible, a mere touch can render a man unconscious, or cripple him, or even kill him?

A. The Way of the Fang.

20. Q. Which staple of the Batcave's décor features in Two-Face's "Almost Got 'Im" (S01E35) tale?

A. The giant penny: Lashed to the oversized prop and flipped through the air, Batman cuts himself free with Two-Face's two-headed coin, saves himself, and then the day.

"So Harvey," asks Ivy, "what became of the giant penny?" "They actually let him keep it," he responds, outraged.

21. Q. Created by Alex Toth for Hanna-Barbera in 1966, which superhero's iconic suit design was appropriated by Bruce Timm for Batman?

A. Space Ghost: "Though limited in detail," wrote Paul Dini in Titan Books' *Batman: Animated* (1998), "Space Ghost still radiates presence and power, and a generation of animators embraced Alex Toth's creation as the last word in superhero design."

22. Q. How many roles did Kevin Conroy voice in his personal favourite episode of *Batman: The Animated Series*, "Perchance to Dream" (S01E26)?

A. Four: Batman, Evil Batman, Bruce Wayne and Thomas Wayne.

23. Q. Who presides over Arkham's kangaroo court of Batman, where the Caped Crusader (Kevin Conroy) stands accused of turning the assembled "freaks and monsters" to lives of crime?

A. The most honourable, most benevolent, most merciful Judge Joker (Mark Hamill) ("Trial", S02E09).

24. Q. What's Baby-Doll's (Alison La Placa) catchphrase, originally uttered with great frequency in her dreadful sitcom *Love That Baby*?

A. "I didn't mean to!" ("Baby-Doll", S03E04).

25. GUEST STAR Patrick Savage

Q. Pioneering composer Shirley Walker's much-loved score for *Batman: The Animated Series* was crafted to seamlessly incorporate Danny Elfman's 1989 Batman movie theme. Which earlier DC TV show, also with an Elfman theme, did Walker likewise score?

A. *The Flash* (1990–1991).

26. Q. Which episode of *Batman: The Animated Series* won a Primetime Emmy for Outstanding Animated Program (one hour or less)?

A. "Robin's Reckoning Part I" (S01E51).

27. Q. What's the name of the hit game Edward Nygma (John Glover) created for Competitron?

A. Riddle of the Minotaur ("If You're So Smart, Why Aren't You Rich?", S01E41).

28. Q. Rather than record each role separately, which is the norm for voice-over work, the cast of *Batman: The Animated Series* recorded their work as an ensemble, all of them sitting in the same room, at the same time, performing together. One of the actors, though, was permitted to stand. Which one, and why?

A. Mark Hamill, as he found it easier to imbue The Joker with the frantic energy the role required if he was free to stand and fully let rip.

29. Q. After the first season of *Batman: The Animated Series*, what key change did Fox Kids demand be made to the show?

A. That Robin (Loren Lester) appear in every episode.

30. Q. What are the full, real names of the villains Roxy Rocket (Charity James), The Clock King (Alan Rachins), Baby-Doll (Alison LaPlaca) and The Ventriloquist (George Dzunda)?

A. Roxy Rocket is Roxanne Sutton, Baby-Doll is Mary Louise Dahl, The Clock King is Temple Fugate and The Ventriloquist, a.k.a. Scarface, is Arnold Wesker.

31. Q. Before Richard Moll won the part, which iconic Hollywood Oscar-winner was approached to play Two-Face?

A. Al Pacino.

32. Q. How does The Joker escape Arkham Asylum in "Christmas with the Joker" (S01E38)?

A. On a rocket-powered Christmas tree, of course!

"Crashing through the roof,
On a one-horse open tree,
Busting out I go,
Laughing all the wheeeeeee!"

33. Q. Which supervillain, introduced as Mr Zero in Batman #121 (February 1959), was dramatically reinterpreted for *Batman: The Animated Series*, transforming him from a gimmicky mad scientist into a far more complex and tragic character whose "frigid exterior [hid] a doomed love and vindictive fury"?

A. Mr Freeze (Michael Ansara).

34. Q. Before Harvey Dent's (Richard Moll) explosive transformation in "Two-Face Part 1" (S01E17), writer/producer Alan Burnett broke new ground for the character by establishing he already had a dual personality. What does Harvey's shrink call his dark, hidden half?

A. Big Bad Harv.

35. Q. What's Harley's (Arleen Sorkin) nickname for The Joker (Mark Hamill)?

A. Puddin'.

36. Q. Until the series was rebranded *The Adventures of Batman & Robin*, what was unusual about the show's original title sequence?

A. There was no title! Everyone, everywhere, recognised Batman, so there was simply no need to use his name anywhere.

37. Q. Which member of *Batman: The Animated Series*' voice cast was its biggest comicbook geek, destined from birth to join the cast, it seems, as the name of Gotham's gloriously gothic asylum is literally hidden within his name?

A. mARK HAMill.

38. Q. At what point in "Perchance to Dream" (S01E26) are Bruce Wayne's suspicions that's he's dreaming confirmed?

A. When he tries to read a newspaper: "The print didn't make sense," he explains. "That's because reading is a function of the right side of the brain, while dreams come from the left side. It's impossible to read something in a dream."

39. Q. Under what lame pseudonym did a young Bruce Wayne (Kevin Conroy) learn escape artistry from Zatara the Magician (Vincent Schiavelli)?

A. John Smith ("Zatanna", S01E50).

40. GUEST STAR Stefan Blitz

Q. Who originally voiced The Joker, though none of his recordings were used?

A. Tim Curry: Officially, he was deemed too scary for the role, mirroring his performance as Pennywise the Clown in 1990 mini-series *It*. Curry, however, maintains he was fired, simply for having bronchitis.

41. Q. Disfigured in an accident, over-the-hill actor Matt Hagen (Ron Perlman) becomes addicted to what experimental compound that, though initially it restores his youthful good looks, eventually transforms him into lumpen shapeshifter Clayface?

A. RenuYu ("Feat of Clay", S01E04/05).

42. Q. Hailed by Paul Dini as "a high point of each episode", what element from *Batman: The Animated Series* was largely the domain of Eric Radomski, described by the artist as a way to "create great drama in a very subtle fashion" and capture the overall feel of every show?

A. The title cards: "Going with the overall retro-Forties feel we were giving the show," said Radomski, "we wanted to treat the episodes as mini-movies. The title cards allowed us to create great drama in a very subtle fashion."

43. Q. Who originally voiced Alfred Pennyworth, leaving after just three episodes to honour a stage commitment?

A. Kiwi actor Clive Revill, who voiced the holographic Emperor in the original theatrical version of *The Empire Strikes Back* (1980) and, in *Star Trek: The Next Generation* (1987–1994), played Sir Guy of Gisbourne in fan-favourite episode "Qpid" (S04E20).

44. Q. With what unusual vehicle does Lloyd Ventrix (Michael Gross) attempt to squish Batman (Kevin Conroy) in "See No Evil" (S01E56)?

A. An invisible car.

45. Q. How much does The Joker (Mark Hamill) bid for the atom bomb up for auction in "Harlequinade" (S02E10)?

A. "How about nothing? Zero, zip, zilch, nada. My personal cheque for bupkis drawn on the First National Bank of Squadoo."

46. Q. What's most notable about DC's *The Batman Adventures* #12 ("Batgirl: Day One", September 1993)?

A. It marked the first comicbook appearance of Harley Quinn.

47. Q. Which cracking two-part episode of *Batman: The Animated Series* was a direct adaptation of "Daughter of the Demon" (Batman #232, June 1971) and "The Demon Lives Again" (Batman #244, September 1972), both by writer Denny O'Neil and artist Neal Adams?

A. "The Demon's Quest" (S01E57/58): O'Neil actually wrote the script for Part I.

48. Q. What's the first line spoken in "The Clock King" (S01E14)?

A. "It's about time."

49. Q. What's the name of Catwoman's (Adrienne Barbeau) favourite cat?

A. Isis.

50. Q. In "The Man Who Killed Batman" (S01E49), what tune does Harley (Arleen Sorkin) play on her kazoo while Sid the Squid's (Matt Frewer) coffin rolls down the conveyor belt, into the acid?

A. "Amazing Grace", most likely as a parody of Spock's (Leonard Nimoy) send-off in *Star Trek II: The Wrath of Khan* (1982).

Acknowledgements

Writing this book took dialling my crazy way up to eleven. For their love, support, encouragement and, above all else, patience, I am forever indebted to my wife, Ruta, and daughters Martyna, Maia and Phoebe. I'm not sure I can reverse the crazy, but for your sakes, I'll try. Maybe I can get it down to an eight.

To my publisher Hannah, who helped me arrive at the idea for this book, thanks for taking the time to do that, also for your faith, guidance and encouragement.

For your wondrous art, Steve, and for always pitching in, I declare you the most excellent, stand-up dude.

Mike, when I grow up, I want to be you. Thanks for all the laughs, for your generosity, and your fabulous foreword.

To my three amigos, Ronald, JK and Sal: I owe you each a Coke.

To my Fantastic Fifty Guest Stars, who took the time to indulge this nerd's mad dream, I'm overwhelmed by your generosity: Howard Berger, Xander Berkeley, Sanjeev Bhaskar, Stefan Blitz, Dave Bossert, Neil Brand, Clancy Brown, Rob Bruce, Bonnie Burton, James Callis, John Carpenter, Steve Casino, Don Coscarelli, Dominik Diamond, Paul Dini, Jeremy Dyson, Ron Fogelman, Mark Hamill, Carrie Henn, Joel Hodgson, Gale Anne Hurd, Louise Jameson, Dave Johns, Sam J. Jones, Sandy King, Eric Lewald, Dan Lloyd, Brad Meltzer, Mark Millar, Pat Mills, Sam Neill, Fabian Nicieza, Julie Nimoy, Phil Nobile Jr, Jerry Ordway, Ben Palmer, Michael Price, John A. Russo, Patrick Savage, Tom Savini, Matt Smith, Yeardley Smith, Ed Solomon, Dan Slott, George Takei, James Arnold Taylor, Lea Thompson, Tony Todd, Josh Weinstein and Marc Scott Zicree.

Appreciation, also, to Tom Baker, Roger Moore, Ray Harryhausen, George Romero, Anthony Julius, Nana Visitor, Mike

Lake, Doug Naylor, Molly Hulnick, Steve Dempster, Julia Lewald, Susan Eisenberg, Steven Scott, Brad Takei, Steve DeVries, Kahlil Schweitzer, Charlotte Cole, Sarah Wray, Sue Amaradivakara, Jamie Keenan, Eddie Robson, Robert Jay Johnson, Elizabeth Kern, Ryan Fleming, Rus McLaughlin, Melvyn Williams, Jonathan Powell, Allan Richard, Samantha Thompson, Jean Danzl, John Robertson, Nadine Rothapfel, Steve Sykes, Trendane Sparks, Liam Mason, Rachael Grant, Mark Harrison, Jennie Rich, Susan Arend, Guillaume Babey and Jonathan Ross...Thank you all.

Finally, mum, I owe you more than I can say. If my life were the opening credits to an episode of *Mission: Impossible*, it's you who lit the fuse. What fun you sparked!